THE NEW TOWN ANTHOLOGY VOLUME 2

NOTHING PERSONAL

CHRONICLES OF CHICAGO'S LGBTQ COMMUNITY 1977-1997

Jon-Henri Damski

fire –)♡(– trap

A Firetrap Press Book www.firetrappress.com

Firetrap Press Books by Jon-Henri Damski

www.firetrappress.com

Nonfiction

Angels Into Dust : The New Town Anthology Volume 1

dead/queer/proud : schizoculture 1

Nothing Personal: Chronicles of Chicago's LGBTQ Community 1977-1997 (The New Town Anthology Volume 2)

Poetry

Poems for the Fo(u)rth Quarter: Virtually Incurable But Not Quite Terminal

Fresh Frozen: First Chicago Poems

My Blue Monk: Poems from Blood and Sugar

Eat My Words: More Chicago Poems from the '70s

Epigrams

Damski to Go

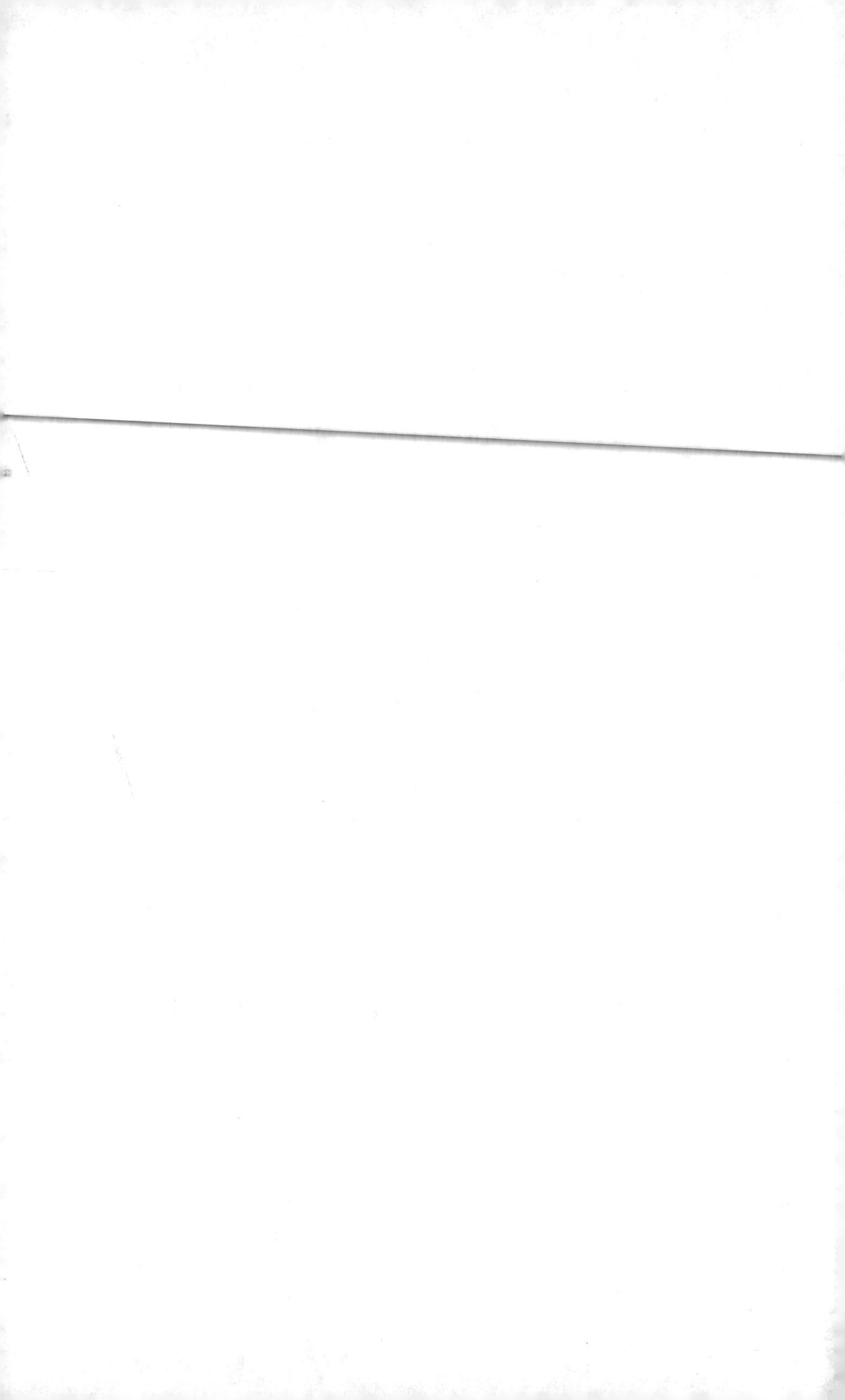

"The ruling passion in man [is] a gregarious instinct to keep together by minding each other's business. Grex rather than sex."

--Robert Frost

Writing in a series of community publications, Jon-Henri Damski was concerned about gay people as individuals and as a community--their emotional, sexual, ethical, political, social relationships with each other across age, gender, sexual orientation, racial, cultural and political lines. This collection of his work is dedicated to everyone whose instinct is to keep together by minding each other's business.

NOTHING PERSONAL

Jon-Henri Damski

fire –)♡(– trap

A Firetrap Press Book www.firetrappress.com

ISBN: 978-1-893143-03-2	First Edition	[paperback]
ISBN: 978-1-891343-07-0		[hardback]
ISBN: 978-1-891343-04-9		[Adobe e-bk.]
ISBN: 978-1-891343-08-7		[EPUB/Sony]
ISBN: 978-1-891343-09-4		[Kindle e-bk.]

Covers & Interior: Design by J. M. Vore, www.johnvore.com

Cover adapted from: (a) front cover: a color photo courtesy Jason Smith, www.jasonsmith.com, of Damski in his Belair Hotel room; (b) along the spine: an undated, unidentified photo from Jon-Henri's New Town Anthology scrapbook and (c) Damski caricature by Danny Sotomayor (also used as a "bullet" in the text); on back cover: (d) a 1979 photo of Michael Orsetti and Damski--and a second color photo of Damski, courtesy of Jason Smith, www.jasonsmith.com. Except for Smith photos and Firetrap logo, all artwork used with permission of Lori Cannon and the Jon-Henri Damski Archive.

The Firetrap Press and Jon-Henri Damski Archives are housed at the Gerber/Hart Library in Chicago, Illinois: www.gerberhart.org

ACKNOWLEDGMENTS

This book could not have been written without the help Jon-Henri Damski received from two decades of editors and friends. I have shadowed him and their work.

If this book were a movie, then Art Johnston--Chicago businessman, activist and friend of Jon-Henri's--would be the executive producer. He flew from Chicago to Oakland, California, in the Summer of 2009, discussed and then agreed to a proposal which enabled four more books to be added to the Damski-Firetrap Press works in print since 1996. Art shared memories, responded to e-mail inquiries and gave me the time to wade into the thousand and one columns by Damski and find one of many possible journeys which became *Nothing Personal.*

The former editor of Damski's from *GayLife* and *Windy City Times*, and co-editor of this book, Albert "Bill" Williams improved the book line by line, correcting what happens when newsprint is clipped, stored for decades, scanned, somewhat recognized by a computer, and formatted anew; he also added most of the footnotes. Bill is a staff writer for the *Chicago Reader*, and his long years of award-winning Chicago writing and service to the community did not stop him from spending many, many hours thinking through this collection with a relative new comer and transient member of Chicago's gay and lesbian community. He's been funny, pointed and amazingly productive under our deadlines. His Columbia College Chicago students are lucky to have him as a Senior Lecturer.

Owen Keehnen, a longtime novelist whose interviews, fiction, reviews, erotica, essays and poetry have appeared in hundreds of periodicals and anthologies worldwide, has also been a co-editor on this book. Owen came into the project fairly early on and played the part of "devil's advocate" as the book grew and developed out of a core series of columns spread out over ten years into a 20-year retrospective.

Work on the cover was advanced by Jon-Henri's pal Lori Cannon as she added her own special sense of Chicago's GLBTQ shaman to the project; as I said to the others, until Lori came on board *Nothing Personal*, something imperceptible (to me) was slightly out of focus.

And then there's a writer named Jon-Henri Damski. Dead, now, for over a decade. Something about him and his work keeps us holding on to him.

John Michael Vore
Publisher
Firetrap Press

Contents

PART ONE

NOTHING PERSONAL: contents

PART TWO

PART THREE

PART FOUR

PART FIVE

NOTHING PERSONAL: contents

PART SIX

PART SEVEN

PART EIGHT

EPILOGUE

preface by albert williams

MINDING EACH OTHER'S BUSINESS | 2009

For 20 years, Jon-Henri Damski chronicled life in Chicago's LGBTQ community, drawing on his background in Classical studies and his love of literature (Whitman, Genet, Burroughs, Algren, Frost) as he walked the streets of "New Town," recording the conversations and interactions he heard and observed in bars and bookstores, in all-night diners where childhood crushes were recollected, and in the chambers of Chicago's City Council where political battles were won and lost.

"New Town" then was the relatively isolated center of an emerging gay and lesbian social world that was expanding into what we now call the LGBTQ community. Writing in a series of publications, Damski produced hundreds of columns that chart changing attitudes about--and within--that community. He scrutinized both "mainstream" and outsider society. He wrote sympathetically about street hustlers, illuminating the causes of their troubled lives while also holding them to account for their own ethics and safety. He celebrated "cross-generational" relationships, delighting in the wisdom older and younger men could impart to each other. He discussed the divisions and the commonalities between gay men and lesbians, "regular gays" and flamboyant "faggots" and "queens," would-be moralists and lovers of promiscuous sex.

Damski referenced onetime community landmarks, long since gone: restaurants like the Hollywood and Jumbo Jerry's, leather bars like the Gold Coast and Redoubt, hustler hangouts like the New Flight, discos like the Bistro and Broadway Ltd., the punk dance club La Mere Vipere and the teen-oriented Joe's Juice Joint. He turned a moral microscope on the difference between ghettoization, gentrification, and what he called "yuppiefuckaction." He contemplated politicians ranging from Presidents John Kennedy and Jimmy Carter to Chicago mayors Richard Daley and Jane Byrne. He invoked the legends and rituals of ancient Greece (Oedipus) and dissected the mythology of modern celebrity (Michael Jackson). And he weighed in on the artists and thinkers who helped shape sometimes conflicting visions of the queer world: Jean Genet and Michel Foucault, Camille Paglia and Mary Daly, Boyd McDonald and Larry Kramer, Pier Paolo Pasolini and Gus Van Sant, Magnus Hirschfeld and Adolph Brand.

Jon-Henri Damski wrote extensively about media coverage of LGBTQ issues, from Roger Ebert's movie reviews to the *New York Times*' longtime refusal to use the word "gay." He was particularly concerned with what he called "the crime of crime reporting." He denounced newspapers like the *Chicago Tribune* and *Sun-Times* for publishing the names of men arrested in raids on "homosexual haunts," ruining their lives even after their cases were tossed out of court. He analyzed how these papers covered the cases of psychopathic serial killers like John Wayne Gacy, drawing a link between gayness and murder that sent "a brutal lesson in sex education" to confused teenagers wrestling with their identities. He chortled about the fact that a homophobic *Tribune* columnist's sensationalized accounts of police crackdowns on a New Town hotel actually attracted new patrons to that hotel by letting them know that where the action was.

The centerpiece of this book is two sets of columns Damski wrote in the mid-1980s and early 1990s about Larry Eyler, the so-called "Freeway Killer" who preyed on young gay men (including friends of Damski's) in Illinois and Indiana. Eyler was finally convicted for the grisly murder of a teenage hustler and police informant named Danny Bridges. While covering the Eyler case (and questioning whether the police had gotten the right guy) Damski grappled with whether Bridges was "an easy mark in a rough trade" or "a wild child" on a power trip; he also peeled away the layers of prejudice evident in courtroom interrogation of another near-victim, a former male prostitute turned AIDS activist.

Gacy in the 1970s, Eyler in the '80s, and Jeffrey Dahmer in the '90s--Damski wrote about all of them, noting the irony that all three men died the same year (Gacy by lethal injection, Eyler from AIDS, and Dahmer by being murdered by a fellow inmate). Yet Damski was fixated on life, not death. He knew that these high-profile tragedies, like the AIDS crisis, helped forge bonds within the gay community, as people came together to defy danger and demand respect from the media and political establishment--and from each other, and from themselves. Even as he wrote about Chicago as a "hustle town," he knew the truth of Robert Frost's statement: "The ruling passion in man [is] a gregarious instinct to keep together by minding each other's business."

an editor's notes by john vore

FROM THERE TO HERE | 2009

I. LISTENING TO DAMSKI I met Jon-Henri Damski not far from the end of his life; he was in his "schizo-culture period," when he used *schizo* as a prefix to describe things weird and/or unusual he would happen across. Hearing him say such things made one laugh, as one felt a slight crack appear between what one normally thought about and the newly fused item he'd given voice to: the *schizo*-thing v. that thing all on its own.

If a queer thing, after being named, still kept showing up, Damski might say of this particular, repeating kind of strangeness, that it was an "Omega-ism"--his neologism which described some occurrence as being notable also because it showed Damski that his muse, Omega Michael Orsetti, was still around.[1]

---

[1] Omega Michael Orsetti died of AIDS complications in 1992. A photograph of Damski and Orsetti from 1979 is on the back cover.

When Damski died, my hand was on his heart. Thereafter, the 2-for-1 Muse Special--this Alpha and Omega team--became *my* guides.

II. LEARNING CURVES This book starts much earlier, in a period of Damski's life when he was beginning to let go of being a professional Classicist and beginning to embrace being a gay writer. In the mid- to late 70s, he and Orsetti and many others in the Midwest found themselves in the midst of a social revolution, when the once-underground lesbian and gay people of Chicago began to come out *en masse*. Damski's writing--and later activism--helped to define this completely new kind of community in America. He called it "New Town."

The name referred to the neighborhood on Chicago's north side then perceived as the hub of the city's LGBTQ community, but for Damski, as one might expect, it also represented something much larger that transcended geographical boundaries.

This is the second book in the New Town Anthology series, the collections of his writings that set out the history of Damski's queer village. The first, *Angels into Dust*, was published in 1997 with Damski's active participation; it was built from a manuscript which had largely been thought about and put together over a number of years by

Damski, as he envisioned the book with other potential publishers back to 1985.

Damski anticipated this present book in a column written and published in the Fall of 1997. We were then exploring the idea of locating what he had written about serial killers who preyed on the gay community--in particular John Wayne Gacy, Larry Eyler, and Jeffrey Dahmer--in the newest book series he had been envisioning, "schizo-culture." We had been talking about the serial killer columns, and I suggested maybe they should be in "schizo-culture"? Their possible inclusion was more of a question aimed at understanding what Damski meant by "schizo-culture."

Damski was facing a serious deadline--his cancer, diagnosed four years earlier, had progressed to the terminal stage. There was little time to give this Editor a crash course. When he died, Damski left behind a file cabinet and stacks of columns, some of which were sorted out into file folders labeled as "New Town Anthology" or "Schizo-Culture."

Reading through columns in the different folders didn't clarify much at the series-level. So, I began to read all of the books he had been reading over the last year of his life. Then I took an entire year to read a book he told me had been foundational for his writing during the schizo-culture period: *Anti-Oedipus: Capitalism and Schizophrenia* by Gilles Deleuze and Felix Guattari, contemporaries of Michel Foucault.

After reading that book, I realized that Jon-Henri's ambiguous and sly references to schizophrenia which one would hear in talking to him, or find punctuating some interviews during the last year of his life...

...I should perhaps pause a minute and let that sink in. Jon-Henri Damski said to different reporters in 1997 that he had "schizophrenia." Now this was duly printed with all the reverence we give to "psychological diagnoses"--and knowing Jon-Henri a little better now, I can imagine him giggling about it back in his transient hotel room.

I also had given the psychiatric label undue reverence, before reading Deleuze and Guattari. I hadn't realized Damski had re-appropriated the psychiatric terminology, refusing to give in to experts' meanings; that he "took back" their word, and extended it as he populated conversations with schizo-prefixed language.

And there was more. Damski heard the word in two languages at once: *schizo* as "broken"; *phrenia* as "heart." Yet Damski didn't see "broken" only as a non-working machine, but rather as something which had broken through a wall, or out of confinement. He liked words whose meanings spread out. Thus, Damski turned schizo into a philosophical and oddly hip-sounding *attitude* outside of the medico-psychiatric ward, meaning something wild. In that last year of his life, at one level, Damski was telling us all that he was wild-hearted.

A careful reading of his columns which remember his muse reveals that Omega had been the person once diagnosed as a schizophrenic; Damski seemed to be further identifying with Omega. By saying to reporters that he, himself, was so-diagnosed, he again appealed to New Towners to open up the "big tent" of queer life, and begin accepting the neurologically diverse among us.[2]

Once reported, his little psycho-drama bombshell in 1997 tweaked two of the "establishments" Damski regularly questions in *Nothing Personal*: the field of psychiatry and the mainstream Chicago press. His friends in the mainstream press added the schizo label to the list of things this dying man had overcome.

---

[2] No evidence exists in the Jon-Henri Damski Archive which supports an actual diagnosis of schizophrenia for Damski--or any extended encounters with psychiatrists--with the possible exception of having been sent to one "for the homosex cure" in the early '60s.

Yet Damski wasn't afraid of death. When he was diagnosed with cancer in 1993, his response was to increase his output and write more, so that when the end came, he would be "in the middle of his work" instead of at the end. He wrote two new books of poetry--and a long essay on Homer's *Odyssey* along with continuing his weekly columns. It would, in retrospect, be the most productive period of writing for him in over a decade.

Damski gave up the ghost not long after finishing what would be his 20th anniversary column: 20 years of deadlines, he often said: never missed one, even at the end.

A wild, romping pathway through his writing was published as *dead/queer/proud*, the first schizoculture series book. This Editor had some serious fun by sharing the work with a...ghost editor named "Not Damski"--the source of a lot of "death" jokes in the chapter titles.

III. '70s CHIC After a break of seven years, in returning to Damski's columns full time, I reread them. Actually I eyed over 700 columns, as I catalogued what he wrote and searched for what might be the companion columns for murderers, and their dead teens and twenty-somethings.

After the arrest of John Wayne Gacy, in late 1978, one could with good reason argue that he was the most famous "homosexual" in Chicago. He eclipsed all that was going on in New Town, and in some news portrayals, seemed to be one of its citizens. Though he lived in the suburbs, New Town was just where he preyed.

In print Damski contrasted the private fantasies and demons of the tourist-murderer with the becoming-public love lives, desires and affections of his lesbian and gay friends who actually lived in New Town. Damski didn't hold back: he was sex-positive and in your face. No apologies.

Looking back thirty years, one has to remember some milestones:[3]

- In 1979, it had only been five years since the American Psychological Association shifted its position on the mental status of being gay: from being mentally ill because one felt some same sex attractions, to being mentally ill only if one was uncomfortable with it.

- In 1979, America was in a "malaise," and American hostages were being held by Iranian revolutionaries. President Carter would soon be challenged in the Democratic party by Senator Ted Kennedy for the 1980 Presidential nomination; and Ronald Reagan would go on to defeat President Carter in 1980.

---

[3] This is the first instance of the "Danny Sotomayor Bullet" in the text.

In 1979, the most famous homosexual in America was probably Truman Capote,[4] who by then was mostly isolated in his New York penthouse, crocked 24-7. Obviously brilliant, he had a high-pitched, lisping voice, and played the ironic wit in talk show interviews. He was a unique and talented man; yet he was so very different from the Americans in the middle of the country, as he had learned more than a decade earlier, while researching and writing *In Cold Blood*.[5]

In Chicago, Richard J. Daley, "The Boss," had died in office, then was replaced by an interim mayor, who was then beaten by Chicago's first female mayor: Jane Byrne.

In Chicago, then, an almost 40-something, popular Greek and Latin professor from Bryn Mawr had come for an academic conference in 1974, where he failed to find a new academic appointment, and then stayed. As he wrote in 1978, he had no money to make it back to either coast--not that he seems to have wanted to.

---

[4] Truman Capote, 1924-1984, was an American writer known for *Breakfast at Tiffany's* (1958) and *In Cold Blood* (1966). The 2005 film, *Capote*, portrayed his life and starred Philip Seymour Hoffman.

[5] Capote's 1966 "non-fiction novel" about the murders of a Kansas farm family in 1959.

From his earliest daily, typed journals in 1974, something about the windy city had caught Jon-Henri Damski's attention: "in Chicago," Damski wrote, "even fags walk like Americans."

IV. PLAYING 'HOMO' Fifteen years later, Damski had become one of the most prominent writers in Chicago's LBGTQ community. In 1989, he wrote a column about how the very notion of a "homosexual" had harmed both gays and straights since its late 19th century inception, at the birth of psychiatry. He saw the term as being--ironically--mostly a conversation between straight men, about straight men, leaving out all women and having little to do with actual gay people. He called it "playing 'homo.'"

Ten years after Gacy had been arrested for killing 33 people, he was still so predominant in people's minds that he was parodied as a gay man with a lover on Chicago's talk radio, for laughs. And even though a Human Rights Ordinance had been passed in Chicago, the equating of homosexuals with pedophiles shows up as the content of their affections--which are then made to seem even more exotic.

As Damski tells it:

"Probably the grossest example of two men playing 'homo' together (without the sex) is the 10-year-old radio act of Steve Dahl and Gary Meier. Steve and Gary impersonate a homosexual couple in the same way that

Amos and Andy used to impersonate Negroes. Four hours a day on WLUP, AM1000, these radio gods play and tempt their audience and each other into believing that they might be a homosexual couple. Gary uses a lisping voice to create a character, Cliff, who runs a 'homo' camp for 'young men and boys.' Steve imitates Gacy in a character called 'Kinko the Clown.' Weekly, they call the Bijou theater to check up on the latest in all-male porn. They read from lesbian S & M magazines on the air. They talk about sex acts so often that their real names could be Oral and Anal."

In this radio farce, Oral and Anal don't love each other, they are a couple because of their shared interest in boys. That a media company could make a business decision to broadcast such ideas says a great deal about the Midwest in which Damski wrote.

V. BOOK NOTES For this Editor to write that Damski focused on serial killers in some columns is short-hand for all the issues which arose when those killers and their New Town prey became known and were portrayed in the mainstream press.

The "gay scene" was new, and some reporters treated "the gay scene" like a freak show of still mostly underground activities, a step removed from the vice squad beat. Yet just as conversations about "homosexuals" seemed to fill a lot of straight men's minds and talk, murder, Damski would argue, was a straight crime. The straight press tried to locate the serial killers amidst the newly forming

LGBTQ community: Damski knew better, wrote down the evidence and threw the search for causes right back.

This argument was not just about how the community was portrayed, or even whether it would be allowed to define itself. Some in Chicago politics would not accept the emerging diversity: police raids increased on gay bars, bookstores and porn theaters and one transient hotel was closed--all attempts to drive LGBTQ life back into the shadows. As Damski often described it, for people who rarely found a physical space in which to be themselves, these amounted to unlawful raids on the LGBTQ home.

This meant that the people and places who were preyed upon by John Wayne Gacy were further victimized--even in their shock and grief. And rather than offering enhanced policing to protect the LGBTQ community, the City of Chicago acted as if it had to protect itself from the LGBTQ community.

Then and now, giving killers too much attention obscures the deaths of five dozen people. Damski regularly reminds readers about "the kids,"[6] as he called them--and one needs to repeat his greatest fear in the aftermath of serial killer news: that gay men would stop reaching out to younger people for fear of falling prey in media reports and in the courts to being "just like Gacy."

As in the radio show, but with real world consequences.

One murdered teenager whom Damski writes about at length in this book is Danny Bridges. While fact-checking Damski, a web search in 2009 brought up some articles about Bridges which give conflicting reports of Bridges' ages at the time of his death.

In newspaper articles Damski himself clipped, when the Bridges' age was reported in error, Damski circled and then wrote the correct age in the margins. He believed such mistakes played into the enduring stereotype set by Gacy: strange man, hidden same sex desires, teen sex playmates, teen victims--all collapsing into a "homosexual" monolith which, as Damski pointed out, confused "homosexual" with "homicidal." Again, because the conversation about gays and lesbians went on almost exclusively between straight men without

---

[6] Damski's use of the word "kid" across 20 years of columns only rarely--if ever--denotes a child according to legal definitions. More often it finds use as a term of endearment between anyone older and someone younger.--JMV

input from women or gay men, this created a situation with great potential for missing the facts. Sometimes, Damski quipped, "News is managed rumor"; at times, this was not enough.

A search through the Damski Archive, and almost three dozen articles from *GayLife*, the *Chicago Tribune*, the Chicago *Sun-Times*, and the Lerner *Booster*--spanning four stretches of time--show that Bridges' age was reported as 16 at the time of his death, in 1984. As time moves forward through events related to the trial of his alleged murderer, Bridges' age gets reported as being younger--especially at the time of Larry Eyler's trial, in 1986. All of the editors of *Nothing Personal* want to acknowledge the discrepancy in the public record, while also noting that we stand by Damski's accounting of events.

Let me take a moment to speak directly about intergenerational affections, from Damski's perspective.

It would take decades before a community of people could form in which more and more age-similar folks could find one another and bond in something akin to straight marriage, in America. "This is new in history," Damski told one friend who has been in a long-term, same-sex relationship since the 70s.

Yet, Damski knew that regardless of the progress in our community--regardless, even, of more social services for teens, and even some which were based in the LGBTQ community--that there would still be kids who fell through the cracks. And some of them would find older men and women who would mentor them.

Damski also assumed that desire exists among younger for older which didn't depend on them being helpless or having fallen through the cracks. That such couplings might involve affection, love and even sexual desire was nothing unusual, completely human and a good thing, from his perspective. One of the many acts of courageous writing one finds in Damski from thirty years ago is his insistence on love across generations as one option among many, even in the face of the negative stereotyping which resulted from news of serial killers.

One of the most prominent reported pairings of older killer and younger victim was made up of teenager Danny Bridges and 30-something Larry Eyler. Years after Bridges' murder, one detective conflated their earlier work with Bridges in bringing down the owner of a nightspot that catered to kids under the legal drinking age (when Bridges may have been 14) and Chicago police work with Bridges in trying to entrap Larry Eyler. The cops assigned to both cases couldn't distinguish between a Chicago guy who, for years, ran a non-alcoholic hang-out frequented by teens, and another who had a recent past which likely included murder, and a longer past with almost nothing to show for it but violence and severe neurological illness.

Damski argues that what blinded them--and many--was the Gacy stereotype, still asserting itself along with a larger Midwest and American anti-sex six-pack of notions which attempt to keep alive the old, pre-liberation norms. Same-sex, wrong. Same-sex marriage: worse. Got bad kids? Throw them into the street, where they'll straighten up. Meaning: wise up, and get away from the recently decriminalized, and more recently de-certified. And of course: any and all affection between generations was evil and "homosexual."

These half-dozen ideas were rolled into one real, killer. And then, Kinko the Clown kept being copied.

VI. USING DANNY BRIDGES Finally, a word must be said about the use of Danny Bridges by law enforcement.

In 1984, Damski underscores the vicious circle in which Bridges' found himself, caught between Chicago and (probably) federal law enforcement and the life path he had chosen. To this Editor, the use of him at 14--and then the retrieval of him from North Carolina in the pursuit of Larry Eyler, when he was 16--seems like an institutionally supported re-victimization.

When law enforcement agencies leverage the mistakes of kids--regardless of the suspect they are after--they insure that a life of lies becomes a legacy of these young people. Many young people get swept up in law enforcement attempts at eradicating the epidemic of illicit drug use in America. These first-time offenders are often then asked to do police work in exchange for a clean record. Only those who do not understand economic deprivation and the allure of drugs for the poor and disenfranchised could think this "fair."

Those familiar with sexual predators know that they use the same tactics, looking for and preying on vulnerabilities, both psychological and economic.

To this editor, tactics which use underage kids displace the real conundrum of law enforcement: asked to "keep us safe"--but rarely given the funds to do the job. In a democracy, we get the government services we pay for. It is yet another sign of how little care we have for our young people that we starve law enforcement, and place good cops in the position of having to lean towards bad means--ultimately, further victimizing young people, and leaving us with law enforcement officials who rarely have the guts to tell us: you get what you pay for.

And to return to the specifics of Bridges: it sickens this Editor to know that undercover Chicago cops knew he was in an apartment with Eyler and did not get him out the night he was murdered. This gives credence to all those who believe that the underworld of illicit drugs, sex crime perpetrators and law enforcement have become, too often, just two sides of the same coin. This in fact was shown to be the case when an "elite" undercover force in Chicago, only in 2007, was disbanded--and several of its members came under indictment.[7]

In such a world, it is not the rule of law which matters, but money.

Years later, some undercover cop tried to justify their use of Bridges as a means. In that explanation, he lowered Bridges' age to show how bad was the guy they were after. Yet that only underscored how corrupt they, themselves, had become. Bridges is, for this Editor, a symbol of a community that asks for help from law

---

[7] In 2007, the Special Operations Section was disbanded and four members indicted on robbery, kidnapping home invasion and other charges. In 2008, the former Special Operations Section was reconstituted under a new name, the Mobile Strike Force. In 2009, 2 of the former S.O.S. officers were cleared after evidence against them was shown to be false.--JMV

enforcement, only to get left knowingly alone in a room in which someone will kill you, cut you up, put you in garbage bags, and throw you in the dumpster.

We refuse to accept, in our 21st century American nation, that we have given up on the fight against violence, illicit drugs and sex perpetrators--we talk the talk, but don't do the walk. And we really just hope we make enough money, some day, to keep our kids safe. Nothing else works. Damski underscores this point time and time again--the difference between our talk, and our walk: what we say we're doing, what we're willing to walk through to make it right. And it is from this place that he insists, at the level of individuals, that we must not leave kids behind.

Slyly, at this level of commentary, Damski disarms readers by first announcing, "nothing personal," here: you can keep (safely) reading.

VII. NOTHING PERSONAL In 1977, Damski began sending epigrams and observations to *GayLife* and *Gay Chicago News*, the two main bar rags, as they were known in those days: a calendar of events plus filler (they would grow into alternative news later). *Gay Chicago News* accepted his submissions first.

One could not, with any assurance, be openly gay and work just anywhere--then as now. Working in a gay-owned business with other openly gay people was an unimaginable dream for most folks, and full of professional, career-ending risks. Damski chose to, as he put it, "live dangerously"--and come out writing under his real name (and soon, using his actual photo) in "two columns" a week for *Gay Chicago*: "Nothing Personal" and "Bits & Pieces"--observations in the first, epigrams in the second.

This book starts with Damski's first "Nothing Personal" column, a defense of queens. If, in Chicago, fags walked like Americans, as Damski had written in his journals--that didn't mean that enduring prejudices couldn't also be found in our LGBTQ community: at times we too easily attacked one another for fear of what the larger society might think about us.

All of us, as Americans, had and have work to do in continuing to create a more welcoming, self- and other- affirming community, where openness to difference means anyone could move in next door to you and share their life.

John Michael Vore
Editor
Firetrap Press
Motel 6-Livermore, CA
Summer, 2009

series introduction by jon-henri damski

THE NEW TOWN ANTHOLOGY | 1997

New Town was never a real place.[8] The name came about as a real estate gimmick to call a neighborhood that was between Old Town, the hippie village, and Uptown, the industrial hillbilly transient home for the homeless in Chicago.

New Town stretched along the Lake from Fullerton to Irving Park and seldom went father west than Halsted Street or Ashland Avenue. In the late '60s and early '70s this area had the feel of a deserted town. Black folks for the first time started to move north of North Avenue and live in the area. Middle class and middle aged white people took flight to the suburbs, leaving burned out buildings, high risers with their parents as senior citizens, and a lot of low rent apartments for young gay and lesbian urban pioneers.

I came to Chicago and lived in New Town in the early '70s. By day, I taught poetry to senior citizens for Truman College. My classroom was in their

---

[8] Adapted from the introduction Jon-Henri Damski wrote for *Angels Into Dust: The New Town Anthology, Volume 1* (Firetrap Press, 1997/2002).--JMV

homes at senior centers and nursing facilities. My standard text was Edgar Lee Masters' *Spoon River Anthology*. At night, and when I wasn't teaching, I wrote and published stories about the lives of folks in New Town, which I thought of as *The New Town Anthology*.

I recognized early on that these people were mostly abandoned souls. Kicked out of their homes, churches, jobs, careers, family, trying to make it on their own with their new openness and lifestyle. A straight history like the mainstream press's who, what, when, where & why-- wouldn't work.

My subjects wanted to remain anonymous, to protect their jobs and life; they didn't want their names in the paper, yet they wanted their stories told, and wanted to know what was going on. I was a low-tech switchboard operator, making connections. My routine was to walk continually, day and night, gathering stories. From one person I would get one story, which would alert me to a theme or situation. Once I heard a similar story from someone else, I took that for verification and wrote it down.

Sometimes I'd write what I heard as dialogue out of Plato, only it took place in a leather bar and was about sex in the park. Other times, I'd write from another person's point of view. We didn't really like authority, so I rarely spoke from my own first person--who would listen? Queens and hustlers--and lonely old drunks--folks who had learned to listen to only their own advice, also needed to see &

hear themselves, to read about themselves and know something like "we" was out there, in a sub-zero winter day, or on a dog day summer night.

Chicago was not like either coast. We were pretty much overlooked by other gay leaders and scribes in San Francisco and New York. New Town could never be a ghetto like Castro, because we never had the concentration, or numbers. We had to adjust to our more numerous neighbors and learn their ways of clout and politics. We had to survive by our savvy and wits. This challenge made us a tough group of sissies.

I wrote these stories as I walked around New Town. My publisher, John Michael Vore, has placed them so that you can read them as though you, too, were walking through a town looking at the scene.[9]

---

[9] The area of Chicago which gave rise to the name "New Town" was recognized as an official gay and lesbian neighborhood by the city of Chicago in 1999, and its center is known as Lakeview East, and informally referred to as "Boys Town." Yet the community also seems more spread out, today, than 10 and 20 years ago: Andersonville, Roscoe Village, Uptown all have large LGBTQ populations.

NOTHING PERSONAL | 1989

[10]I have never thought that I was the voice of the community; the trouble was that until New Town was big enough, I was sometimes the *only* columnist. Early on I'd write from different perspectives, or show two people debating to stay *out* of my own voice. Still, people would stop me on the street and tell me they agreed with what I'd written. I once wrote a column about two guys discussing backrooms and a few people came up and said I was completely correct, even though I presented more than two sides of that issue.

In LGBTQ journalism, you must remain an advocate for freedom. We are still fighting for equal recognition of gays and lesbians inside a dominant society that wishes we would just go away. We are still fighting for our lives.

Even with all our acceptance and credibility, we cannot assume the luxury of pseudo-

---

[10] Adapted from a two-part series of columns Damski wrote in 1989.--JMV

objectivity. This was my life! I didn't write a line which did not have my gay body inside that line.

Gay Chicago was my starting place in gay journalism, and I am still thankful to Ralph Paul Gernhardt for giving me my start, and to Dan DiLeo for being my first editor. Ralph and Dan helped me work out my early assignments and strategies for the column. Just as we kept "gay" in the title of the magazine, so we used our full and real last names. Up until the early '80s most gay journalists used pseudonyms. And almost none ran their real-life pictures with their columns. What would your mother think? What would the fag-bashers do?

Later, at *GayLife*, I took my direction from the editor-in-chief, Albert "Bill" Williams.[11] To watch Williams scan a line of your prose was to behold a genius at work. No editor has ever understood my words and their subtexts better than Bill. He challenged me to take on broader subjects and aim for a wider audience. He got my focus off the street and into the full politics and social scene of Chicago.

---

[11] Williams was managing editor at *GayLife* and *Windy City Times*. A senior lecturer at Columbia College Chicago, Williams is also a staff writer for the *Chicago Reader*. Damski's posthumously read endorsement is what lead to seeking out Williams in 2009.--JMV

Now that I look back at it, violence was a common theme in many of my early stories. Gangs controlled Broadway and Surf, Barry, and Cornelia. You took your life in your hands to walk down Halsted. Touche on Lincoln was an isolated outpost.[12] You did not safely walk down Diversey to Touche, you took a cab.

One of my first stories for *Gay Chicago* concerned a shocking act of daytime violence. I was going to the Hollywood restaurant, then on Diversey, at noon for Sunday breakfast. In front of me, coming out of the restaurant, was a balding guy in a high school jacket two sizes too small for him. He was holding hands with his lover. Four teenage gang-bangers attacked the guy in the jacket, yelling about his "colors." They called him "sissy" and "fag," while his lover looked on helplessly, frozen in shock. They knocked the guy's glasses off, sending them splattering, and left the guy dazed on the sidewalk. We sympathetic onlookers didn't know what to do. In those days if you called the cops, they too might beat you up. Or just laugh it off.

At the same time this bashing was going on, around the corner on Clark a cop was writing a parking ticket in front of the Steak 'n' Egger (now Greg's Snack and Dine at 2737 N. Clark). I

---

[12] Leather bar.

wanted to ask this cop for help, but didn't know how he would respond. Later I learned that this same cop was gay. He was Paul Damico. Later Paul and I became good friends, but on that corner that day, he seemed to be on the other side.

Also at the same time, two doors south of the cop, a bus was loading passengers out of Dion's pizza parlor. They were members of the Illinois Gay Rights Task Force (the word "lesbian" had not yet been incorporated) going on one of their first trips to Springfield to lobby the state legislature on behalf of a gay rights bill.

In those days I also learned to keep my personal opinions out of the story. That's why the original title of my column was *Nothing Personal.* When I met Joe of Joe's Juice Joint, for example, I personally thought he was a mean drunk. He told blowhard stories that were impossible to believe, stories about his fast days as the power behind the governor of Florida. He enticed kids with checks that would bounce. He dominated every conversation, until you never wanted to talk to him again.

But that was just my personal view of Joe. When I stepped back from my dislike of him, I observed that kids liked him, liked his big talk and fantasies, his pretentious lifestyle, forgave him his bounced checks and other sins, and actually took tender care of him. His kids mothered him and stayed with him at his joint, stayed by him when he went to jail, and were there to greet him when he came back. They loved the guy as best they could. And they paid their final respects when he died soon after jail, a broken and battered man.

That's why when I used Joe as a model for my stories, I didn't write about the mean drunk. I wrote about the reversal. How the kids actually took care of him. How they were his private counselors in "transitional living." How they would give one straight story to the police and social workers, keeping their true feelings and love for him hidden. They knew the system had set him up. They knew they were expected to testify against him. But they never really betrayed him. One of them was always there, even in his jail cell, bringing him chicken soup.

PART ONE

chapter one

OVERHEARD: STRAIGHT MASQUERADES | 1977

The world hates fags, so fags have to hate other fags.

"Flaming fags!"

"Damn Queens!"

No one, it seems, can keep their resentment to themselves.

"Look at that stupid Queen. Why does she have to be so obvious, so loud, so embarrassing? She is giving the gay movement a bad name."

Society has also said as much. If gays will closet their Queens, then the rest of us can slip into the mainstream.

A tempting offer?

Whenever there is a discussion of homosexuality on WGN 720, some anonymous medical student calls in and says he doesn't approve of Queens, the "flagrant kind," and like the moderator, wishes they would stifle themselves.

Are Queens really that offensive?

Queen Sally always offends the waitresses at Ricketts. How can you wait on a fake woman? "He wanted me to call him 'her'-- the nerve."

The male nurses snicker when they bring Queen Mary in for her routine bout with suicide. "She doesn't know a vein from a tassel."

And this: "Queens, of course, are no help in democratic politics. If you get them up and get them registered, still they will probably vote for The Man because he is a Man. Something like Blacks in Mississippi voting for the white sheriff."

Most gays don't date, know personally, associate with, or even say hello to Queens. They don't turn each other on. Most gays wish Queens would keep their poses private, confined to the bedroom and the dark.

So why not limit gay liberation to the practical, to the mainstream gay, the guy who fits in during the day and comes out Friday night? "Let the Queens go the way of all freaks," some say.

But this safe approach--a straight masquerade--won't work. For even if you are partially gay, closeted gay, hidden gay: the risk is the same and the risk is total.

Queens cannot hide. They carry the risk of all gays on their person. They also show obvious vulnerabilities. And that's what mainstream gays find hard to forgive.

And if "regular" gays think they can separate themselves from Queens, they are kidding themselves. Society's compromise will not be genuine until all are free, including Queens. As Bob Dylan once said: if you sacrifice your Queen, you'll just be a pawn in their game.

chapter two

GODS & MEN (...AND LESBIANS) | 1978

Lesbians and gay men, like apples and oranges, are supposed to be part of the same fruit salad, but they don't seem to mix.

Lesbians and gay men--outside of some thin and quasi-rational words about civil rights--have nothing in common. They don't hate each other, they don't love each other, and they don't often know each other. They don't play together, and they don't live together.

About the only thing gay men and lesbians have in common is their exclusiveness. Gay men usually come to terms with the female in them, and lesbians know their masculine side. Each is a, more or less, self-sufficient sexual package. But this sexual independence keeps them from needing, or paying much attention to one another.

Obviously, there is little sexual attraction between lesbians and gay men. No matter where their minds are, or even if both are insightful and love to converse with each other, their bodies are not playing the same game.

Also, American social customs of the last hundred years have pretty much determined how each shall behave. Lesbians can touch, hug, and kiss in public, but they can't be in a man's world of business and own taverns, bars, banks, and discos. Gay men can own the world and franchise it, but they can't touch, kiss, or hug in public.

And now after the great post-Victorian sexual revolution in America, the '80s are coming and men can discretely hug and kiss in public, as long as they are not in a fireman's uniform. And gay women can own banks and bars and baths. Except, years of exploitation and male dominance leaves them either without the capital or the will to exercise their new right.

The real life difference, then, between gay men and gay women cannot be glossed over by coalition rhetoric, or the gratuitous use of "brother" and "sister." If you believe gay men and gay women are part of the same "family," then you might as well also believe in the family of man, and say with a straight face: Poles and Blacks are the same.

It just ain't in the cards, or our history.

In fact, historically, the difference between gay men and gay women is even more dramatic.

Lesbians can derive their origin from Sappho, a real woman, a real poet, and a gal who probably had more balls than the whole Spartan army. But gay men invent their origins out "of thin air." They say they are Greek gods, descendants of Apollo, the mythical patron of poetry and dance.

What it comes down to is this: women, even gay women, know where they come from; while men, either because of their vulnerability, or self-delusion, must have heroic origins and divine creators. They can't just be what they are, they need a god on their side. And that is probably why gay men and gay women seem to stand apart like earth and air.

chapter three

MEN & BOYS | 1978

As everyone knows, men are men and boys are boys. Also, as everyone knows, boys grow up to be men, and men are supposed to look and act older than boys. That's all baby simple.

The common assumption is that you start out as a boy and grow up into a man. Boy first and man after, such is the natural course of events. But experience is perverse, and does not seem to follow nature's plan. It is not unusual for some boys never to grow up, never to look like men. Senator Church[13] is still baby faced, despite his seniority and power. Andy Warhol[14] is still considered a boy-wonder, even though in simple fact he is a shrewd business man.

On the other hand, some males, like Richard Nixon, were never boys. Richard Nixon was a

---

[13] Senator Frank Church (D-Idaho) was a member of the United states Senate from 1957-1981; his Senate Select Committee investigated the use of the C.I.A. and F.B.I. in domestic spying.

[14] Andy Warhol, 1928-1987, was an American-born painter, printmaker and filmmaker, and a leading proponent of what came to be known as "pop art."

man, even when he worked as a teen-ager in his father's gas station. He pumped gas with a tie on.

Whether one is a man or a boy does not depend so much on age or looks, as on fate and temperament. And contrary to common belief, some males stay boys all their life, while others are really men from the start.

All boys, then, do not become men.

In the gay world, moreover, the difference between men and boys is more pronounced, and takes on an added twist that causes much sadness and anxiety. There is a great and undeserved premium, in the gay world, placed on being a boy, or looking like a boy. Boys have been worshiped from Narcissus to Dorian Gray. Gays seem to want, or want to be, the perpetual boy.

This excessive boy worship has caused two kinds of pain. A lot of gay men hate themselves, because they look like men, and are in fact men. They feel a loss: "I don't have it anymore." "I've lost my youth."

Sadly, this sense of loss makes men, who are familiar with and comfortable with Haydn, Purcell, and Sibelius shuffle off to disco joints snapping their fingers to music they abhor. While other men try wearing key chains and a red bandanna, hoping somehow someone will mistake them for Mick Jagger.

Then, there is the other kind of gay pain, felt by males who, either by curse or fate, are fifty years old and still look like boys. They wonder when anyone will ever take them seriously. "When will I grow up?" "How long can I go on with this disguise, carry off a boy's face in an arthritic body?"

Consequently, there are a lot of mixed up gays. There are a lot of lovely men, fascinating men, beautiful men who would give up anything, including their soul, to be a cute boy. And there are a lot of fifty year old boys, who would like to crawl out of their skin, and fit into something more mature.

The net of all of this is: each of us is in some way locked into his skin. His fate. If we take a gentle look at ourselves and our friends, we will see that some are predominately boys and some are men, having nothing to do with age, or growth. And if we accept our type, then we can relax with it. And, who knows, maybe some day men and boys will learn how to enjoy themselves and each other.

chapter four

OVERHEARD: VIOLENCE IN NEW TOWN | 1978

"I don't like what's going on in New Town. It scares me."

"What do you mean?"

"All these beatings, the violence I read about in the gay and straight newspapers."

"Have you ever been attacked?"

"No. But now I'm scared I might be. I don't wear my jewelry anymore when I go out. A friend of mine knows a guy who was attacked up near Montrose. They cut his arm with a broken bottle. And now he has lost the use of his right arm."

"Was he attacked because he was gay?"

"No. They wanted his money and jewels. But I have heard and read about Blondie, and the gangs that beat up gays in New Town."

"But the police arrested Blondie, didn't they? He's been put away."

"I don't know. I've never read that. I just know there are a lot of toughs out beating up on gays."

"OK. But if you never have been attacked, and none of your friends ever has been attacked, why are you scared?"

"It's reading about the violence every week, headlines in the newspapers. And in our own gay newspaper. I'm an American. I work in advertising in the Loop. I'm 43 and look much younger. I'm in good shape. I can pass in most crowds and no one ever knows I'm gay.

"But, the other night on Clark Street, a kid was walking with his girl friend and they both called me 'fag.' It scared me. How did they know?"

"Perhaps it was because you were a single male walking alone in the gay ghetto. A . . . lucky guess."

"Yes. But that means I'm not safe on the streets anymore. They know."

"You don't have to play it alone. There's whistleSTOP."

"Yes. I went to one of their meetings. And I just didn't feel comfortable. They are not me. I mean the people there. Most of them seemed to be unemployed, or fully occupied in gay causes. I couldn't identify with them. It's good they are protecting themselves, but I just didn't feel they were protecting me. I really couldn't trust them."

"I see your point. I don't know if I can trust them either. I know they are working for the cause and think they are doing right. And somebody has to do it, be our leader, talk to the police, etc...."

"I've been on the streets all my life. There always is violence. A year and a half ago, my friend got beaten up, a broken arm, by a fag hater and owner of a well-known restaurant in New Town. He has sued and prosecuted the man. He tried to get his story published in the gay newspaper. They wouldn't publish it. A minor incident, a personal affair, they said. But now, they are publishing all kinds of stories, beatings of both gays and straights, both inside and outside of the ghetto. Gay violence has become the new wave fad in journalism."

"I agree. And I suspect they are over-reporting it."

"And another point. Frankly, all these imperatives turn me off. 'If attacked, do this. Don't do that! Call this number! Take down that number!' It's like going to bed with a guy who keeps saying: 'Turn on the lights. Turn off the lights. Don't kiss me on the lips.' It's the imperative attitude of our leaders that turns me off.

"And, ironically, I think they've got their story out of focus. Just as we are winning our sexual freedom, just as homosexuality is being tried, practiced, or tolerated by the majority of the young, a few impotent thugs come out to bully and bluff us. And what do our leaders do? Embellish the boogie man stories and scare us back into old morality."

chapter five

OVERHEARD: PAINULTIMATE | 1978

"Pain is jaded. And anyone who mixes pain with sex is sick."

"God, I wish that were all there was to it! I used to think that way too."

"You mean you're into pain?"

"Yes. I dig pain. It may seem 'sick' to you, but that is the way I get off."

"Gee man, you could have fooled me. You don't look like one of those S&M boys. You're clean, smooth-featured, a sharp dresser. In fact, you look like a basketball player."

"Yea, sure, I'm the Jack Armstrong type, the All-American Boy. And, I did play basketball in college, and golf in the Army.

"It may sound crazy to you, but I liked the Army. I couldn't wait to get out of high school to join. I wanted to go to Nam, but instead they sent me to Germany. The Captain liked me, kept me in his office, and put me on the Army golf team.

"It was in the Army, that I realized I got a sexual charge out of taking orders. I need a sexual partner who takes me over, barks out commands, and is in full charge. Because if he is firm and strong, then I have no doubt that he likes me. And I know I can please him, because I do exactly what he says."

"OK. I can understand how it is a relief to have a strong, macho lover. Someone to lean on, someone you can trust. But why would you let anyone hurt you, physically?"

"You have to understand, you are confused like I was at first. There is no pain in the actual hurting, just in the expectation.

"Pain comes in trying to avoid pain, running scared. As I did at first. Bill was my first rough partner, and of course, I was scared of him. My mind was running faster than my body. I couldn't imagine, or rather I imagined all sorts of things he might do to me. But once I settled into him, and just let him do what he did, responded with my body and did not try to anticipate his moves, the scare went away. I was relaxed. I did anything he said, and felt no pain whatsoever.

"Oh, the next day I was sore all over. And there were bruises. But I was completely satisfied, because I knew I had tested my body, put my whole body on the line, and let it become the instrument of his will. And, since he knew what he was doing, he rewarded my trust all the way. He made no false moves. He didn't hurry. We could have stopped anytime. He wasn't mean, or doing it like a bully for some cheap thrill.

"Since then I have done it from both sides, master and slave. And now I know your head has to be clear to do it. No hesitation, no tricks, no poses, just straight flat out force. And if you are mean or petty, the sexual energy will not flow.

"Flow is the key. To get your white flesh, red blood and the blue bruises flowing. And in the act itself, there is no recollection of pain, anymore than the ballet dancer feels pain on stage. There is just the thrill of the total discharge of the whole body."

"That's bullshit! It's guys like you, with your sex and violence games that cause wars."

"Wrong! In the modern world, wars are caused by guys like you, in knit suits, tinted hair, with computer minds, who would never dream of inflicting pain, because they are so dumb, they don't realize that pain is the ultimate dream."

chapter six

OVERHEARD. THE LOVE OF STRANGERS | 1978

"There is one thing my lover and friends cannot give me. The thrill of meeting and having sex with a stranger."

"And is that why you go out cruising every night?"

"Yes."

"Isn't that just compulsive and degenerate behavior?"

"Well, it would be compulsive, if it were something I wanted to stop doing, like smoking. But I don't. And, it would be degenerate if I did it when I didn't enjoy it. But I don't."

"Yes, but how far can you go with a stranger? Don't you just keep repeating the same experience with a different sexual partner? You make no real commitment. You just have a series of half-hour, or one-night stands."

"I'll agree it's not like love or friendship, it's sex pure and simple. In fact, I would call it an art, because to do it right, you don't do it by impulse, but by skill."

"What do you mean?"

"Well, I can remember a time when I was cruising in a shopping center, where all the guys go. It has lots of mirrors and windows, so you can watch each other up close without looking directly at each other. You just sort of stare each other down, like two stalking animals. I like to feel the vibrations.

"Anyway, this guy I was cruising comes up to me and says: 'Let's go to my place.' I can smell immediately we are into each other. Ten minutes later we are at his place, and right off we're doing things my lover of six years is still too embarrassed to try. But here we are, two strangers, satisfying each other completely.

"I don't know if he likes cats better than dogs, or if his mother is dead or alive, or if he is, or wants to be, an architect. I just know him as another body. And for the, moment I feel totally committed to his body with my body. It's primitive, raw, simple, but satisfying. And from it, I get a thrill, a feeling of being loose, of being released from myself. I like being uncivilized for a change. We are for that moment two unknowns fully knowing each other."

"But isn't it dangerous. What if you pick up a freak or a murderer?"

"Of course it's dangerous! That's part of the thrill. But I am not afraid of myself, and therefore I don't fear strangers. If you have any doubt, let him go. After a while you get good at it."

"I'd still be careful, if I were you. It only takes one bad time, and you're done for."

"No man, you miss the point. You are the danger, you are the stranger, and you are the one you have to fear or love. For, if you don't love yourself, you can't love a stranger. And if you can't love a stranger who can you love?"

chapter seven

AN ADMITTED HOMOSEXUAL | 1979

John Wayne Gacy[15] is, as the newspapers report, "an admitted homosexual."

He also is "suspected" of mass murder. He is "alleged" to have molested, strangled, and murdered as many as 32 young men and boys.

The horror of the grim sex and murders has been reported with great caution. Everything he might have done is either "alleged," or "suspected ," or reportedly "confessed."

But no newspaper has been cautious in reporting that Gacy is an "admitted homosexual." This is the only declared fact about Gacy that all the papers seem to state without hesitation.

Call someone a murderer before trial without saying it's "alleged," and he'll sue your ass

---

[15] John Wayne Gacy, 1942-1994, was convicted and later executed for the murder of 33 young men and boys between 1972 and 1978, when he was arrested at his home, outside of Chicago, Illinois. Twenty-seven of the bodies were buried in his crawl-space; 2 under his garage and driveway; 4 more were found in the Des Plaines River, west of Chicago.

off. But call him an "admitted homosexual," and make that charge sound like some great crime, and then everyone in society will understand what he has really done wrong. And he won't be able to sue.

For in our society, to be an "admitted homosexual" is to be a sexual criminal.

All the laws for consenting adults, all the movements for gay rights, and all the liberal commentators who say being gay is no different from being left-handed, have not changed the gut reaction of the majority.

If you do sex wrong, then you can be assumed to do anything else wrong too.

You may be living a comfortable, bourgeois, quiet life with your lover in the suburbs. You may think all those dirty fags who get beaten up in the city are getting what they deserve for living so screamingly open. But then you, too, get hit in the stomach with the whopping headline telling of sex crimes in the suburbs.

And in all the initial blurred stories of how many bodies are here and there, one fact is stated without doubt: John Wayne Gacy is an "admitted homosexual."

Yet, ironically, the one fact all reports are so clear about, was the one central fact that John Wayne Gacy never was clear about.

He really never was able to admit to himself or his world that he was a homosexual.

Sure, he admitted it once in an Iowa courtroom. And they promptly sentenced him to ten years in jail.

But none of his fellow prisoners recognized him as "queer." He made no homosexual advances in the homosexual setting of prison. In fact, when most of his fellow prisoners heard he was in for sodomy, they thought it was some kind of mistake, he must have been drunk one night. That's all.

He carried on regular sexual activities with each of his two wives. But when he tried to tell his wives about his homosexual desires, they were shocked. And soon he was divorced.

So, every time he "admitted" being a homosexual, he got punished.

Could he tell his neighbors? Could he tell his fellow Democrats? Could he tell, as a clown, his audience? No. Could he say: "Well, folks, your precinct captain is a homosexual."

Sure, a few would admire his courage, if he had told. But then a few months later, he probably would be replaced. "You know John, we really need a family man in that position. You know how things are."

To admit that you are a homosexual still means: That you will probably become an outcast in your family, a sinner in your church, and a pervert in your society. In short, a sexual outlaw.

Gacy, of course, is too banal and too grim, too horrible and too extreme, to be much of an example to anyone about anything.

He is a super-victim. He can't draw a straight line between murder and suicide, between heterosexual and homosexual. He kept trying to bury his homosexual present, in order to preserve his heterosexual future.

So forget Gacy. What about the kids?

Yes, indeed, what about the kids. What about the many thousands of kids still out in the suburbs who are wondering about their own sexual orientation. They, of course, have just received in the media a brutal lesson in sex education. And now it is going to make it even more difficult for any of them to admit to themselves, their family, or their friends that they are homosexual. For admitting homosexuality now is seen to be on a par with confessing mass murder.

So even more kids will grow up feeling they have to repress their life into a closet. Forgetting that to try to live in a closet is very much like living in a grave.

chapter eight

CHIC TOLERANCE | 1979

It is becoming chic and fashionable now in some circles to tolerate homosexuals. Even *Time* magazine says homosexuality is a private affair, and should be nobody's public business.

To make homosexuality a strictly private affair is an attractive proposition. It appeals directly to our sense of individuality and narcissism.

If two guys want to own a condominium, and they have the money to pay for it, what does society care how they carry on in their urban enclaves. Let them even have a couple of token representatives on the city council. As long as they keep their sex quiet, discreet and private.

On the surface, this chic tolerance seems fair. But besides being patronizing, this attitude hides two serious misconceptions.

First, after years of pinning the wrong names on homosexuals as freaks or sickies, society just can't get up and run away as though nothing had happened.

It's like the bully who quits in the middle of a fight and says: "No hard feelings."

Society at large will have to stop using homosexuals as their easy target of fear and hate, before any real change of attitude happens. And to confine homosexuals to their own pleasure islands and urban ghettos is not a policy of real tolerance.

Second, chic tolerance fails because it views homosexuals as some kind of social eunuch. You have nothing to offer society, so stay in your bedroom. That's where you belong.

All societies have defined homosexuals as useless people. Homosexuals do not reproduce their species, they do not have children and raise families. They make no useful social contribution. Therefore, even in the best of societies, they have no rights to share in the goods of society.

True, some lesbians are mothers and do fight in the courts to keep their children. Some gay men do father and raise children. But in the main, society is right: Homosexuals don't reproduce the species, and don't raise families.

Many homosexuals, in fact, feel very ashamed, embarrassed and somehow inadequate because they don't have children.

This marks them off from the rest of society. No one to care for. Thus, because they can't pass on their family line, they feel that they are making no real contribution to society.

Often gays, in fact, resort to noticeably flamboyant and near hysterical behavior to cover their sense of loss and inadequacy. Sometimes it gets so lonely being single, that a single gay will play at being his own family: Play being mother, father and kid.

But the trap in this argument is in accepting the definitions of society as given, and as true. Reality is both a given and a gift. Homosexuals don't have children. That's a given. But they have a unique gift: They seem to possess an almost prophetic understanding of the family and society.

Psychologists just now are recognizing that homosexuals are absolutely different. That is, they can be both asocial and sane. And being outsiders, they reflect not so much what is wrong with themselves, but what is wrong with the conventional society and family.

Sociologists just have recognized that the family not only is the most loving and supportive institution in America, but also the most violent. Thus, homosexuals as a given, don't share in full family love; but as a gift, they also are free from traditional family patterns of violence and aggression.

As a given, homosexuals do not participate in the conventions of society. But, as a gift, they truly are free from those conventions. Conventional art, music, biology, psychology, and politics all have forms based on the family with its tradition of the one-man dominance of the father.

Homosexuals live free from that traditional dominance, and thus can create from their own experience new forms, new ideas and new fashions and directions.

Call it fate, or call it God. Or, call it arbitrary chance, being a homosexual is not a little private matter. And it's not just confined to the bedroom.

Too long society has wanted to reduce homosexuality to the frivolous. Homosexuals can be cosmeticians, but they cannot have a cosmic mission.

Granted as a given: Society will usually choose its leaders from the family--people who will reproduce other people in a conventional way.

But as a gift: Homosexuals don't have to participate in that conventional charade. For their chief function in life is not simply to reproduce the species. Indeed, if you look at the whole process on a more evolutionary scale, you might find that homosexuals are the guardians of the species.

chapter nine

FIRST PERSON: OLD MAN SEX | 1979

"Gays fear growing old more than dying.

"At least that is the way I have always felt. If I grow old, I'll lose my sex. And, if I lose my sex, by definition, I'll no longer be a homosexual. Thus, I'll lose my identity, too.

"As I say, that's what I always thought, until I had an unlikely encounter with an old man named Reginald Carter, or Reggie, as he liked to be called.

"I am 29 and I've only been out and openly gay since college. When I first came out I tried to make up for lost time. I was heavy into the gay scene, and particularly fond of chicken.

"I spend all kinds of money cruising, dating and chasing guys younger than me. I always said I would never go to bed with anyone older, anyone who did not have a pretty face. Not even for money!

"But, to be honest, with the kids I struck out a lot. I have more rejections than an amateur poet.

"But sometimes I'd get lucky. Date a pretty one for a while, till he tired of me. We split. And I'd be back in the scene again.

"Weekend after weekend to the bars. And, if no luck, to the baths. Where I never let the drunk old men come into my room.

"That was my weekly routine, and I knew I could go on a few more years, until old age hit me.

"Then, as I say, I met Reggie. He was waiting for a bus at Chicago and State. A man between 57 and 65, wearing an old suit coat he must have gotten second hand. He had five cigars in his pocket and a scuzzy beard. From all I had ever been taught, he was a bum.

"Why we started talking baseball, I'll never know. And then he sat next to me on the bus. He had a roving eye and a twinkling charm, and one of those deep sea-captain voices that fascinated me.

"When it came time for me to get off, I said I was going to get coffee. He asked if he could come along and I said OK.

"Really, I had nothing else in mind. He was nice and all, but he reminded me of my sexless grandfather.

"He saw me cruising a young guy in the restaurant. He winked. As much as to say: 'Try something better, try me.'

"Of course I didn't get the young guy. And Reggie cut right through my pretense. He said, 'Chasing that stuff, you sure must like to get your heart broken.'

"Then he asked if he could come home with me. I said 'OK, But no funny stuff, Old Man.'

"He said that I had a lot to learn. That he was not into funny stuff. That his generation had manners and that he knew how to respect my wishes.

"And at my place, we talked more. He told me about growing up Catholic. But he never could square with the church because they told him he could be a homosexual, but it would be a sin if he committed a homosexual act. He said it was just like those religious fanatics who had taken over Iran--they kill the queers first.

"As he talked, I forgot he was an old man. I didn't see his old man face staring at me. I felt a warm presence instead.

"Obviously, he wanted me. And I enjoyed being wanted. I felt like I was the young guy I was always chasing.

"Like I was becoming my dream.

"It was so easy. I opened up to him as I had never opened to anyone before. With young guys, I played like I was in a movie. Tried to make them. Make it. Never let it happen.

"But with Reggie it happened. He took me 'around the world.' Except, when we started, I told him I wouldn't kiss him on the face.

"Reggie made me realize that young guys, despite all their macho pretense, only have oral and genital sex, not full body sex.

"Reggie had me so worked up, I never even knew when he came inside me.

"He idolized me and I enjoyed being on the receiving end of someone else's dream. And, of course, I reciprocated. I gave him all I had too.

"I could see the thrill in his eyes. He was alive.

"The next day, when he got up to go, I kissed him on the mouth. His old face did not embarrass me anymore. He thanked me. He said I had done an old man a 'good trick' and God would see that I got justice too, someday.

"That last look in his eyes I will keep with me: So peaceful. I had seen one man at least, face old age, and accept life's situations.

"And I know I will be able to do it too someday. Sure, I'm still out cruising young guys. I haven't lost all my taste! But I am, I must confess, a little less afraid of old man sex."

chapter ten

FAGGOT CHICAGO | 1979

Now that the *Sun-Times* is writing freely about gay Chicago, it's only fair to do a column on faggot Chicago.

Gays learn what they do from faggots. Gays do what faggots do, but they try to make it seem more respectable.

Straights are also fascinated by what faggots do. They also want to know what faggots do, but because faggots are dirty, straights never want to interview or come in direct contact with them.

So straights are always learning what faggots do third hand: by watching and interviewing gays. And that is why a series such as in the *Sun-Times* is positive and supportive of gay life, but it contains some distortions of what is actually going on in the gay community, because it censors the dirty part, the faggot element.

Reading the *Sun-Times*, you would think that gay Chicago is a one bar, one bath, one church organization, one newspaper town.

So naturally a fag rag like *Gay Chicago Magazine* gets scant mention.

True. A lot of liberals and ex-hippies and nervous gays don't want *Gay Chicago Magazine* on their coffee table. *Gay Chicago* might burn their straight cover, as well as their table top.

But Ann Landers has no trouble with us. She reads and recommends us. Because that lady knows mass markets and trends. She knows that the gay community is not just one big committee or club or congregation of leaders; but it also contains a hard core element of street people: the faggots.

The fault with the *Sun-Times* series is that while it clears up many old myths about gays, it also creates some new ones.

Trying to be so in the know about our world, they invent a glossary of terms and say: "Fag hag - heterosexual women who hang out with gay men."

Fag hag is an ugly word, ten times worse than spinster; and anyone who uses it is going to say things that are either very cruel or ridiculous.

Parents, who can just barely cope with the fact that their son is gay, will now, because their daughter hangs around with her brother's friends, have to think their daughter is a fag hag.

Jane Byrne[16] has a lot of gay men hanging around her. Does that make her a fag hag?

No one is going to understand gay terms, gay politics, and gay movements until they figure out gay life derives its energy, and direction from women and faggots.

A faggot is not gay by the luxury of choice: sometimes gay and sometimes not. A faggot is queer from the get go: it's the way he looks and the way he is.

No hiding the fact.

A faggot knows you cannot wait; you can take your freedom now, because it's yours to take.

Faggots don't have to wait for City Hall, or a proclamation from the White House.

A faggot has no time to wait. He is a faggot whether his parents know or approve, whether his society knows or approves.

To have fair standards and human rights will help the non-gay treat us better. Will help them.

But a faggot cannot wait for them, for he must be the way he is now.

If that means you are a dirty transsexual, and that some nights you have to walk the streets turning tricks for $6 and a cheeseburger; well, that's the way it is, and that's the way you are. A faggot can handle that!

---

[16] Mayor of Chicago, 1979-1983.

Faggots don't take crap. They don't even try to make sense out of bad theology, or cheap politics.

They know you cannot exist being a homosexual without doing homosexual acts.

They know that the same politicians, who ten years ago were telling Blacks you can't legislate morality, are now trying our morality.

They know that a self-proclaimed city hall chaplain and an ex-mayor are not going to keep a faggot from his freedom. I mean: it's nice that pair get along so well, go hand in hand together, play religion and politics together, share tax shelters and campaign committees together.

But, we would wish that they would have the good sense to realize that their jogging suits and jogging shoes were designed no doubt by a faggot.

Faggots are like roaches, indestructible and everywhere.

No matter how elegantly you try to picture gay life, they will always be around.

Faggots are like Jean Genet; they can take the worst situation and turn it into sainthood.

You can neither give nor take away their dignity and freedom.

For: if you are a faggot and the world comes down hard on you, you don't turn a cheek, you turn both cheeks, and make sure you get a good fuck.

chapter eleven

OVERHEARD: BACKROOMS | 1979

"I don't like backrooms!"

"You mean, like they have in police stations?"

"No! Like they have in some of our bars."

"But not for long. Did you hear? Mother Carol[17] has closed her backroom, and says it will stay closed forever."

"Good! Backrooms are bad business and bad sex. Straights aren't allowed to carry on like that in their bars, and it's not right for us either. We've come a long way: you can do anything you want as a consenting adult: behind closed doors, and we don't need orgy rooms in our bars. They are illegal, and I agree with the law: they are out of place."

"Who doesn't agree?"

"Yes. There is absolutely no justification for having a backroom in a bar. Look. We've got bookstores, and baths. Those are the places for that kind of stuff. It's only greedy bar owners who

---

[17] Popular and well-known Chicago bar owner.

let it happen in their bar. That's their way of keeping their customers in their place all night. That's all. Pure greed."

"O.K. You're right. What can I say?"

"Of course I'm right. Backrooms cannot be justified. No way. Look: not even our radical gay activists will touch that issue. All our leaders are unified on this point. None of them condone what was going on in the bars. Our only protest is the way the police overreacted, and used unnecessary force on the patrons coming out of the bar. No one will defend what was going on in those bars."

"Phil, have you ever gone into a backroom?"

"No, why should I? I have a lover."

"I have a lover too, But I've been in backrooms. I've even been in one with my lover."

"Well, at least you were with your lover and not getting a disease from some stranger."

"Sure, there's a medical risk."

"Oh, Jerry come on, there's a medical risk, a legal risk, and a lover's risk. What lover will tolerate that kind of promiscuous behavior for long?"

"Not many, I guess."

"You guess? None! Can you really justify sex in a backroom? A momentary experience that won't mean more to you than taking a shit."

"Well, I could say I did it because it was fun."

"'Fun'? Oh, come off it Jerry. You did it because you were drunk, loose and horny.

"You think you see a pretty face, or an ass you want to grab. You follow him into the dark room and play grab-by grabby, slobber a couple of kisses that reek of poppers and stale beer--and suddenly you're in heat. And you have sex. Fifteen minutes at the most!

"Then you crawl out of the backroom and see your partner in the light. And he, turns out to be just like you:a wrinkled-face, thirty-eight year old aging architect. Big deal! You call that fun?"

"Well, you've got me there."

"No Jerry, I'm sorry, that's where I draw the line. Sex between consenting adults. Yes. Sex in backrooms. No. Never."

"Phil, have you ever done sex when you weren't consenting and weren't an adult?"

"That's a stupid question! What do you mean?"

"I mean you articulate everything very well. And you're very legal and precise."

"Jerry, and I'm also very practical."

"Yes, practical, right, adult, proper, sure!"

"Well, what's your point?"

"Point? Damnit, I have no point. I can't justify backrooms. I'm not the devil's advocate. And I can't penetrate your legal mind either."

"Well, don't try."

"But, there is something more to this argument--I know."

"Say it then."

"How about: no one is free, until everyone is free."

"Nice rhetoric, bad politics."

"No, Phil, not rhetoric. Not politics. Not social. Just layers and layers of shame."

"You're not making sense."

"Shame! Society hates gays. They are ashamed of us. We fight their shame, and win a few rights. We can have a loving relationship. But not in public. We can share condominiums, wear furs to Superman, and act like a proper married couple. But all behind closed doors."

"So?"

"So, there is more. That's all. You see gays are also ashamed of other gays who play around in backrooms, are perverted. And we turn on them like society turns on us."

"So. Can't free everybody."

"No, you're right. The heat's on. And we've got to keep things down, I know that. But still. . . "

"Still?"

"Gay sex is not like straight sex! It can't be put in boxes. We can't use straights as models or parallels. And someday we've got to open ourselves to the idea that just as a commercial, artfully done, can be as good as a movie, so a momentary experience, tastefully done, can be as good as a life time."

chapter twelve

WHO'S SICK? | 1979

Question: Who's sick?

Answer: The person who has the disease.

Question: Who has the disease?

Answer: The person who is dis-eased, not at ease with himself.

Question: Then, does that mean, if you are a homosexual, you are sick?

Answer: Only if you are dis-eased, that is, not at ease with yourself.

Question: But how can you tell? Who knows?

Answer: That's the tricky part. As everyone knows, homosexuality is perverse. That means its pathology is also perverse.

If you have a cold, diphtheria, glaucoma or athlete's foot, you are the one who suffers the discomfort, therefore you are the one who is sick, diseased.

But if you are a homosexual, you feel no discomfort yourself until society intrudes and calls it wrong.

Homosexuality is perverse, because it is a disease that society, not the individual spreads and communicates. Society makes you ill at ease, sick over it; but you are not sick with it.

So we end up with a near comical situation where the people who have it, the homosexuals, are not sick; and the people who don't have it, but are worried about having it, or getting it, are the sick ones because they are least at ease with it, and thus most dis-eased by it.

So homosexuality is a perverse disease that strikes the non-homosexual worse than the homosexual. And the consequences are always comical and sometimes fatal.

Norman Mailer is a good example of a non-homosexual. No one has ever accused him of being one, and he has continually confessed and advertised in all his writings that he is not a fruit.

As a kid, Norman wore what all you Jewish and Irish kids wore: little Lord Fauntleroy Suits. He looked very foppish. He grew up at the time the American melting pot was in; and every Jewish and Irish mother imitated the Queen of England and dressed her son like the Prince of Wales.

As a young man, Norman left Harvard to become the great American novelist and joined the army as a cook. He scored big with *The Naked and the Dead* so he was on easy street at 25.

During the '50s, he slummed in Hollywood and Greenwich Village, invented the concept of the White Negro, toyed with the existential hero and stabbed his wife; came up with his Reichean theory of orgasm being the great it (which really is another way of saying love is rape); bullied and mocked Adlai Stevenson for being too soft and too fey; and dismissed James Baldwin, Gore Vidal, Truman Capote and Tenn Williams as impotent freaks; that is, men inadequate because they couldn't, wouldn't or didn't have sex with women.

During the '60s, Mailer did his best and worst; his *Armies of the Night*; and his great dud, the moon shot autobiography. But even in his best work, he never caught on that the army of the night was made up of mostly fairies. He went through another series of wives and women, finally confessing at the end of the decade that he was a prisoner of sex.

The '70s found Norman going deeper into alimony and debt, and back to his mother.

Sadder yet, after all his wars of conquest, he still knows nothing about women. He never caught on to how much his scenes and heroics bored them; how they were tired of the jerk who couldn't handle himself, who was never at ease with himself, who was either excessively brutal or excessively sentimental.

And then the knock out blow: all the women liked all the fairies better, like Gore and Jimmy and Tenn and Truman better than Norman. They would rather be a companion to a queer, than bed partner to a fake.

Norman never did figure out that a self-centered Hercules, even with all his labors and feats, is a gigantic bore. If he had wanted to be that self-centered, he should have been more gay about it, and let the Narcissus inside himself out.

That's exactly what Gertrude Stein had told his literary father Hemingway years ago, when she predicted his ultimate conflict and suicide.

These big tough propagandists for the American male fail, always fail because they can't love themselves, their homosexual selves. Their gigantic systems fall on top of them and we see them for what they are: not tragic heroes, but comic failures who can't handle themselves; cannot be at ease with themselves; men who are always calling us what they are: inadequate and immature; always calling us homosexuals when it is their problem, their disease.

So I ask you again: who's sick?

chapter thirteen

HOT BODIES AND BROKEN HEARTS | 1979

"Wow, Francis, do you see that one--he's hot!"

"Greg, how can you see anything in this dump--the cigarette smoke is burning my eyes."

"No Francis, he's hot, and a butch number, too. Look at those tight Levi's."

"Swish, swish, swish--he looks like another stuck up queen to me. Why is it every little queen you cruise is suddenly a butch number?"

"No. Francis. He's hot. Look how he just sits there with his hand wrapped around his beer bottle. Boy, I'd sure like his hand wrapped around my beer bottle."

"You're just horny, Greg."

"Of course, why do you think we come here. To meet guys, don't we--you know, to get together."

"Oh, I suppose so, But it's all so boring. Hot bodies and broken hearts. These hot guys are all the same, cold inside. They go home alone, and we go home alone. Same old thing. I don't even try anymore."

"Maybe that's your trouble, Francis. You're too cynical."

"Maybe. But I'm not a fool like you, chasing after what I can never have, getting my heart broken all the time."

"Look at him now--he's looking at us. Look, he sees me."

"Wise up, Greg, with those spaced-out eyes, your Wonder Boy isn't seeing anything. You're fooling yourself again."

"Oh, I've got to go over and talk him. But I don't know what to say. Oh God, do you think he will--he's so hot--like me? What should I say to him?"

"Tell him you're a Libra from San Francisco, and you're looking for some balance in your life."

"Oh, God, Francis, he's going to go, he's leaving."

"No he isn't. He's just going to take a piss, he'll be back."

"Good, good, you're right. I'm going over there now and I'll be sitting next to him when he gets back. He's so hot!"

"You're the one who's hot, Greg. He's cold, if you ask me. But go ahead and get your heart broken, if you want. I'll wait for you here."

"Well, Greg, back so soon? How did it go? As if I didn't know."

"He said his name was Bill or Phil, he mumbled so I couldn't tell."

"Then what?"

"He said he was from Fargo, North Dakota, and he had been to every bar on the near north side, and that he and his friend had been tossed out of lesbian bar ..."

"Real macho men, aren't they?"

"Let me finish. And that his friend had slipped in a mud puddle coming over here, and was changing his clothes and would be back soon."

"A brilliant story teller! What else did he say?"

"Oh, he said he was a Capricorn, born on the cusp."

"Oh, a horny old goat ..."

"What?"

"Go on, finish your tale."

"No more. Then he just stopped talking; went dead, like his recorder had shut off. He just sat there and stared off into space. I made a few more efforts at conversation, but he just looked more bored. So I came back."

"Well, that's your hot butch number for tonight, I guess."

"God, Francis, why does this always happen to me?"

"Because you cruise guys who are out of your class. Cheap nothings, the hunky hitch-hiker type, little egocentric brats. You cook gourmet omelets for them in the morning and all they want is a box of Total.

"Greg, here you are, one of the leading authorities on oriental art in Chicago, and every weekend you come to this sleazy bar panting after spaced-out runaways from North Dakota. I don't understand it."

"Balance, Francis, balance! I hate my type, all these pseudo-intellectuals living precise, measured lives. The phonies I have to work with in the week. I come here to get away. I don't want to be the authority, the father, the one who knows it all. And these spacy kids let me get out of myself, into them, and feel something firm again. It revives me, Francis."

"Maybe. But someday one of those hot bodies is going to tie you up and do you real harm."

"Cut the superstition, Francis. You've given up. It's easy for you to stay within the confines of your professional world. Never trash, never test your dignity. Always play it safe. OK. That's fine for you."

"But I've got more fire inside me that wants out. And these hot bodies, even when I don't get them, keep me burning. Do you understand that?"

"No. Not really."

"You see, Francis, I'm not afraid to get my heart broken. I'll take my rejections, but I also will get my moments. I'm not giving these kids my long-term love, access to my Swiss bank account. We just exchange a little momentary heat in a very cold world. It's my way of keeping the fire burning and stay alive. Don't you see, Francis."

"No. Not really."

chapter fourteen

"SLEAZE BUCKETS" | 1979

We, that is, homosexuals, or as they like to pronounce it on television, HOmo-SEX-U-als, are more and more in the news.

We are in the news because they want to know about us.

Often, journalists report on our activities as though we were a sub-species, a sub-culture, or some subterranean night crawlers from another planet.

The rule is: when talking about homosexuals, keep your distance. Never expose your own sexuality. Hide behind your objectivity. But this rule and style of reporting often breaks down, because in matters of sexuality, there is no clear and fixed distinction between them and us.

When you are talking about homosexuality, it is hard to tell who is them, who is us, and who is hiding. The traditional canons of objectivity fail.

People are always saying you can't be a little pregnant without eventually showing it. True. But you can be a little gay without ever wanting to show it. In fact, that's the state most people live in.

And so, since there is always a little bit of us in them, journalists have difficult time with us.

Most journalists, when talking about homosexuals, get their facts right, but err in interpretation. For straight facts often lead to queer interpretations.

Roger Ebert in his review of *Nighthawks*[18] (*Sun-Times*, Oct. 16, 1979), for example, has all his facts right, but his quasi-objective and distant point-of-view distorts his interpretations.

For Ebert, Nighthawks is a movie about them (gays)--for them. And his conclusion is: let's hope nobody is like them.

He keeps his critical distance from us and our world, and he dutifully reports in his liberal family newspaper that gay is sad, and gay is bad.

Factually, he is right: *Nighthawks* is a dull, uninspired, two-star movie. It has left town after a week at the 3 Penny.[19] Even with foreign kudos, it couldn't hold an audience: gay or curious.

Jim, the school teacher/nighthawk, is an anti-anti-hero: so ordinary that he stirs little more than a yawn. Sure, he does the best his lukewarm

---

[18] 1978 independent film.

[19] Art-film theater on Lincoln Avenue, now closed.

British flesh will allow, but he has a difficult time keeping a stiff upper anything.

The movie is so ordinary, in fact, that it begs all kinds of interpretations. And a critic can't just say, "well, folks, that was one I slept through." So Ebert fills in with gratuitous interpretations and musings on gay life.

For Ebert, Jim is a victim, his haunts are gloomy, and his life, dead end. And the last and only good thing you can say about the movie is that it was playing at the 3 Penny, and not at one of those male "sleaze buckets" on Clark Street.

For Ebert, Jim is a victim because he cannot find an "Enduring Relationship," which according to Ebert is the "social epidemic" of the 20th century.

But: male homosexuals have been having and surviving transitory relationships for centuries. It's nothing new for us. That's why we are probably better able to cope with this urban situation than most self-proclaimed, married-again monogamists.

True, among homosexuals you will not find too many American Gothic, til-death-do-us-part couples. In a gay "marriage" it's more likely that both partners will be holding a pitch fork.

There are millions of couples in New York, Chicago, and London who have discovered that an exclusive, one-on-one relationship is not essential. Many of us don't even have an enduring weekend together.

But that does not mean life is a horror show. It means we have changed our expectations, or totally abandoned them. And for us it's not a dead end; it's a life cycle on speed.

Further, to call homosexual haunts gloomy is a prudish cliche. Gloomy for whom? That's where we find other guys, our sex partners, our sun shine.

It might seem sad to you, an outsider, because you are not there for what we are there for. But the wait is worth it, honey; the wait is worth it! For when the arrow hits the target, you scream inside like a Zen master.

And as for "sleaze buckets": I remember the Newberry Theater,[20] now a parking lot on Clark. Cold seats, fat men, leaking roof, stink bombs, and the projectionist sleeping at the switch.

Who used to go there? Dirty nighthawks. Sure.

And kids from the suburbs. Who found out about the all male sleaze bucket from reading Roger Ebert's *Sun-Times* movie section. And since they never read about an all-male anything else,

---

[20] A gay porn theater.

they would flock to the Newberry, often for their first coming out experience.

Yes, I remember one kid, in his early twenties, arriving at the Newberry on a cold, rainy Friday: going to the bathroom, showing a half of dozen men what he had to offer: and then, leading them, like a good shepherd, down in front to the cement floor, and while another dozen men watched, he made sure there were a lot of satisfied customers at the Newberry that night.

And all the while he performed, there was a movie going on above them. *Duffy's Tavern*, with a couple of long haired blond kids making it on a pool table, while the Stones rolled on in the background. Talk about *Apocalypse Now*. Talk about a real movie experience.

So, Mr. Ebert, do keep your critical distance: for if you were to slip into one of the sleaze buckets on Clark Street, and review one of our movies, it just might turn out to be a living experience.

And if you looked down beneath the screen, I just don't know who you would recognize.

chapter fifteen

SOMETIMES | 1979

Sometimes I get upset by what I see going on in the gay community. Not always, but sometimes.

Being gay for me has always been a privilege and most of the time a pleasure; even when it is a pain, I secretly enjoy being different.

But sometimes I get upset.

I don't think diseases and addictions are cute or fun to spread.

And if you become hooked on being gay, until it becomes your addiction, that's wrong.

Oh I know, even heroin for some is harmless. Keith Richards could sleep with death and wake up the next day reborn.

But, when I see a kid burnt out and prematurely senile, scuzzy, all his teeth gone or black, with sickly yellow hepatitis skin; with scars and gashes on his arms from dumb attempts at suicide with a coat hanger, my stomach turns. I get upset when I see kids trying to make their gay identity their sole existence. When it becomes their only habit. Trick and party, drugs and sex and always on the empty run.

I get upset when I see kids living in isolated rooms; barren, self-imposed jail cells. Rooms without plants or animals or things to care about. With no space for the internal growth of the soul.

I get upset, because I know that your cock will not endure alone; and that your brain is your primary sexual organ.

O.K.: to drop out of school is not wrong; schools being in the mess that they are, so anti and so authoritarian. In fact, to drop out is probably a positive rebellious act.

But you cannot drop out of learning, drop out of growing and self-teaching, without destroying the roots of your own curiosity and freedom.

The body can take waste and abuse; but the mind won't function in disuse. Fortunately, a way out is easy.

Across the street from the Abbott Hotel[21] there is a public library; across from Bughouse Square,[22] there is the Newberry Library;[23] and

---

[21] Transient hotel popular with gays.

[22] Park known for cruising.

[23] Esteemed research library.

within blocks of the bus depot, there is the Art Institute, and the City Colleges are open to any citizen of Chicago, high school graduate or not.

So, being gay doesn't have to be your only habit, your only problem, your only way of being. Thus, you should be able to come out of your gay experience with something more than an expanded asshole.

Another thing upsets me: If sex is not mutual, sex is dumb. Sex cannot be done one way. If you've ever been a good fuckee, you'll never be a good fucker.

And there is no one dumber than a fist fucker who doesn't know what it is like to be a fist fuckee.

I know it's cute and "in" these days to wear your red hankie, left pocket. And say: "Oh no I'd never let anyone do that to me!"

I'll do unto you, but you can't do unto me. That's raw hubris, an act of total violence, all commandments broken.

Oh I know, there are receivers of the fist who say the experience is near nirvana.

But Nirvana is dead.

You meet a doped up kid at a bath for twenty minutes and fist him on the spot. You are not a proctologist; you have no rubber glove. And you have no interest, or commitment, beyond the twenty minutes.

But if there is a speck of bacteria on your hand, or if your fingers slip, or one of your nails is chipped, you can damage the soft tissues of his colon forever. So that for the rest of his life, your twenty-minute lover will have to wear one plastic bag to shit in, and one plastic bag to piss in.

Fist fucking is a violent act, in a way as horrible as abortion; and surely infinitely worse than leaving a woman pregnant.

So, one-sided sex is wrong.

Gay sex is not wrong because it happens in a glory hole, behind a bush, or in an orgy room; gay sex is not wrong because it is often brief and repetitious; gay sex is only wrong when both guys don't share the moment they have together. Brevity only means that the quality of feelings have to be stronger and purer.

A final thing that upsets me: A kid's mouth on a man's cock does not offend me.

A man's cock up a kid's ass does not offend me.

Sex for money does not offend me. People barter sex and money in almost all social relationships. Who hasn't read the marriage contracts of Jackie O?[24]

But when a man reaches out to a kid with genuine care, when he exposes his soft side, and the kid just uses him to get money, dope, a stereo, and drinks, that offends me. When a kid becomes a human Acujack, and stays with his "customer" only as long as a cigarette lasts; that offends me.

And, if the old troll whispers even a mild complaint, then the kid uses that as an excuse to beat him up, tie him up, slash him up--for he's just an old faggot anyway--that offends me, that is evil.

And on the other side: Men who use their official position to trap and hustle kids; when they are, or pretend to be, counselors, law officers, doctors, priests, only to get into a kid's pants, that offends me.

And by far the worst of these are men who sell God and hustle kids. Their churches are fake, their credentials self-invented, and their doctrine perverted.

---

[24] Jacqueline Kennedy Onassis, 1929-1994, was married to John F. Kennedy, 35th President of the United States; Kennedy was assassinated in 1963. In 1968, the former First Lady married a shipping magnate named Aristotle Onassis, with whom she remained until his death in 1975.

Even if they do not have sex, they force the kids to suck their dogma. Their act is cheap, dishonest, and evil. So pardon me. But sometimes I get upset by the things I see going on in the gay community.

chapter sixteen

THE ST. JAMES FAMILY | 1979

A gay family? Impossible. Gays don't have families.

A gay family that gives a baby shower. Double impossible! Gays don't have babies.

Well, the St. James Family does!

When I first heard of the St. James Family, I thought it was pure hokum. An embarrassing spin off from the disco hit *We Are Family*.

That a group of gays could get together and call themselves a family seemed to me very suspicious. It must be a cult, some kind of sex ring. Or a ship of sentimental fools.

That two mature Taureans in black leather jackets with cock rings on their epaulets, could call themselves Mom and Dad, and have a group of fifty children--who also called them Mom and Dad--seemed silly, forced, and unnatural. And that this so-called family would have its headquarters at Mom and Dad's on St. James Place, the shortest street in Chicago--a street previously known for its millionaires, hospitals, and black hookers--only added to the craziness.

But, after watching them for over a year, I have discovered that the St. James Family is a mixed group of warm individuals, who are learning to cope effectively with separation and loneliness in a big city. They have put together a unique association that preserves the best traditions and conventions of a healthy family; yet, which also allows each member of the family to be gay, different, and free.

Even if you have never seen the St. James Family, you have probably heard them, because they are a merry bunch of hard laughter. The Dutchess, alone, can keep the whole family laughing until they want to be chained. You have probably heard them kidding each other, and judging the hunkiness of strangers as they pass, while they eat their Thursday night dinners, or their Sunday breakfasts at the Random House.

Or, you may gave seen them at Darche's, Robert's Lounge, The Baton, El Jardin's, Dion's, The Gay Pride Parade, roller skating near the lagoon, or marching en famille into the Columbus Hospital to visit one of their own; or parading en masse, down Clark Street in various costumes to one of their family parties on Fullerton.

The first most striking thing you may notice about the family is that nearly a quarter of them are women. Everyone in the family is gay, in spirit; and each works openly for gay rights. But sexually, all you can assume about the family, is that the majority of males are homosexual, and that the majority of females are heterosexual.

The second thing everyone always notices about the family is that they have strange sounding names like: Princess NoNookie, Aunt Laura, Clyde, Golden-Rod, Farmer-John, Navy Brat, Connie Continental, Judi's Straight Man, Enchilada Sue, Contessa, T. Bitch, Aunt Gabby, Debbi Dimples, Esther Rose, Closamae Monaise, Chatty Cathy, Bubbles, Dego Dick, Tallulah, and Sister Titanic (so named, because she is always likely to go down). From their names, about all you can conclude is: if it sounds like a girl, it's a boy; and if it sounds like a boy, it's a girl.

Third, just as you can't have a real family without a real Mom and Dad, so the St. James Family has a real Mom and Dad in Bob and Bruce.

Twenty-one years ago, when Bob and Bruce got together, all their friends said it would never last 90 days. And their marriage would never produce anything. Well, Bob and Bruce have been an openly gay, one bedroom couple, long before most of us dared even to use the word gay in public.

They have shared about everything you can share in a gay relationship; both have worked, both have cooked, both have fought for their rights, and for the rights of all people to be themselves. And now, after twenty-one years, at a glance, they know what each other is thinking.

Dad is a perfect Dad: handsome with a beard and supremely patriarchal. He can trace his mystical ancestry back through the American Indians to the ancient Kings of Jerusalem.

And there is nothing half-way about Mom's past either. She can tell you about what it is like to have your first gay experience at 14 on a fire escape in Normal, Illinois; and she can tell you how she got through the Korean War by being a fox, without ever having to sleep in a foxhole. Mom can do Edith Bunker in drag so well that she makes people come up and ask for autographs.

Mom and Dad are a real modern couple: completely capable of reversing their roles. This year, for example, Mom works and Dad cooks. In fact, Mom and Dad seem so comfortable together that straights in their neighborhood do not feel awkward calling two men Mom and Dad.

As in any family, when quarrels arise, father always knows best. But the reason Dad knows best in the St. James Family, is that he listens to Mom (at least, the next day).

Although Mom and Dad, with their warmth and conventional wisdom, set the tone of the family, they are not the center of every event. Aunt

Laura, for example, was in charge of the family for its super-trip to Great America.

What makes the family work? If you listen to Dad, or read their coat of arms, you might think it's love and understanding.

That would be nice, but a little too ideal. Frankly, not everyone in the family loves each other all the time; and surely, not everyone in the family understands each other.

If you have a big problem, the family can't necessarily be a big help. If you are suicidal, need more than $35, need a lover to go home with for the next twenty years, the family can't help. But, if you don't like living alone in a single room, don't like to have a cold for five days with no one caring or bringing you chicken soup, then the family can help.

The family is good at practical caring. Good at the old plain virtues and natural excitements. They care enough to ask: how are you. They care enough to help you move. They care enough to remember your birthday. And they care enough to make sure you are never alone on a Sunday or a holiday.

About the only thing all members of the family have in common is their healthy, voracious appetites. They love to eat.

That is why, when they get together, they often talk about simple things like food: Mom's beans, Mona the Maid's pumpkin cheesecake, Dad's turkey soup, Tallulah's chocolate-chip mint cake, Bubbles' blueberry pie, (Navy Brat's cakes too, except I've never known him to bake one), and Ione's black olives and homemade wine.

Sure, someone from the family can be seen almost anywhere gays meet; and three of the family went to the march on Washington[25]. But the St. James Family is not a social-political organization with formal rules and regulations. Nor is it a club or fraternity with initiations rites.

The family started out a year or so ago, as a party of six, at a table for eight, and now it is a party of forty or fifty, at a table for Mom, and a table for Dad. Some of the original members bitch and say its grown too big, too fast. My God, who are these people who say they are in my family, out singing Christmas carols on Clark and Diversey.

But they miss the point.

The St. James Family has grown, simply because it meets the practical needs of a lot of gay people in Chicago. For there is no warmer feeling than to know that there are fifty people out there, who don't care if you are gay, but who do care for you.

---

[25] March for Gay Rights, 1979.

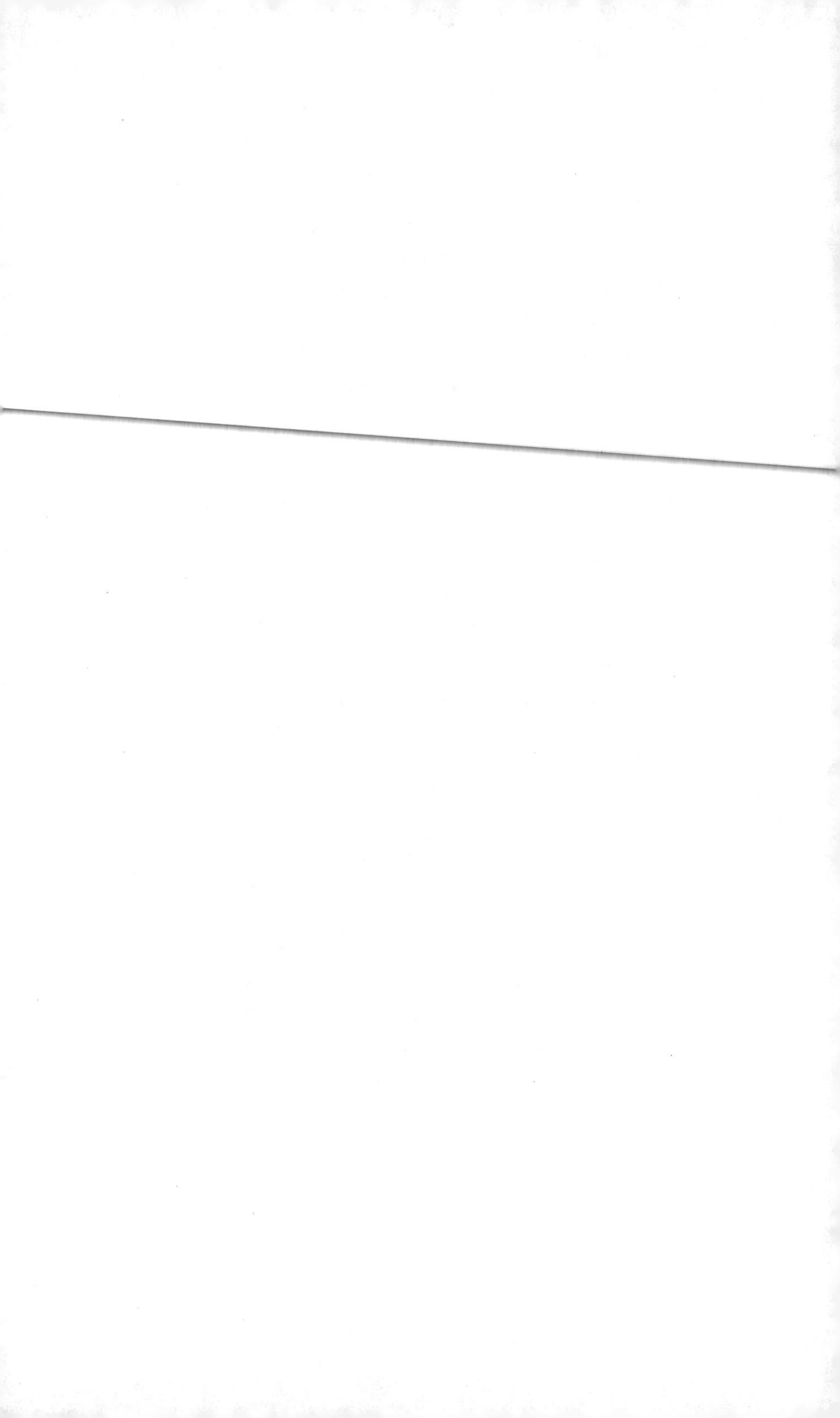

PART TWO

chapter seventeen

OVERHEARD: "FAT HEAD!" | 1980

"I'm 56, and all my life I thought I had a weight problem.

"Well, I have: I've been a fat head!

"You may know me, but you don't know who I am. Just say that I reside somewhere in Chicago, and that I have a good job in hospital administration.

"Oh, my name is Archie. Or, at least that's the name I was born with, and the name my mother always called me. But it's the name I hate. In school I was known as Arthur, and my friends called me Art.

"I've never had any problems being gay. Except: I've never told my brother. He's 61. And no one at work knows. What I mean by no problem is that I'm not like my college chum Paul, who got arrested for exposing himself in the Bus Depot in Ames, Iowa. Nor have I gone to a Doctor about it. That's what I mean by no problem.

"My problem isn't being gay, it's that I've been a fat head all my life. I mean in the way I've chosen my lovers and friends.

"It all started for me in school. I mean little school, in the fourth and fifth grades. I had a crush on a little guy in our class named Tommy. He was either a year, or a year and a half older than the rest of us. He was rebellious, always picking fights with the big kids, and talking back to the teachers. I liked his hot temper.

"He was frail, left-handed, cute, a tough little kid; no boyish fat, he seemed like a little stud even then.

"That summer our family went to Colorado for vacation. I rode horses and played cowboy, and saved all my allowance money, and with the silver dollars my uncle had given me, I bought a real man's cowboy hat.

"I loved that hat so much I took it to bed with me every night. Then, when I got back to school, I gave that hat to Tommy. I don't know why. He never gave me anything. He never fought the big boys for me. In fact, two months later, I never remember even seeing much of him again. And I can't ever remember him thanking me for the hat.

"He just took it, that's all. And I didn't really get to be friends with him. When we were eighteen, he went off to jail, and I went to college.

"Mikie and Lesley were also in my class. They liked me, I know. But they were so dull. They didn't know how to wear their Levi's. How to roll them. They didn't even wear Levi's! Mikie wore thick glasses, carried lizards in a jar, knew all about biology, and nothing about sex.

"Lesley was, as his name implied, a little on the fairy side. He wore green on Thursdays, or whatever it was that gave it away in those days. So we were never close, because I didn't want to be seen with someone like that.

"I still have my crushes and choose my lovers just like in grade school. By now, I have known hundreds, if not a thousand Tommys; and I never have given even a return phone call to the Mikies and the Lesleys.

"What a fat head I've been! If a guy likes me, I'll have nothing to do with him. But if he abuses me like Tommy, I'm in love with him.

"I can't tell you the money I've spent on my Tommys. Clothes, meals, loans never paid back, airplane tickets, skis, rent, dental bills, electric guitars, stereos. Sometimes I feel I don't have a house, I have a warehouse.

"And it always ends the same. No thanks. That's what I get. Let a kid stay with you till he gets a job, let him burn your coffee pot and rugs, smoke you out of house and home, till he finds a job or a new Sugar Daddy and leaves you. And no thanks.

No deposit. No return. I might as well have slept with a coke bottle. What a fat head I've been!

"But I had the money to spend. And if I didn't get real love I got some real sex and real excitement. So I don't have a lot of regret over my Tommys. Where I've really been hurt in life is not by Tommys, these false lovers, as much as from my false friends. People who have given me nothing but aggravation.

"You see, I'm a nice guy and I always try to be fair and give people the benefit of the doubt. Treat them like I'd like to be treated.

"I voted twice for Adlai Stevenson and cried when he lost.

"I voted for Jane Byrne and cried when she won.

"I'll probably vote for Anderson[26] this time. I have no quarrel with the world. I like all kinds of people. I'd like to see Bert Parks stay on as MC of the Miss America Contest.

"But my friends take advantage of me and my doctrine of fairness.

"I was in a small investment club with Harry and Steve. I put up most of the money, and they lost it. Now they blame me because I won't put up

---

[26] Former U.S. Rep. John Anderson (R-Ill.) ran as an independent in the 1980 presidential campaign.

any more money. They say I'm cheap. I say I want my $15,000 back. And they make me feel guilty.

"Then there's Roger and Bill, they are always stealing my Tommys. They call my house and make dates with my boys, with no regard for my feelings. They treat me like a closet midget.

"I now realize you can't treat everyone fair. Give an asshole the benefit of the doubt, and you'll make him a bigger asshole.

"The clue is: if a guy keeps saying he's your friend, you're the only one he trusts etc. and you keep trying to balance things in your mind, while he is always rude to you and makes you feel uncomfortable in your stomach, then you should know you've not got a real friend.

"Don't try to play an ethical chess game with people, if you don't feel right about them in your gut, forget them.

"For example, I've known Peter for six years. I always have to call him, he never comes to my home or office. When he was sick I helped him with his bills.

"But when I was in the hospital, he was down in Miami with one of my ex-Tommys, and neither one of them even sent me a card.

"What a fat head I have been! You know right away when someone is rude to you. You don't have to go along with it.

"There have been so many people good to me that I don't have to put up with assholes.

"What if they don't like you then? So what if they don't like you now, that's why they are rude to you now, dummy!

"It isn't that hard to feel. Pay a little more attention to people who feel for you now and avoid the rest.

"False friends have no feelers, no guts, no insides. They are just like a TV voice box, but with no soul. Sure they will take your bets on the Cubs, talk about the old times and the old movies, their trips to New York. Even seem fascinating for a while.

"But they are only voice boxes, they have no feel for you.

"Well, I don't want to bore you with my life story, telling you what you already know; the point is: a false lover will not hurt you as much as a false friend.

"You can fake romance, because of its brevity, but you can't fake friendship, because it has to go a long time.

"So I'll probably still waste a little more money on another Tommy or two.

"But never again am I going to waste a New York second on a false friend."

chapter eighteen

GACY ON DEATH ROW | 1980

John Wayne Gacy is now on death row.

He who lived like an executioner shall die at the hands of an executioner.

Gacy used to brag about his famous rope trick. Now he'll learn that the State of Illinois has a famous chair trick that will fry his brains.

Even those against capital punishment find an exception in Gacy's case.

Not only did the jury from Rockford vote death for Gacy, they were totally unmoved by his lawyer's psychological plea for insanity.

Despite Gacy's last clowning around in court, his telling the judge he didn't know if he was an onion or a piece of Swiss cheese, while he winked at his guards and smirked at his prosecutors, the court bought none of it. They simply decided that this clown will never again get away with murder.

It is a decision that we all can live with quite comfortably.

They say nothing clarifies life like death. So with the trial over, and Gacy on death row, we should be able to think about him in simpler terms. We can stop talking about him, in guarded legal and psychological language, and simply ask: Why did he do it? What kind of man is Gacy? And what about his victims?

I would like to make three observations, two of them are not my own. They are speculative. But I offer them not asking you, to agree, only asking you to think.

Why did Gacy do it? Kill 33 young men and boys?

My senior citizens, in a class on Contemporary Thought, came up with the best idea why Gacy did it.

"Mr. Damski," they said, "don't you realize he did it for the thrill of it! It's not homosexual, it's not psychological, it's that some guys get a thrill in killing. Like the Boston Strangler, Gacy did it because he enjoyed it, got a thrill out of it."

My class is predominantly women, ages 62 to 96. I was stunned by their insight. But senior citizens have minds that are tough and alive, they can cut through the bullshit; they have lived through enough to know how things are.

Sure Gacy is a monster, and what he did is evil.

Most of us read murder mysteries and go to movies. He acted out his own thriller.

Death and love, love and death in fantasy often go together. Our ego is always telling us: "Find me someone who will love me to death."

Death is the flip side of love. Read western literature, read Shakespeare: the word love, and the word death often mean the same.

So all of our elaborate psychological theories about Gacy being a driven man, sick, a compulsive monster, and a homicidal maniac, living a sinister life, cruising lurid homosexual haunts, bagging boys in his crawl space, and sleeping upstairs on top of the corpses--all our theories that make exciting reading miss the point: Gacy did it, and did it repeatedly, because he got off doing it!

Okay then, what kind of man was Gacy that he would get off on murder?

After the trial, I was discussing Gacy with my friend Omega Michael, and I was asking the usual questions: do you think he was sick, psychotic, neurotic, did he have gene damage, brain damage, etc.?

And Omega said: "No, no way, Gacy is not sick. He's an animal, a manipulative animal with a brute soul. He is always a clown, and he is always conning us.

"Look at him now, smiling, calm, calling in the prosecutors telling them, 'No hard feelings, boys,' Telling the press he hates to be alone on his 38th birthday.

"What's he think we're going to do? Send him a kid?!

"No, your senior citizens were right. not only did Gacy get a thrill out of what he did, he is enjoying every moment of the publicity: he's clowning with us, faking heart attacks, getting all our attention, making headlines, becoming the crime of the century--he is eating it all up and he is very pleased!

"How many fathers get mad at their kids and really want to give it to them. Pow! But they hold back. Gacy didn't. He's all animal. He gave it to them, and got a total release from it."

Personally, I don't like either of these ideas. They disturb me. But I think they come close to telling why Gacy did what he did, and what kind of man he is.

For six years, he did get away with murder! At least 32 times!

There is no punishment on earth for what he did. There is no multiple death for his multiple murders. It's horrible he has gotten away with all that aggression.

Death row and the death penalty are not enough. Will he go off to Hell, and live like evil men do in the pictures of Hieronymus Bosch? Or, will he go no where, and mock us for eternity?

Finally, what about Gacy's victims? The young men and boys.

The papers and TV have favored the prosecutor's side. They focus on the 15 year old Robert Piest, the last victim. The good kid from the suburbs.

But 11 of the 33 victims have not yet been identified. No parents or friends come forth for them. And at least half of the 22 named victims were not all that good, or pure.

They were runaways mostly, like hundreds of others living on the streets of Chicago. They failed at home, church, and school. Or more accurately: home, church, and school failed them.

Some of them are hustlers. They prey on gays. They are little street clowns themselves, who pretend to like, or sexually tease older men, so they can get money to buy drugs and take out girls.

And some of them were bad kids, running around with bad company: kids who have jumped completely over the Wall. They are the kind of kids who listen to Pink Floyd, who tells them: "We don't need no education."

And for many, Pink Floyd is right: the Chicago Public School System sucks! It is corrupt from the janitor to the superintendent. The teachers who make the biggest impression on kids are sadistic, and the rest are indifferent. And the good teachers are forced to shut up.

Some of these victims listen to Black Sabbath and were eager to try the occult and the kinky. They were looking for someone who could really do it to them. And Gacy did.

Nobody wants to face it: but some of these victims, with their teasing and hustling, virtually picked up Gacy. But the saddest thing about the whole Gacy mess is that many good gays, I could almost say "straight" gays, don't want to have anything to do with kids anymore. Too much risk!

For if you even try to be friendly with a kid, and you piss him off, because you tell him he ought to get a job done, or watch his dope, he can always turn on you and tell the police you're trying to hit on him like Gacy.

A lot of gays would make good teachers, counsellors, and social workers, because they have a compelling need to love kids; but for their own protection, they will be driven away from helping kids.

So, while Gacy sits on death row laughing at us, because he is going to escape here, the rest of us stay here too scared to love a kid.

And that's the real crime of Mr. Gacy.

chapter nineteen

COPS & GAYS | 1980

Cops and gays will probably always be at odds.

Even in a society like ours, where each year we all celebrate our independence, still, in the main, gays are not free to be cops, and cops are not free to be gay.

Cops and gays have a deep, mutual suspicion of each other that amounts to an innate and incurable prejudice. Most cops think all gays are faggots. And faggots are weak, skinny, limp-wristed, no-account, boy-girl sissies that can be toyed with like toothpicks. Many gays think all cops are pigs and bullies. And that all cops are out to hassle, intimidate, harass, arrest, and get them.

The game of cops and fairies goes on in all the streets of America; and there is visible evidence to support the prejudice of both sides.

There are some outrageous sissies, who do swish by and taunt and tempt every policeman they see. They want the cop either to arrest them on the spot, or take them home. And there is a minority of bully cops, who at the sight of someone they even suspect is gay lose all their professional cool. And they say things like: "Forget it, it's just another faggot getting beaten up."

In fairness though, probably college professors, and surely bankers, are just as prejudiced, as a class, against gays as are policemen. But because some gays and cops are more often seen confronting one another on the streets, cops, unlike professors and bankers, are less able to finesse and hide their prejudice.

Some police departments, like San Francisco, openly recruit and hire gays. But in the real world, even in San Francisco, a known gay cop is looked on suspiciously by his gay friends as some kind of undercover agent. And if a gay cop has to do his duty and arrest another gay, he is made to feel like he is a turn-coat and a betrayer of his kind.

Most police departments, like Chicago, will have their superintendent and P.R. men saying: "We have no policy against hiring gays." But then, on a force of 12,000 "men" no one can ever find, or name one.

Cops and gays have one strange link in common: they have to keep secrets.

Secrets are a cop's business; and being secret about it, not telling anyone, has, in the past, almost been synonymous with being gay. And if you are a cop, who is also gay, you have to be very secret. You have to live, not just in a closet, but behind a glass shield. Everybody is always watching you, looking for your secret. As a cop, to keep your gay life secret, you may even have to beat up a few faggots, so none of your superiors, or your wife will suspect.

When you are Black or Latino, all your cards are always face up on the table. The prejudice always shows. But when you deal cops and gays into the same game, most of the cards are held face down. No one ever knows for sure who is what.

J. Edgar Hoover,[27] the most famous cop of our time, lived most of his life, with his mother; he had a constant male companion whom he ate with everyday and made Assistant Director, and to whom he left his car, his home, and his personal belongings when he died; he never married, of course; he confessed to one mistake of passion in his life, that of falling in love with, and doing a favor for Tallulah Bankhead: a most outrageous female female impersonator.[28]

---

[27] J. Edgar Hoover, 1895-1972, was the director of the United States Federal Bureau of Investigation from 1924 until his death.

[28] Tallulah Bankhead, 1902-1968, was an American film actress whose first film was directed by the gay director, George Cukor. She also starred in films for Alfred Hitchcock and Noel Coward.

J. Edgar wore platform heels long before either Elton John or Kiss made them popular; he had his desk raised so he would always seem taller; and he was erotically obsessed with the way "his men," "his boys," dressed, groomed, and wore their neckties; "his men" were kept in fashions woefully out of date just to please their Director's own personal sense of interior design; and today, even in death, his gross building that he forced on the capital, stands in the middle of the porn belt and adult theater zone of Washington, D.C.

That was J. Edgar Hoover, the most famous cop of our time, who if not gay, and not homosexual, led a life that was very odd.

Ironically, gays and cops have an attraction and fascination for each other that is not easy to explain. They often relate to each other in the realm of fantasy.

Many gay men would like nothing better than to have cop for a lover. A cop to serve, and a cop to be their special protector. Many gays are turned on by uniforms, guns, handcuffs, a man who knows how to use his strength and power, knows how to show his masculine sensuality. Yes, many gays would like to have a real cop, for a real lover.

And many cops are more than routinely fascinated by gays: even the Marilyn Monroe sissy type. The pressure and frustration of being the big tough hero, a marriage growing stale; years to go before the pension comes; tired of doing society's shit work, dealing with scum bags and garbage; and training yourself not to feel: not to see how people on the streets suffer.

Yes, there are cops, who would like to put down their blue armor. Would like to have a young man lie next to him; and bring out of them something their wives can't do as well: bring out the young man still inside them to have and to hold. Hercules should, now and then, sleep with Narcissus: for the sanity of both.

Back in the real world, however, cops and gays are not allowed to act out their fantasies together. That's why they more often act out their frustrations, and make war, not love on each other.

A couple of weeks ago, in Milwaukee, a cop put on a towel and went around playing a very strange game of "search and seizure" in the dark hallways of a private men's gay bath house. After he had felt and seen enough, he called in his buddies and they rounded up 25 men. They detained them for several hours before hauling off five of them to the station.

It reminded people of an earlier raid in Milwaukee when the cops asked questions like:

- "Do you like to be the top man or the bottom man?"

- "Do you like to suck dick?"

- "Or do you like to get it in the ass?"

Of the remaining they arrested a couple of the more closeted ones for previous parking violations. The raid intimidated the whole gay community of Milwaukee, and everyone that heard about it was angry.[29]

Cops do have the power and authority to be irresponsible. They can make your life uncivil and miserable for 24 hours, while they play games, and enforce, not the law, but the superstitions of society.

We can be detained. But we sissies cannot be stopped.

We will get our lawyers and our money together; and sometimes we will suffer a few hours of harassment and intimidation. But we won't be stopped.

For we know, and we have read what it says it Article IV of the Constitution of the United

---

[29] Over a decade later, these same attitudes in Milwaukee cops would lead to horrific outcomes with the case of Jeffrey Dahmer. See Damski's commentary, beginning on page 347 with "Dahmer be Damned!" and continuing with "Cops Who Played God" on page 353.

States: "The right of the people to be secure in their persons, houses, papers, and effects, against unreasonable searches and seizures, shall not be violated."

When we sissies go to our private bath house, it is our home for those few hours, because society will not let us live and be ourselves anywhere else. And when cops lay a hand on us there, it is our person, our gay person they violate, when they try to search and seize us in our "home."

So, there is one new thing that cops will have to learn about gay people: We sissies don't have to make a declaration, or raise defiant fists: we have grown tough and independent in "our gay person": and no cop in a bath towel is going to come into our bath house and take away our constitutional rights, or our bodily commitment to be a free, gay person.

chapter twenty

OVERHEARD: OUTDOOR LOVE | 1980

"Doug, I'd like to hear you explain why you think you need to go to the park two and three times a week and have sex right there in the bushes, outdoors, and in public?"

"Explain, Bruce? What is there to explain? It's my theater."

"Pretty silly theater, if you ask me, where you can at any moment be hassled by the cops, or be beaten up by fag hating punks."

"Yes, it involves some danger."

"Some danger? What about the time those four Latinos found you giving a blow job to a guy and chased you both all over the park?"

"Yeah, but I ran to the yacht club and hid in a boat, and they never found me."

"Okay then, what about the time the cops came into the bushes on horses and took all your names. You were scared for weeks that they would come and arrest you, or tell your boss at work."

"You're right those things happened to me. And I have heard of some guys really getting the shit knocked out of them, and the police forcing gay guys to give them head and never tell about it.

"But in six years, those were the only two bad things that ever happened to me personally. I know the danger. It makes me cautious, but it also gives me a hard-on almost as soon as I walk in the park at night.

"The park is my theater, and danger is my stage cue. It turns me on."

"So, Doug, when you go to the park at night you are just thinking of your own turn-on, your own little personal gratification. What if people see you? What if a young kid sees you? That just brings everything down on all us gay people. A lot of us more respectable gays are trying to win our rights, and your adolescent antics in the park--the way you think you have to play cowboys and chicken in the dark and be big tough sexual outlaws, is only going to keep all of us down, all of us from getting our rights. Do you ever think of that, Doug?"

"Yes, Bruce, I do. I don't want rights, I want freedom, mine and yours.

"Are you going to wait until America, the sexual hang-up society, says it's right? That's bullshit! It may be rude and in bad taste, but I want my freedom indoors and outdoors, and right now."

"Freedom to fuck in the park? Psychopathic behavior is freedom? No, Doug, I could only consent to things like that being done in private."

"Behind closed doors?"

"Yes... "

"And closed minds!"

"No. But you should show some respect: decent guys are trying to win their rights, and all you want to do is go fuck in the park. Why there?"

"Because I came out there! Bruce. Because that's where it happened to me the first time: Where I learned to do it, and where I've learned to love to do it.

"The first time. It was an early April night, I was 15, and a real loose guy with sky blue eyes, long black hair, and a big flat nose that was fun to touch, wearing a Rolling Stones tour T-shirt , yellow gym shoes, came by, got off his bike and sat next to me.

"It was getting dark, and we talked about everything, looking out over the smooth pond. He touched my leg, and asked if he could see it.

"See what? I don't know what he was asking.

"He started to zip down my pants.

"There was this smell of bicycle tire on his hands. That and the smell of pine trees, dirt, and wet grass made me feel at one with him and the outdoors.

"I loved the way he kept softly rubbing my eh...and under my crotch. I got real excited, and he went down on me. That was it! For me, my first.

"He let me kiss his hands. And I licked them, I licked the tire smell right off them. Then he rode off.

"And that kind of stuff still turns me on, more than any bedroom. It's my theater!"

"Okay Doug, you were lucky, you had a nice first coming out gay experience. But theater? You're getting to be a 26 year old man, it's time you grew out of these teenage fantasies.

"Besides, what kind of theater is it? You never get to know anybody. You hardly say two words to them."

"The other night I said four words.

"I saw this muscular young Italian-looking kid by the statue smiling at me. He had his hand on his cock, rubbing it inside his Levi's.

"But at first, I wondered if he was a fag beater tempting me. His age and signals were ambiguous.

"He hesitated a little too. He probably thought I was a vice cop.

"We danced around each other gesturing for about five minutes.

"Finally I went beside him, let my leg rub his, and said, 'Quiet night.'

"Eighteen minutes later, he said, 'Suck it.'

"Those were the only four words we spoke. But I tell you Bruce, for those eighteen minutes I devoured that kid, and he possessed me.

"After I shoved poppers up his nose, he went wild. Hands and fingers in my mouth, he was all over me.

"I kept looking behind him on the statue wall where they had written in Puerto Rican gang script the letters, F.K.O.: Fag Killers Organization.

"That excited me more. Because we did it on their turf. We fucked under their sign, and conquered. This kid stranger and I didn't go and petition for our rights, we didn't kiss some closeted politician's asshole, we didn't go down to Springfield, we went down on each other, outdoors, took our chances, fucked, and took our freedom.

"That's my theater, Bruce."

"Theater, Doug? Pure self delusion, cheap self gratification. You got your rocks off in a park with a teenager. So now you are a life-time member of Psychopaths Anonymous."

"You don't know what you're talking about, Bruce. I gave my whole self to that kid out there, and he gave me, for those eighteen minutes, every inch of his love.

"That's something you never forget: you feel it forever!"

"Just pathological sex. If it were so satisfying, why do you keep going back for another try?"

"For the luxury of it all, Bruce. I've had so much of it I want to share it, share my riches.

"Can you understand that, Bruce? I go back only for memory sake. To remember the dream. When I do this one, I remember what it was like for that one. And I remember everybody I've been with every time I do someone new. It's my way of passing it on, and saying thank you. Thank you everybody!"

"You do get theatrical, don't you Doug? But in my book, what you are doing out there in the park is sex, pure sex. And there is no love in that kind of encounter."

"Wrong, Bruce! There is no love for you in that kind of encounter. People who put sex and love in different boxes are just voluntarily schizophrenics.

"For me, love and sex are always the same. It's the same quality of feelings. Your character shows, shines on like a crazy diamond, in everything you do.

"Eighteen minutes or eighteen years, it doesn't matter how long you have been together with somebody. Your character shows.

"Don't you see, Bruce? That's how I show myself. That's how I love, and shine with my outdoor men in the moon."

chapter twenty-one

AN ERRONEOUS PROCESS | 1980

"Coming out" has often been described as a trauma, a tragedy, a triumph. A ritual, a birth rite, a time to discover yourself and to assert your gay rights. In short, a serious process.

I would like to take an opposite view and propose that "coming out," the whole thing, is an erroneous process. Something much more human, and much less serious than we usually take it to be.

"Coming out" is an erroneous process in three senses of the word erroneous.

First, the whole coming out process is erroneous from the gay point of view, because it is something in a free society no one should have to do at all. You should not have to go underground, and feel like a borderline criminal to be yourself.

Why should a mature lawyer hesitate before entering a gay bar, for fear that one of his clients might see him?

Why can't two men or two women rent a one bedroom apartment? Do they always have to have a second bedroom for show, and for the landlord's conscience?

Why should society intrude upon your private affairs, and tell you who to love and who not to love?

Second, the process of coming out and being gay is erroneous from society's point of view. It is deviant behavior. "They" say, society says, it is not right, true, or proper.

Even if it is not a sin or a crime in some states anymore, the majority will still say that it is a big mistake to be gay. Your parents and friends, fellow-workers and well-meaning advisors will still think you are doing something erroneous, that is, making a big mistake coming out and being gay,

But, the bottom line on any conflict between what society says is right, and what the experience of gay sex is really like, is always determined by whose ass is, or is not, getting kissed.

If Tom and Gary kiss each other's ass in bed, and give each other a rim job, and Tom places a hickey, a three-day love tattoo, on Gary's ass and both get up the next morning feeling totally released and totally together; and Tom goes off to be a damn good computer operator, and Gary goes off to be a brilliant classroom teacher, both guys, being perfectly healthy and sane, and neither of them have any urges to rape any children on the way home from work, but both are happy and gay and love to kiss each other's ass, tell me then: how does society lose?

It doesn't! Tom and Gary are said to have engaged in a social, deviant behavior because they will kiss each other's ass, but they won't kiss society's authoritative, symbolic ass.

All over this country, every hour of the day guys and gals are doing gay sex and finding that they do not lose their eye sight, or their ass the next day.

Society, however, still extends the old masturbation taboo to cover gay sexual activities. You do it, and your cock will fall off. You do it in the road, and we will take you to jail and cut your cock off.

So, when two guys or two gals do actually have sex together, and find it to be their health and pleasure, of course they become more radical, question "society's values," and then stop kissing society's ass, because they each have one of their own to play with.

Yes, when you find society so wrong about something so close to you as you and your sex, you do become suspicious and more radical.

And if you are forced to be more radical, your mind also opens to see words in their more radical or root sense. "Erroneous" is from the Latin errare, and in its root sense means: "to wonder about, looking for something."

That is, perhaps, the best description of what coming out, cruising and being gay is all about. It is a life long process of "wondering about, looking for something." It is being curious all your life.

And if people think you are a "curious person," because you never quite grow up, and you always stay curious and cat like, what's wrong with that?

Yes, being gay is erroneous, and your behavior is at times childlike and unpredictable, because you are always on the go, wandering about looking for something.

You never do become that fixed and final person, that finished product, that grown up adult. You stay erroneous your whole life. Your whole life is a charming and delightful mistake.

I think people become gay out of curiosity, and for no other real reason.

Like philosophy, and poetry, and music thinking about being gay begins as something erroneously wonderful.

You are looking for something, and there is Timmy, your buddy, sitting on your bed next to you. You like his smile, his curly red hair; he likes your hands and your blue eyes. You touch each other, you feel each other. You play with each other.

That's how it starts. And it is always specific. It is not something in nature, or in psychology. You like Timmy, and Timmy likes you. You like to please Timmy, and Timmy likes to please you. In the beginning you are not even conscious that it is sex, or even the same sex.

You have to find out later, when "they" tell you: it was sex you had with Timmy, and it was wrong, and it was the big mistake of your life; and if you continue you'll lose your ass.

In truth, the whole thing is erroneous and should not be taken too seriously. To err is human, as they say.

And if to err is human, then to be erroneous, to spend your life wondering about, looking for something, for something you never really have to find, is the most human thing you can do.

That is why some day, it may be recorded, that gay people are the most humane. That being gay is wonderful. A wonderful mistake.

Of course, some gays do carry their behavior too far; they won't associate with women, if they are leather men; or they won't associate with men, if they are leather women.

They get stuck in their poses, and they lose their curiosity: they don't keep looking, moving, going: everything is fixed and settled for them. "I'm a dyke, don't tread on me." "I'm a slave, tread on me!"

The whole process of loving and coming out is erroneous, so you've got to keep going, exchanging your self.

You might prefer blond, blue-eyed kids, who have nothing to say in the morning. Well, try someone your own size sometime; try an old man, you may really learn something. It may be fun to talk when you get up. It may even get you higher up. And women are fun too. If you wake up with one some morning, you won't lose your gayness.

Life is a parade. Don't get stuck trying to be one person. Each one of us is a parade of selves, a camp of people: a child, a boy, a girl, a dress, a pair of pants, a lover, a leaver, a chaser, a chasee, a good guy, a bad guy, an ass to kick, an ass to kiss.

Yes, each one of us is a whole parade, marching through an erroneous process.

chapter twenty-two

BEFORE PSYCHOLOGY | 1980

Before psychology, everyone was clear about what everybody had: everybody had a body and a soul. Our normal condition is a psychosomatic: soul and body, body and soul.

Today, we often sneer at the Victorians, the ancients and other old-fashioned people, because we believe they were repressed, and they didn't use their body in sex as many times as we think they should. And then some neo-Victorians, today, are worried that we are living dangerously, because too many of us are using our body too often in sex.

Both miss the point.

Granted: we are living through a time of easy vice. Some guys do have sex everyday, or every six hours, and keep penicillin at home in their refrigerator. This loose behavior is not actually dangerous, however, because it doesn't risk or expose anything, like your soul.

It can become a numb dumb habit, but it does nothing for the soul other than make it a curious adding machine in a numbers game. But sex is more than a game of body counts.

We snicker sometimes at the Victorians, at the old-fashioned ladies like Sara Teasdale, Willa Cather, and Emily Dickinson, who seemed to find more glory holes in heaven than in bookstores. But these crafty Victorian ladies lived before pop psychology, and they would not commit their bodies to anything or anyone that did not also take their souls.

From our modern high tech towers, we look down on them and say: what those women needed was a good lay. But these quaint women tasted states of melancholy and desire deeper than can be explored by our jokes and our psychology. They left their souls to us in the body of their works. In their poems and their short stories.

Our crude jokes about them only give away our smaller sense of humor, and our smaller sense of soul. Before psychology, people had a larger sense of humor and a larger sense of soul. In fact, before psychology, people used to think your humor was your soul. A strange, but still workable idea.

Humors are the bodily fluids that determine the balance and temperament of your soul. The four basic humors are: blood (red),yellow bile, black bile (spleen) and phlegm (throat). The flow of these "humors" or fluids determine the makeup of your soul and personality.

John Kennedy could be called sanguine, because he seemed outwardly so red-blooded and bright looking. His ruddy brightness also indicated a shallowness of soul, not much depth. A charmer, more personality than person. Lincoln was full of melancholy, black bile, a deep and sad soul. An oceanic person. Nixon seems like a yellow-liver-gizzard. A jaunty rubber soul, that is always able to bounce back.

Mary Tyler Moore's humor is green, stolid and phlegmatic. Her humor is deeper than her jokes on the Mary Tyler Moore Show: hence she can also be a nice bitch in Ordinary People and in ordinary life. Her top side humor and charm hide a lot of pain; but her stolid soul is tough, and can survive many breaking points.

Modern psychology has never been quite able to live up to its name. Psyche/logia means to render an account of the soul. But because the soul is so unscientific and so unverifiable, the soul is often lost or forgotten in psychology.

Melancholia, for instance, if it is your humor, there is not much you can do to change it or cure it. It is not subject to behavior modification. Pop physiognomy might tell you to smile more. But after you leave the mirror of self consciousness, you will sink back into your natural melancholic humor.

Psychology does not promise and cannot give you a new "me," like a new car, new home, or new stereo. Psychology is useful for temporary clarification. Psychoanalysts can work like your private classroom, where you are the star pupil. But after psychology you come back home to your original humor.

When our high tech world of ideas and pop psychology fail us, we might then want to use some old Victorian artifacts like the concept of the naked soul.

No me, no single body can absolutely live with itself alone. Others help. And not just with their bodies, but also with their souls. It is as if we all come here with a missing element, and missing humor, a missing part. We are a wanting self. We lack and desire at the same time. And we want and are wanting a lot more than just a body: we are not just body snatchers, we are also looking for a soul mate.

When you are predominantly homosexual, this quest for a soul mate is even more vital and critical. Two guys sucking each other's cock or two women sucking each other's tits, has its narcissistic mode: you feel almost like you are doing yourself, when you are doing someone who is the same sex. It feels total, like the ultimate in satisfaction. It is about as close as one body can get to one body: one body be one body.

But that kind of total experience, even repeated often for verification, is not enough. We want more. We are a wanting self: we want a body and a soul.

The soul is the body behind the body, the body most invisible, and seductive. The body most alive when it shares a thought and not a genital. The body gives you clues to what can be. Chase a pretty face, find a model. But find a soul, behind even a less than model body, and you'll know what is. And your soul mate may not be one single person, like a wife.

Sex as sex is an old and ancient sport. Those who have mastered the game have tacitly recognized, like any other major sport, you've got to be willing to play some games at home, and some games away from home.

The body and soul makes you want both. One partner, many partners. For staying home with one captured person does not guarantee you will get that one person's soul; anymore than having a new body to play with every night, means you really get a body.

It takes some combination of both. Something from the middle. When you know what you are doing, moderation is the most dangerous way. It means, you want both, and will have both. You've got to feed a hungry body, and keep a hungry soul.

It also means you have to have a sense of humor larger than a joke, and some knowledge of science before psychology.

chapter twenty-three

DO-GOODERS AND DO-BADDERS | 1981

Most people want to do good in the world. Some people so obviously want to do good in the world that we call them do-gooders. Other people, however, are in such a mess in their life that no matter what they want to do, they cannot really do good.

We have no name for this messy kind because we always want to think positive about people. But we could call them "do-badders."

Many gays, because they are single and have above average intelligence and incomes, often have a great urge to help a friend, a kid, or a refugee from the street. So gays often turn up as do-gooders, and just as often get stuck in some do-badder's trap.

The do-gooder's intentions may be honorable and above-board, or slightly below the belt. No matter. Whether the do-gooder thinks he is going to get sucked or not, he will probably get sucked into the do-badder's mess. Then the do-gooder, after getting burned and ripped off, will often turn bitter and swear never again will I help a kid.

We all get caught trying to help in some way, at least a couple of times in life. It's like getting the crabs. Do-badders are like parasites, they look for a good host to snuggle up to, cling to, and live off. And sometimes you're it!

The do-gooder, do-badder trap has everything to do with character, and nothing to do with age, sex, or race. You can be a 50-year-old trying to befriend a 16-year-old Cuban refugee, or a 19-year-old trying to help a younger buddy.

The initial mistake most do-gooders make is they let impulse and chance rule; they don't consider the limits of their own time, money, and energy; they don't know what they can give and they take less care in picking a friend to help than in picking a house pet.

There are two kinds of do-gooders: the Jimmy Carter type and the Hubert Humphrey type.

Jimmy Carter thought because he was bright in school, always had the best ideas, the right ideas, was a brownie-point, four-point super-achiever, scored high on his college boards, worked harder, jogged harder than any other 56-year-old, was a clean, born-again Christian, that he could easily do good and help people.

Yes, Jimmy Carter was a good man, a self made man, a self made Christian and a self made President. But inside his soul, he had no fire, nothing to give: Jimmy Carter was a taker, not a giver. He appropriated everything good in his family, stole the good and ripped it off for himself. And he lorded it over his little brother Billy, whom he forced to play the sad role of a lazy redneck.

Jimmy was the good boy. Billy was the bad boy. Jimmy was clean. Billy was dirty. Jimmy was the saint. Billy the sinner. But Jimmy forgot that a saint can't help a sinner, they live worlds apart. Only a sinner can help a sinner.

Cleanliness is no where near Godliness. Jimmy was all good, but he had no humanity, no shit, left in him. No connection to us, and that's why he couldn't do us any good.

Hubert Humphrey was the other type of do-gooder. A real giver. He gave his time, his mouth, his ideas, his heart to anyone and everyone. In the end, he gave his hair, and his teeth, and his colon, and his body to medical science.

Hubert Humphrey gave so much of himself away all the time, that he was somewhat of a mess himself. That's why he couldn't help the rest of us, because he was a mess like the rest of us.

Hubert Humphrey ran a shabby office, had a fourth rate staff, ate too many cherries with red dye, drank too many Manhattans, and had the same kind of backers and supporters that now appear in pictures with Frank Sinatra.

Hubert Humphrey was a do-gooder, yes, but he knew he was surrounded by do-badders. And he let himself be taken by, and eaten by them, he didn't care, he just kept on coming and giving.

So unless you are willing to give that much of yourself, practically let people eat you alive, you will never make a real do-gooder.

If you are gay, you will also have to face the sex issue. If you help a kid, they will say you are doing it for sexual reasons.

As far as I'm concerned, all philanthropy has an erotic root. Cecil Rhodes[30] came back from South Africa with his diamonds, and his asexual lifestyle, and set up Rhodes Scholarships for bright young men, so he would always have young men around him. Behind his largesse was his love of boys.

So, if you take a kid off the street, and you tell him you have no sexual motive at all, you're just a Florence Nightingale with a big heart who likes to help kids, the kid won't believe you. Nor will anyone else!

---

[30] 19th century British imperialist in South Africa who founded the DeBeers diamond company.

The first question the kid will ask himself is: "Why is this old fruit helping me?"

So you might as well be honest from the start: "Yes, kid I am a fruit. I enjoy sex with young men. Obviously I would not have picked you out of the crowd, if I weren't attracted to you.

"No, kid you don't have to go to bed with me, to stay with me. But I do expect some affection from you, at least as much affection as I would get from a dog from the pound."

Tell the kid you do gay sex and enjoy it. You do bad shit too. It's what makes you human, healthy and whole.

Let the kid deal with you on your terms. Then you won't be pushed into dealing with him on his terms, and get sucked into his mess.

Don't let him tease and blackmail you with his bisexual confusions. Be straight with him: if he wants to learn gay sex firsthand from you, you will teach him. But it's his move, not yours. Let him think it out for himself and make the first move.

Innocence, like wisdom, is something acquired late in life. Kids are not innocent. They do everything adults do, they just don't want to be responsible for their mess.

If you are going to teach a kid anything, you will teach him to be responsible for his mess.

If he goes to a Ted Nugent concert, and hears his rock idol sing "Wang Dang Sweet Poontang," "Yank Me, Crank Me," and then leaves the concert with a girl wearing a No button, what's he going to do? Obviously, he's going to do himself, or one of his buddies.

These kids are into bad shit just like you: Don't pretend to be a saint, and don't let him lay guilt on you, because you do bad shit too. And some of these kids are real bratty do-badders. Their own home, school, church, and country couldn't straighten them out, so why should you.

If you sign on to help a kid, keep your gay sex and desires in the open, so he can't blackmail you. You probably will not succeed in every case, but neither do parents and grandparents.

And if you learn to give, without counting your losses, like Hubert Humphrey, you'll come out maybe not winning the first prize, but not being a loser either.

chapter twenty-four

LEFTY | 1981

Lefty, last January, quit his job.

In fifty years, it was the only thing Lefty had ever quit.

Except in 1948, he quit trying to be a major league ballplayer, as his father wanted him to be, after he got hit in the chest with a line drive, while he was trying to become a pitcher for the Sacramento Bees in the Pacific League.

Lefty was not a quitter, much more a joiner. He signed right up for the Korean war when his country needed him. Even though going to Korea meant he would have to postpone his wedding to Helen, the girl he had always thought he was going to marry. Helen was not the waiting type, however, and she married a beer salesman from Fresno, when Lefty was in Korea.

Lefty always looked and seemed ten to fifteen years older. That's why people even his own age would always lean on him. His buddies in Korea treated him like a trusted father: they would let him hold their money, and they always came to him for advice about dating, or when they wanted to talk to someone kind.

He liked drinking with the guys in Korea. In his camp his buddies were known as Lefty's "boys." But there was nothing overtly sexual in the way they got together.

Lefty was wounded twice in Korea, and spent several months convalescing in Letterman Hospital in San Francisco. Then for about eight years, he drifted around the country, using some of his disability benefits, and cash he would pick up from odd jobs.

After Korea, it took him ten years to settle down. He liked to drink and play the horses, he didn't want to wear a grey flannel suit. He liked playing with his buddies. He could never figure out why men in peace time jobs never seem to have as much fun as when they go to war together.

Lefty always thought he was going to get married. Even today he carries Helen's picture in his wallet. He still shows her picture to strangers in bars, and he never corrects you if you get the impression that he is going with Helen.

As far as Lefty sees things, he's not queer or gay. The few gay activists and peace protesters he argued with during the Vietnam days horrified him. To him they were freaks. Rule one: you've got to serve your country in time of trouble. Rule two: you've got to maintain your decorum at all times. If a couple of guys do something in private, who's to know?

There are a lot of decent ladies out on the streets, and Lefty thinks it is wrong to shove your "queerness" up into their face. As he is fond of saying: "You don't walk across your mother's garden in motorcycle boots!"

One day in the early '60s, Lefty was arguing with a guy, a "freak" in a bar, and the kid turned to Lefty and said:

"Hey Pop, where do you get off slamming on us freaks, when you're just a drunk drifter."

That kid woke Lefty up. In Lefty's mind he still thought of himself as being a fresh young kid out of high school ready to go to his career in baseball with the boys of summer. Even though he was technically approaching 40, he still imagined he had his whole life ahead of him.

So after the shock, Lefty came to Chicago in the early '60s and got a good job as a manager-maintenance man in a 64 unit apartment house.

Seventeen years ago when Lefty took over running his apartment, the units were occupied mostly by Jewish widows. Today, the building is mostly filled with junkies, blacks, and drag queens.

Seventeen years ago, his boss and his wife, the owner of the property lived in the apartment above him. Today, their nephew, a lawyer in Miami, is never around, he just gives Lefty his orders on the phone.

Seventeen years ago, Lefty got his apartment and $500 a month. Today he gets his apartment and $750 a month.

So for the last seventeen years Lefty has repaired air conditioners in the summer time, shoveled snow in the winter, hassled with tenants on a daily basis, broken up fights, been stabbed twice, been called everything from kike to queer, fought with the inspectors, paid off the precinct captain, worried with Abe and Sophie, the original owners, about Abe's heart and her diabetes and their no good nephew who would someday inherit it all.

But for the last seventeen years, no one has called Lefty a drifter. Drinker, yes. But not a drifter. He has not left his place, his building, his station, for even a day-off.

Does Lefty have any pleasures in his life?

Yes. One. When he was 37, Lefty discovered, by drunken accident, in a Y in Ann Arbor, Michigan, that there was another way to do it. He fucked a boy, instead of a girl. The first time he did it, he thought to himself, "Well, it's just like sticking it into a girl's pussy, and who will ever know the difference?"

Lefty also discovered that it is much easier to find boys than girls because runaway boys are always playing big man on the streets, and are always needing a place to stay the night.

Lefty never had any second thoughts about what he did in sex with boys. In his mind, even though fucking boys became a regular habit with him, he still never thought of himself as not being straight. Even after he bought Michael a guitar so he could become a rock star, Lefty never knew that Michael two weeks later traded his guitar with another guy so he could become a drug dealer.

Lefty's friends tried to warn him about Michael and his drug problem. But all Lefty could see was how young and pretty and thin Michael. was. How Michael looked 20 even though he was 32. The way Lefty had been taught when he grew up, if you took drugs, it would turn you into a contorted monster. He had no idea that some people actually look "better" on drugs. So, since Michael didn't look bad, Lefty couldn't believe that Michael was a drugger.

After Lefty quit his job in January, he thought two phone calls later could he could get another job.

Besides he had some money saved, and as an ace in the hole, he thought all these kids in the past he had helped when they needed some money would pay him back.

Lefty first used his savings, and he didn't make his two phone calls till March. Then he discovered: those owners of the other buildings, who had always wanted Lefty to come to work for them, suddenly had no jobs.

"Tight budgets." "Not hiring now." "Looking for someone younger."

By June, he was completely out of money. Walking the streets, like a runaway kid needing a place to stay. But who takes in a 53 year old kid?

Craig, Tim, and Michael did not have any more money now than when Lefty had first helped them: And they thought it was rude of him to even suggest or ask them for his money back.

Michael twice promised to come and take him to dinner. But he never showed. Partly because he was too high. Partly because he couldn't believe that Lefty, a big man, an old man like his father, could be in trouble. And because, he had never really cared for Lefty. He had used Lefty for a place to stay, and Lefty had used him to get off. End of their commitment.

Some of Lefty's friends are now worried about what he might do. But, of course, no one wants to take him in. Who is going to help a 53 year old kid? A boy-fucker who doesn't believe he is gay?

A couple of Lefty's friends asked him on the street if he had thought of suicide. Lefty's answered that he wasn't a quitter, he had never quit anything in his life.

And I guess he's right. Until last January, when he quit his job.

chapter twenty-five

FIRST PERSON: INTIMATE ACTS | 1981

"Hello, Jeff."

"Eh?"

"Hello, Jeff. Can't you say hello?"

"Oh, hi."

"You walked right past me coming in the bar, and I know you saw me because you turned your head away to pretend you didn't know me. Is it too much to ask, a friendly gesture, a hello?"

"No, but I'm with my friends now."

"Oh, and your friends won't let you say hello to your other friends?"

"No, but I'm with them now, can't you see?"

"Yes, I see. But you were with me 45 minutes ago in a bookstore across the street sharing the most intimate acts two people can share--there I was getting your love, passion, tenderness and affection, warm kisses behind the ear, and now 45 minutes later I cannot even get a 'hello' out of you?"

"Yes, but I'm with my friends now and what would they think?"

"What would they think if they saw you talking to me, an older man."

"Yes."

"Well, what would they think if I told them how you met me, and how you know me?"

"That's private. I don't talk to them about that I do when I'm out tricking."

"You can't tell your close friends about the guys you've been close to?"

"No, I just don't want them to know my business."

"Oh, so being with me was a business? Do you do this business often? Are you a hustler?"

"No, you're getting me wrong. I don't want to hurt you, but how could I tell my friends I had been with someone like you?"

"Because I'm 44 and you're 22?"

"Yes."

"Because I wear slacks and Pendleton shirts, and I'm not a clone of a clone like your tight circle of friends over there? Look at them. Britannia jeans, camouflage T-Shirts, and now like every other young person here: the clone's headband. That's not a circle of friends, that's a chain of clones in a look-a-like contest."

"They are not clones, they are nice guys after you get to know them."

"But who is there to know?"

"What do you mean?"

"If they dress alike, talk alike, smell alike, taste alike--what thrill is there in going home with a look-a-like?"

"We're just out at the bars, we don't go home with each other. We're just out for a good time."

"Boring! And, if you come over to talk to someone like me who is older, yes, but different, an individual, all your clone friends will evaporate? What would they do if you told them exactly how you met me, and what we did?"

"They wouldn't understand."

"If they are true friends and not silly clones I think they would."

"But how could I tell them?"

"Tell them, like you would tell any-one, tell them straight out, like Jimmy Piersall tells about baseball.

"Tell them, I didn't go after you in the bookstore, you chased me. I was ready to go home, and you asked me to stay and be with you.

"Tell them you were attracted to me, younger guys can get the hots for older men, too."

"They can?"

"You did. And, probably a lot of your other friends do too, but they don't know how to break out of their clone's closet, and talk about it.

"Tell them how you overwhelmed me with your tenderness and affection, how you hugged me, rubbed my back and cheeks, and licked me all over like an excited puppy.

"The only reason I responded so well to you was because of your tenderness. Sex is the easy part, you never expect, in a bookstore, someone to give you the tender feelings that poured out of you. That's what excited me. That's how I was able to make, or let, you cum twice. And as you said it was the first time you had ever been able to do that!"

"Yes, that's true. You are a good teacher."

"No, Jeff, I'm not exceptional. There are a lot of good men better than I am. It is just that you let yourself go with me. You went deep, intimate, you were hot, but you were also tender. You let all your feelings out. And that's why it was such a great release, and effortless the second time. We didn't try, we let it happen."

"I've got to get back to my friends now, they will be wondering about me."

"You still don't feel comfortable being seen with me, do you?"

"Well, to be honest, no."

"Well, I won't embarrass you much longer, but do you at least see whose fault it is?"

"Yes."

"Nor will I make you confess. But so many young guys try to make the older fellow feel that it is his fault. That being older is creepy. When that's not true at all; when you are young it's hard to break out of your circle, people won't talk about you if you stay in your circle of clones.

"And that's true. But the reason they won't talk behind your back, is that there is no one, no individual there to talk about. You may have a pretty face or a nice ass, but they don't talk about you individually, because there is no individual there. One pretty face, one soft ass is like another."

"I really should get back to my friends."

"I know, but you get garrulous when you get older, because you have things to say.

"Jeff, I am old enough to be your father, but I won't be your father tonight, anymore than I was your Big Daddy in the bookstore. You can go now, but I would like you to think about your behavior tonight.

"Being rude to me coming into the bar and not saying hello, right after we had just shared some of the most intimate and tender moments possible between two people, really cut me off.

"If I see you chasing me in a bookstore again, I'll say to myself that was one tender kid, and I will keep you in mind like a hot dream; but I would not touch you again, because I am afraid you will flip out on me again, turn me off again. Your unfriendly gesture, the no-hello, makes me never want to be tender or intimate with you again. You can't switch it on and off so fast.

"But forget me, Jeff. Here's the real problem: It's not that I won't be there the next time you want someone to be tender with, it's that you won't be there. Switching yourself on and off like this, you are going to break the knob on your emotions. You won't be there. You will find someone you want, and no tenderness will come out. Your feelings will have evaporated, you'll just be a sex clone. A face with a head-band. And all your intimate acts will be empty gestures."

"I've got to get back to my friends now!"

"I know Jeff. Good-bye Jeff."

chapter twenty-six

FIRST PERSON: HUSTLER EYES | 1981

He had hustler eyes. He had finally gotten the disease.

I was coming out of out of the Golden Nugget where I get my Sunday morning french toast, and again I ran into Paul coming back from his night's work, needing a cup of coffee to come-down on, and a bed, this time to sleep in.

This time I noticed that Paul had that familiar glaze over his eyes that many hustlers get. And it's not from the drugs or the sex, it's something that comes from hustling itself.

Hustlers have to see what's going on every moment to survive. Two seconds can make the difference between the right choice and the wrong choices. Who's a John, and who's a killer.

Your eyes always have to be on, even when you are sleeping with your client. Rock stars lose their hearing from the noise, hustlers impair or lose the function of their eyes: too much heat and pressure on their brain. One day the system snaps. They get hustler eyes: a glazed look, like they are wearing shades, even when they aren't wearing shades.

I could see it in Paul. I looked at him: "Hello, is anyone in there, is there anyone behind your wall, Paul?" He would look out, but he didn't really see anyone. Non-contact eyes.

"Do you have a place where I could crash for a few hours?"

"Sure, come to my room, I've got a new Styx album on tape."

At my place, we went to bed, but we didn't have sex. After the first couple of times, we never had sex. I had become too much of a friend to be his John, but I was not enough of a friend to be his friend or lover.

The times we did sleep together, we would usually wake more interested in breakfast than each other. So we got up for coffee, not each other.

When I first met Paul, he looked like a young, fresh Tom Petty: long blond hair, parted in the middle, little, thin arms and little slim body, but long fingers that could wrap around a big guitar. Paul's head seemed larger than his body, and he had a very attractive sunken torpedo look, that made you want to sink your torpedoes in him.

His other head also seemed larger than his body. He had all the necessary manners and illusions to make a good hustler.

He came from a family of hustlers.

His two older brothers, Tim and Booth, were drug dealers. Booth used to brag that he went around San Francisco bars raising hell with Jimmy Carter's nephew.

His father was in real estate. Or I should say, sold mineral rights to parcels of desert land where there were no minerals. His father knocked up Paul's sister Pam when she was 15, giving her at once her first sexual experience, a social disease, and a two year stay in a mental home.

Paul's mother was a survivor. She had moved the five kids and her loud-mouth husband from Rockford and made sure they all went out on the streets, hustling to be good providers for her.

The kids played along with her. The whole family would get together for events like Mother's Day and give Mom big presents: usually envelopes filled with cash. They would take their family picture together.

Paul's mother never discussed how her boys made their money. Nor was it ever discussed that Paul's family was a family only on holidays. I guess that's why Paul liked talking to me.

Although I was gay, Paul treated me more like his straight older brother, someone to talk and tell his secrets to.

Early on, I remember him asking, did I think it was wrong that he did sex for money?

I said do it neither for love nor money. Do it because you enjoy doing it, and for no other reason. Otherwise you'll lose it. Money and sex has nothing to do with it. It takes brains and style to be hustler.

He just smiled, reached down, squeezed his cock, and said: "I've got what it takes. I've got what guys want. I know how to make them want it. And I know how to give it to them."

Bully for you, Theodore Roosevelt, I said. You are a real grand illusion going down the river Styx, a male chauvinist hustler.

One moment you ask me if it's right or wrong, and the next you put on a cocky little boy's act.

I said hustling takes brains and style, not love or money. You get out there and you put on yourself. You can't cheat. You have to know who you are. And you've got to give, baby! More than you ever get back. But you don't mind, because you are being yourself, you say what you feel and do what you feel.

A good hustler is a romantic figure. He's out there pleasing others. He's out there giving his whole self away, because he knows he has the style and skill to bring it all back the next day.

Dumb hustlers steal and rip off. Give me, give me, give me. They'll sell their soul for a broken TV set. Then, there are all those creeps who claim to be ex-hustlers. Dumb. They really believe that hustling means stealing. And so, they stole for a time, and now they think they don't do it anymore.

Never trust someone who says he's an ex-hustler. He's still hustling you with all his talk about being an ex-hustler, he's hustled away his whole soul. All he is telling you now is that he lives with no style.

Once you got it, you never lose it. Your soul, style, your self, you keep, all that.

What you've got to worry about is the burn out. When the lights go out. On the streets you go through so much, you see so much, that you can't see anymore.

You see too many people getting hurt. Fucked over. Your eyes close! You don't want to see anymore. That's the danger in hustling. You get so high, and so aware, that you don't want to have another look.

You get hustler eyes. You look out, but you don't see anything. And people look inside you, and they don't see anything.

That's the way Paul struck me, when I saw him again. He had those hustler eyes. Like he had died years ahead of his time, like he had seen everything once, and now didn't want to see anything ever again.

chapter twenty-seven

JAMIE AT 19 IS NO MORE | 1982

Jamie, 19, was a quiet guy with soft features.

But a month ago he did a very hard, noisy thing to himself. At his folks' home in Barrington Hills, while listening to "Eye of the Tiger" on his headphones, Jamie walked into his father's game room, pulled a gun from the shelf, loaded it, put it in his mouth, and blew himself away.

He was not a survivor.

He wrote a note telling his folks it was not their fault, the pain was too much. He also told them to give his things to Leon to pass out to the other kids.

Who is Leon? Leon is a 41-year-old man who "manages" a video game emporium in New Town. His relationship to Jamie? None. He just knew Jamie as that quiet kid who sometimes scored 84,000 on Asteroids. The kid he had talked to about Tron. The kid no one could reach.

Jamie's mother, manager of a suburban bank, knew Jamie was going through a difficult passage but felt he would come out of it. He did stay in his room a lot, and he was always hooked into his music. But kids grow out of that. Sure, the other kids teased him a lot in school. He had all of their equipment but was no sport: He played in none of their games. He gave his skis and mitts and balls away to strangers.

They used to tease him on the bus coming home. He would just come in, slam all the doors in the house, and go to his room. He never talked about it, to his sister or anyone.

He was a gentle soul. He never fought back. Jamie's father, who works for the county, hated grounding him. But he had been told: Either keep your grades up, get your own money, or you can't go out every night playing games.

Jamie was their first born son; they did everything for him. He seemed not to care for their material things. He gave everything away, to anyone who would ask. He never got into the spirit of being materialistic.

Kids at school were perplexed by Jamie's generosity. He was such a soft touch: If you liked his hiking boots, he would give them to you. He gave away his calculator to a kid in his math class. They teased him, but they never meant him any harm. They just wanted him to watch out for himself.

Was Jamie "gay"? Some openly gay kids in his class thought so. But openly gay people are often too quick to impose their way on everyone else. Jamie was shy, inward, a pastel spirit, more soft than effeminate, but you could not say he was gay because of his fey disposition. Jamie never "came out" anything; he never materialized.

He liked his games and his tapes. He would buy all the latest cassettes, record what he liked, and then give the new cassettes to anyone who happened to be around. His mother let me play his last tape, and it was not suicide music.

Side A had "Eye of the Tiger," Frank and Moon Zappa's "Valley Girl," selections from the Kinks tour, Simple Mind's "This Earth that You Walk Upon," Tom Verlaine's "Words from the Front," "Coming Apart," "Days on the Mountain," and Peter Baumann's "Realtimes" and "Repeat, Repeat."

Side B: Donna Summer's "Love Is in Control," Diana Ross' "Work That Body," Stevie Wonder's "Pushin' Too Hard," and then the only unusual sequence, "Eye of the Tiger" repeated three times, ending with the Police's "Spirits in the Material World."

His mother says that Jamie wore his headphones everywhere, even to bed. Once on a trip to Lake Geneva his batteries went dead, and he threw a fit. His mother said: "You would have thought he had lost his air supply."

No one recalls ever having a sex or drug experience with Jamie. He did, however, have one dangerous habit. When he was younger, his parents did not want him to drink. So he went to their liquor cabinet and took less than a shot out of each bottle that was there, so they would never notice any liquor missing. He called the mixture his "suicide drink."

Jamie's only other passion outside his tapes was video games. He would spend six to 10 hours a night playing Asteroids and Space Shuttle at Leon's emporium. For Jamie, the noisy ghosts in those machines used to come alive.

Leon says he has never seen a kid get so intimate with a machine. Jamie and his machine would vibrate together like they were dance partners. "Jamie gave his body to that fucking machine--if that machine had been another person, they could have arrested him on a morals charge."

Leon is gay. But he never laid a hand on Jamie, or on any other kid who comes to his emporium. His boss knows he is gay and thinks that's good because he won't bother the girls. And if he as much as "talks funny" to a boy, it's his job. Leon takes a lie detector test twice a year.

As Leon told me: "A guy like me working with kids has to watch himself. It's made me cold and impersonal. When I heard about Jamie, I was not surprised. I felt a hopeless chill. He was such a gentle spirit. He didn't belong in this world.

"Sure, I used to watch him at his machine. I wanted to go over and hug him and ask him home. I wanted to daddy him and love him and help him through. But they would have had my job. They would have called me a 'child molester.' I know the score; I keep my distance from these kids. If they don't get love at home, that's not my fault--I can't give them love here, either.

"Did you read *Newsweek* this week? They want every guy who works with kids to take a special test, and if he shows up 'homo' don't let him even work around kids. They think everyone is a child molester just because they can't love their kids. I mean, you don't want to love your kids, so send them out of the house, send them to see *E.T.*, that bug-eyed Buddha from outer space. The kids in *E.T.* can say 'penis breath' and pinch Elliott's mother on the ass, but in real life, if I tell a kid I want to hug him or that I love him, wham bam, I'm locked-up for dirty talk as a child molester. So our young Jamies have to be satisfied by movie fantasies, with celluloid pedophiles like E.T."

Leon has a point. Jamie left earth unloved, but not unwanted. He was a spirit who could not materialize himself in this material world.

chapter twenty-eight

THE CRIME OF CRIME REPORTING | 1982

Rape, murder, and prostitution, in our society, are crimes, or criminal acts. People who rape, murder, or prostitute themselves are criminals. These are easy truths: you need only an open-and-shut mind to follow them.

But, then, a naive kid might ask: "What exactly is a crime?"

Most criminologists, sociologists, and legal experts--relying on the standard quick but circular definition--would say: "Oh, that's easy. A crime is anything punishable by law."

Homosexual acts, even between consenting adults, are still punishable by law in many states--not in Illinois, but, for example in Wisconsin--and therefore are "crimes." And even in places where homosexual acts between consenting adults are legal, because of the hangover of past repressive laws, many people think homosexuals are criminals.

That is why, in our society if you catch a thief, or a murderer, or a rapist, and if you also reveal, truly or falsely, that he is a homosexual, you can get the public to believe that the poor guy has committed a double crime.

Even more outrageous, if you arrest a person for one crime and then describe him in a newspaper or on TV as "being a homosexual," he may get off the charges for which he was arrested--he may not be punished by the law at all, may not in fact be a criminal--but he will be punished by society, by his wife, friends, and boss for being a homosexual.

If you are caught in a forest preserve holding hands with an undercover cop and are arrested for "public indecency" and your name appears in a local newspaper and you are a high school teacher, you can be summarily dismissed from your job, even though you are never punished by law.

Also, if the *Sun-Times* names you as one who frequented a so-called "known hangout for homosexuals," you will be punished by those who see your name listed, whether or not you are in fact a homosexual and whether or not you have committed any actual crime.

Rape, murder, and prostitution are serious crimes in our society; to he charged with them you have to be caught in the act. There is the law protecting you: due process, a trial, rules of evidence, and a set procedure that must be followed to determine your guilt or innocence.

A homosexual, however, does not have to be caught in the act: he only has to be caught in the accusation. Merely to have it reported publicly that you are a "homosexual" (or "self-confessed homosexual") will in many cases make you look like a criminal in the public mind.

Crime, or *crimen*, originally in Roman law--on which, supposedly our system of jurisprudence is founded--meant "charge or accusation." In Chaucer, Shakespeare, and Milton, and in all our dictionaries until 100 years ago, crime meant accusation.

Today, for the homosexual, crime is still the accusation: All you have to do is accuse someone in our society of "being a homosexual" (shades and shadows of Oscar Wilde); no acts need ever exist or be proved; you've caught a criminal, lavender-handed.

Call someone a homosexual in print or on the air, and you have committed the perfect crime; you make your subject a criminal. You are the offender, he the victim; but he gets punished by fag-beaters and the homophobic middle, while you get protected--rightly, I agree--by freedom of speech.

Accusation is the perfect crime. It is the crime that dares to speak its name and raise its ugly head all too often in crime reporting. It is done almost on a daily basis in the newspapers and nightly on television.

News reporting, in our society, has long enjoyed making homosexuals into criminals and criminals into homosexuals. With a few healthy exceptions, this kind of reporting is still the standard practice of newspapers and television stations in Chicago.

Let me examine in great detail three recent examples of crime reporting in Chicago: the anti-prostitution campaign against the Abbott Hotel; the convicted murderer who seems to claim that because he was the victim of a "homosexual rape" at age 13, he had the right, the right of revenge to have sex with and kill perhaps as many as 32 gay men; and the "Jack the Ripper" mutilation murders of females, which may have occurred, according to a *Tribune* news analysis, because the killers may have engaged in "homosexual conduct" among themselves.

Recently, at the prompting of community leaders on Broadway and Belmont Avenue, the Abbott Hotel has been the center of an anti-prostitution movement. Robert Wiedrich, *Tribune* columnist, wrote two strong anti-vice pieces. Mayor Byrne met with over 200 citizens protesting at the Carmelite school across from the Abbott. Then, the City Council surprisingly passed an ordinance, long buried in committee, to license hotels and motels like bars (at $75 per year). The ordinance states that hotels and motels can be temporarily or permanently padlocked if they tolerate acts of "public disorder" (prostitution).

How has this anti-prostitution movement, carried on in the heat of the mayoral race, been reported in the news and on TV!

The CBS local affiliate (WBBM-TV, Channel 2) did an exceptionally professional, sensitive, and well-edited mini-documentary in the middle of its nightly news on the Abbott Hotel. The station restrained its language, used the word "homosexual" only once--properly so--and for the rest of the program made it clear that the "crime" being investigated was prostitution.

The young students across the street from the Abbott, who can see into the loosely curtained hotel, used the word "prostitutes" when describing what they saw (or thought they saw), and never said "homosexuals" or "perverts." The TV crew showed nine city inspectors arriving at the Abbott along with the beat cop, and gave the Abbott's owners equal time to respond to the preliminary charges. It was a fair and tactful job of reporting an inflamed situation.

Many in the gay community have known for some time that things going on at the Abbott were not very "gay," and that it would probably be curtains for the Abbott if its managers did not get better shades and curtains for their rooms and if they kept running what appeared to be an "adult bookstore without walls."

Bob Wiedrich, in his two *Tribune* columns all attacking vice at the Abbott, could hardly restrain himself from using the word "homosexual" in nearly every paragraph. He called the Abbott a "homosexual haven" and treated the whole affair as though "homosexuality" were the real crime being committed at the Abbott, not prostitution.

Ironically, however, just as all drugs have side effects, so all loose crime reporting has humorous consequences. Last week, three men were nabbed around the Abbott Hotel looking for "pick-ups." They told the arresting officer that they were hanging around the Abbott because they had read about the action there in "Bob Wiedrich's columns in the *Tribune*," according to another *Tribune* column, "Gold & Sneed INC."

Once again, loose crime reporting helped create loose public morals, helped set criminals on the loose. Wiedrich did not confine himself to the facts and the actual crimes; he interjected the allure of sexuality. And his readers, not caring what kind of sexuality he was talking about--male, female, or epicene--came pouring in from the suburbs and the South Side looking for "pussy."

Wiedrich helped make victims of these people--bad news reporting is not, after all, a victimless crime--and yet he goes unpunished for his offense.

Such were the immediate results of crime reporting on prostitution at the Abbott Hotel.

chapter twenty-nine

MORE CRIMES IN CRIME REPORTING | 1982

> "The news media should not pander to morbid curiosity about details of vice and crime..."
> --Code of Ethics (1973) of the Society of Professional Journalists (Sigma Delta Chi)

The editors of the *New York Times* still gag on the word "gay." They refuse to use it.[31] They insist upon calling gay people "homosexuals." Calling gay people "homosexuals" is equivalent to calling black people Negroes. And what the *Times* says is "fit to print," the other news services take as fit to copy.

Only a distinguished local paper, such as the Lerner *Booster*, regularly uses the word "gay" in its news stories. The Lerner papers, of course, are closer to the truth, and thus more accurate, because they are "local," closer to the communities they write about.

---

[31] The *New York Times* refused to use the word "gay" as a synonym for "homosexual" until 1987, according to the Gay & Lesbian Alliance Against Defamation.

Bob Wiedrich, *Chicago Tribune* columnist, is such a balloon-head, even when he uses the word "gay" he gets it wrong. In two recent columns, he attacked "homosexuality" as if that, not prostitution, were the crime around the area of the Abbott Hotel. In a third column, focusing on the kids at, the Carmelite school across the street from the hotel, he wrote: "It would break your heart if you could read some of the [children's] letters in their entirety. They reveal an acquaintanceship with a seamier side of life to which children their age never should have been exposed. Words like pimps, prostitutes, hookers, gays, and drug pushers were used as though they were everyday vocabulary."

Wiedrich uses the word "gay" and makes it sound equal to scum.

The more standard practice in crime reporting is to use the word "homosexual" and make it sound equal to crime. Homosexuals sound like criminals, even when they have committed no illegal acts. The word alone is the accusation, thus the crime.

Oh, I know, editors will say "homosexual" is the proper term, the older, more traditional word--that's why we follow the New York Times and correct all your press releases that say "gay" to "homosexual." Wrong! Check out John Boswell's *Christianity, Social Tolerance, and Homosexuality* (page

43): " ... gay probably antedates homosexual by several centuries."

Editors, predominantly white males, use "homosexual" in news reporting and crime stories because it fits more comfortably in their numb, puritanical minds. It protects their innocence; who cares if it defames our experience? Who cares that the word "homosexual" is used to distort the truth and accuracy of almost every crime story?

The wire service stories about convicted killer Bruce A. Davis, the alleged "Menard ax murderer," made him out to be a homosexual maniac. The news was filled with homosexual overkill. The "facts" of his case were copied and re-copied without anyone thinking about what they were saying: As a teenage paperboy, he was "homosexually raped"; in 1971, convicted of the murder of a Catholic priest; escaped Menard, allegedly killing a prison employee with an ax; returned home to West Virginia; re-arrested; confessed to hating "them" (homosexuals); told deputy sheriff he used to take "them" to dine, to their motels, have sex with them, then shoot, stab, strangle, kill them. Preferred to take out "professional men"--doctors, lawyers. End of report.

So the average reader might read: Boy has "homosexual encounter" (rape) at 13, which so disgusts him that he goes on to have a life filled with more "homosexual encounters," which end in him having homosexual sex and killing his homosexual partners. Homosexual kills homosexuals. So what?

The irony is that neither Davis nor his alleged victims, in any true or accurate sense, think of themselves as "homosexuals." Davis has the defense: "I am not a homosexual." And in a narrow sense he is correct: He is a man--or, more accurately, a male-child--with a homosexual problem. He was 11 in West Virginia when John Kennedy was spreading sex, charisma, and his father's money to beat Hubert Humphrey and win the nomination for president. Homosexuals were not covered in the news; like all rape victims, Davis as a boy had to live both with the horror and the thrill of the crime. He had shared the forbidden act, the homosexual act, and therefore must be in some way a homosexual, too, and a criminal like all the other homosexuals. So he might say: "What the hell. I'm there in hell already, I might as well go out and have murder with my sex."

Davis' victims are not homosexuals either. They are gay people, and gay people, if a reporter will dig into the real "stats," are seldom violent toward one another. A gay person can end a love, get a divorce, just by walking across the street away from his partner.

When Channel 7 (WLS) got a copy of the Davis story for their happy talk horror show, we got to see a strawberry blonde mouthing the most horrible words: "homosexual rape," "ax-murder," "Catholic priest stabbed"--the bland and incoherent babbling of a balloon-head. So most people would think, "Omigod, Gacy is loose again."

There is nothing either rational or poetic about television justice. The news is the scare part designed to grab and seize, rape your mind, until you get the commercial part. Television news, when done in the happy talk style, is just a way for balloon-heads to release their own erotic energies by re-enacting verbally and imitating the crimes they imagine we commit. Fade to lavender boys!

The most perverse and probably least accurate piece of "homosexual" news reporting was done in a recent Sunday "think piece" in the *Chicago Tribune* by Bonita Brodt. She tried to analyze and explain how Robin Geeht, a family man, could became the Satanic mastermind behind the bizarre mutilation and murders of several Chicago area females.

Brodt made sure the *Tribune* never will be out-positioned or out-hyped by other news services on this "crime of the century" story. OK. the police now are thinking Geeht may be responsible for only a couple of murders, and the *Sun-Times* has the story on page 56. Still. Brodt got the *Tribune* out front by linking Geeht--over the objections of his brother, family, and neighbors--to Charles Manson, Satan, and Jack the Ripper. Geeht and his gang of "slow learners"--teenage boys who, Brodt reported, used to go in and out of Geeht's house at odd hours of the night, a la Gacy--would pick up women, some of them loose women and prostitutes, drug them, slash them, rape them, mutilate them, cut off their breast(s), and then kill them. The boys also performed Manson-like Satanic rituals in Geeht's attic, leaving parts of slaughtered animals and humans remaining on his altar.

Why did these nasty, evil boys do these nasty, evil things to the females they picked up? After five columns describing vice in morbid detail, Brodt offers us the final solution: "There also have been unconfirmed reports of homosexual conduct among the men arrested." That's it! They were homosexuals! Obviously, that's why they mutilated and murdered women!

An "unconfirmed report" is either a perverse truth or an outright lie. You can say about anyone--arrested for murder or speeding or libel that there is an "unconfirmed report" that "he slept with his mother when he was a lad." Perverse!

more crimes in crime reporting

A quick and reasonable way to stop crime would be to stop these crimes in crime reporting. The real murderers are not getting away with their crimes nearly as much as the reporters are getting away with calling them "homosexuals," thus making it seem like they are double murderers who have committed a double crime.

chapter thirty

THE CASE OF WILLIAM THE FAG BRASHLER | 1983

Chicago magazine[32]--by hustling quiche and fur fashions to real men, by pushing pork ribs on people who have forgotten their Leviticus, and by promoting FM tuners to people who already march around the city listening to their own boombox--has managed to inflate an FM program guide into a successful city magazine. It rose to prominence in the '60s, when magazines were supposed to be "relevant," and it has survived into the '80s by keeping its editorial copy mostly neutral or irrelevant.

Just as you could argue, however, that there is food value and nutrition in a chocolate mousse, so *Chicago* magazine often does publish breezy political commentary or genuinely humorous pieces on Chicago history. But, at its worst, *Chicago* magazine can be both liberal and patronizing, slick and smarmy.

---

[32] The glossy *Chicago* magazine published a story about the gay and lesbian community by novelist and reporter William Brashler.

In *Chicago*'s February issue, the editors had the good sense to let blacks talk about blacks in Chicago politics and Hispanics talk about Hispanics in Chicago politics. Had they also had the good sense to let a gay talk about gays in Chicago politics, they would have had a fresh, new story. They would have learned that pols are coming to mingle with gays--that the Mayor, the county party chairman, the campaign managers of all the mayoral candidates, and all the aldermanic candidates came to speak to the Gay Dems. They do not think we are a joke, they think we are votes and a political force to recognize.

Chicago magazine, however, still thinks we are a closet joke. They did not bother to come and see what is actually going on in the gay community. Instead, they assigned contributing editor William Brashler--a blatant, one could almost say a flambe, heterosexual--to write about gays and pols in Chicago.

Brashler spilled out two pages of bad history, bad jokes, and embarrassing self-exposure, so that even a casual reader would know that Brashler had agreed to a topic not just beyond his reach, but absolutely beyond his grasp.

Brashler begins his thoughtless "think piece" with three jokes that aren't funny:

"This is the city of the big shoulders, not the lisp."

"Its leaders can be weak-kneed, lily-livered, fat-headed, but not limp-wristed."

"A Chicago politician can survive any attack and weather most scandals, but he cannot be soft."

Brashler speaks to us like Big Buddy, an older brother; we are not supposed to think that these things are what he thinks--he is just telling us for our own good.

This is the way it is in Chicago, kid, and this is your "enduring political tradition." Face it: If you are gay, you can't be a pol in Chicago. Then, after three more columns of this same kind of verbal fag-bashing, Brashler leaves us with a cute and swishy last hurrah: "The careers of politicians, at least in the eyes of Chicagoans, end not with a bang but with a swish." Thanks, Big Brother!

Brashler prides himself on his "street knowledge." He says elsewhere that you can't be a good fiction writer or a good reporter unless you get your knowledge "from the streets and not the classroom," unless "you have done your homework." Writing about gays and pols this time, Brashler stayed home and let the words fly through his word processor. He did not come out on the street and see us. He just stayed inside and decided to speak for all gays, pols, and Chicagoans, thus insulting all three groups with his irresponsible writing and remarks.

We should believe him, he tells us, because 10 years ago he used to go out as a police reporter on the "fruit patrols." Then our happy voyeur used to witness gays getting arrested in bars, on the streets, and in public parks. He even used to watch while men who spend "longer than 26 seconds to relieve themselves" got busted for loitering in public men's rooms.

Big Brother Brashler sure knows what he is telling us: He was a voyeur on a "fruit patrol" 10 years ago, he has seen action in a men's room. That Police Supt. Richard J. Brzeczek has restricted "fruit patrols" and instituted a new policy toward gays, admonishing his men to concern themselves more with crime and less with prejudice--all this has escaped the notice of our street-wise reporter.

Brashler would rather sit at home by his word processor and tell us what used to be in Mayor Daley's mind. We learn from Brashler that Daley backed no losers and no bachelors. Daley wanted only married men in his party. That's why, Brashler tells us, "Otto Kerner, Bilandic, and Jim Thompson got married."[33] Is

[33] Otto Kerner and James Thompson were Illinois governors; Michael Bilandic was a Chicago mayor.

Brashler saying what he is implying--that Kerner, Bilandic, and Thompson were "soft and gay" and only got married under "Daley's aegis" to hide their softness from public view?

Brashler puts imaginary pink triangles on all our pols (both the living and the dead).

We also learn from his scattered remarks that "spontaneous acts of sex are now occurring in Bridgeport" because Daley (the censor) has been dead for six years. Also, while doing research for his famous--but no longer read--biography about Sam Giancana--a book, according to one reviewer, filled with "breezy sociology and ex cathedra pronouncements on 'dago' traits"--Brashler discovered that even the goons in Capone's gang used to engage in "homo hijinks."

Other Brashler discoveries: Edmund Muskie,[34] while not a homosexual himself, suffered the fate of a homosexual pol when he cried in public because his wife had been slandered. Chuck Percy[35] won his last election despite the fact that he became weak-kneed in public and "pulled a Scarlett O'Hara and swooned." Jane Byrne, "Attila the Hen," is not "soft." And Ted Kennedy may be a "philanderer," but he has never been caught--like the gays

---

[34] 1972 Presidential candidate.

[35] Former Illinois senator.

harassed by the "fruit patrol"--with his "decorum down."

While Brashler manages to put his sweet lips on all pols living and dead, he saves his most venomous kiss of death for Harvey Milk.[36] He tells us not to worry, Chicago is not like San Francisco, we will never elect someone like "the aptly named Harvey Milk." Brashler does not explain his tasteless joke. Why is Milk "aptly named"? Did being an openly gay councilman make him like a soft ice cream cone? Besides, I always thought drinking milk would make you homogenized, not homosexual!

Brashler also thinks it is a great laugh that Dan White, Milk's assassin, used "the Twinkie defense." Big laugh! What if, Brashler says, a Chicago defense lawyer said: "My client killed a Twinkie. So?" Does street-wise Brashler have any ear for homosexual slang? Does he know what he is saying? Let's reopen the case, we have new evidence here. White killed Milk over a "twinkie." Did White kill Milk because he (White) was eating a "twinkie," or did he kill Milk because Milk was eating a "twinkie"--his "twinkie"? Were Milk and White just two old chicken hawks feuding over their "twinkie"? Tell us, Big Brother.

---

[36] Gay activist Harvey Milk, elected to the San Francisco Board of Supervisors in 1977, was assassinated in 1978.

If William Brashler ever again wishes to become a serious writer, he will have to stop going around Chicago streets like a blind Narcissus. He always writes about men--ballplayers, pols, gangsters--and yet he never knows he is really writing about himself. He is dumb, like Hemingway. As Gertrude Stein would say, "He doesn't listen while we are talking." And he doesn't listen, because he thinks the we in that sentence refers to two dykes. Gertrude and Alice, while the we really refers to the double part of every man's soul, his male and female part.

Until Brashler opens up to his "gay" self, ironically, he will have no real manhood, humor, or humanity. He will just go around town a pathetic loner, verbally fag-bashing sissies, telling dirty jokes about gays and pols, and earning himself the twisted sobriquet: William the Fag-Brashler.

chapter thirty-one

QUERELLE: ART, LIFE AND DEATH | 1983

Only in Chicago did *Querelle*,[37] Rainer Werner Fassbinder's last film, receive an adults-only rating. There was no frontal nudity, and 30 seconds from the scene showing Nono fucking *Querelle* in the ass had been edited out to ensure an "R" rating in America.

But the Chicago Film Review Board--a censor body almost unique to our city--run by the Chicago Police Department, and supervised by Sgt. John Vrdolyak, brother of Fast Eddie,[38] our "acting mayor"--saw what they thought was lurid penetration, and declared the film "adults only."

---

[37] *Querelle* is Rainer Werner Fassbinder's film adaptation of Jean Genet's novel *Querelle de Brest*; the 1982 movie starred Brad Davis.

[38] Attorney and politician Edward Vrdolyak, a Chicago alderman from 1971 to 1989, was the leader of a Chicago City Council bloc opposed to Mayor Harold Washington in the mid-1980s. In 2008, he pled guilty to federal wire fraud and mail fraud charges.

Of course, as reviewer Gene Siskel[39] pointed out, the board was being "homophobic." Yet having seen the film three times and having read the original 1947 book by Jean Genet a couple of times, I would not be too harsh on our police censors. They are not dream interpreters. Probably most all of the film, except the title and the one famous simulated ass-fucking scene, washed right over their pedestrian intellects. They were exercising the same kind of associative thinking which made two cops recently describe the Gold Coast as a "punk bar" on North Clark street ("You know, the place with all the motorcycles ").

I am sure they looked at the title and ran. *Querelle*? How do you say it? And translating French into native Illinoisan, they probably sounded it out and said, "Queer-elle," and assumed it meant "little queer." Or, if by chance they heard someone say it correctly, then it must have sounded to them like Mick Jagger on downers singing, "Oh, Car-rol," and their bulldog ears would have immediately detected a girl's name for the male lead.

Besides, our police board must protect us from seeing blue-eyed boys from Milwaukee like

---

[39] *Chicago Tribune* film writer Gene Siskel died in 1999 from complications following brain surgery.

Brad Davis[40] playing sailor and getting fucked by Italian brothel keepers.

Querelle in French means "quarrel," and the film causes a brawl or dispute, however it is seen or imagined. Even those who have not seen the movie have views about Fassbinder and his tricks--artistic and otherwise. And behind all this quarreling sits Mother Genet like the sweet flower--or is it weed?--that she is. Laughing, no doubt, at the Chicago police, and smiling maternally at Fassbinder's efforts.

The last time Mother Genet saw the Chicago police in person was in 1968 at the Democratic National Convention covering the event for *Esquire* magazine, along with William Burroughs and Terry Southern. Genet was right here in our town, supporting those who were throwing shit--both ideological and real-at the "pigs" in Grant Park. Back in her room at the hotel, she could look out her window and meditate over the beautiful pigs--the handsome German, Polish, and Irish men in leather with their eggshell blue helmets.

Genet, like many petty criminals, has either had a crush on or fallen in love with every policeman she has ever met. They take her breath away. As she says in the book (quoted in the film):

---

[40] Actor Brad Davis died of an intentional drug overdose in 1991 after a long battle with AIDS.

The police represent the only "supreme moral authority in our society."

She loves them. Even more than thieves, the police get their hands dirty. They are always into the real shit. As she once said: "They kill with their own hands," not like lawyers and judges "at a distance and by proxy."

Next to murderers, Genet most frequently celebrates cops, particularly when they are like Mario in the movie--faggot cops in leather living both inside and outside the law.

Jean Genet would never appear on a police review board. She respects the police's art too much. In 30 seconds they must decide between life and death. Nor, out of a sense of fair play--as one artist to another--would she ever allow the police to review even 30 seconds of her work, which fantasizes the quarrel between life and death.

Fassbinder's curse was that all his life was too real and all his films too artificial. *Querelle* is a totally artificial event, a stage of mirrors, which accurately translates the mood of Genet's world, where everyone is a homosexual and the heroes are faggots--but he misses Genet's final deception. Genet is pro-life and still living; Fassbinder is neither.

Genet is a born trickster. Also a born bastard. Thus, he has every right to live like a real bastard, and does. Fassbinder could only aspire to be a phony bastard. Hence his limit, and his rich artificiality. Fake psychosis is a more crippling disease than real psychosis.

Fassbinder was born in the spa town of Bad Worishofen, the Palm Springs of Bavaria. His father was a physician. His mother was well known for translating Truman Capote into German. Maybe she read *In Cold Blood* to her son too early. As a growing lad, Fassbinder would make statements about how he hated his bourgeois parents. Kill or be killed. "Love is colder than death." So he killed himself; they won. At 14, he told his father he was in love with men. And his father said: "Fine. But why go out with such low life? Why go out with the butcher's son, when you can date a nice boy from the university?"

Genet built a series of petty crimes into a life of fantasized crime, an imaginary Class X felony. He never murdered anyone--not like Jack Henry Abbott, Norman Mailer's writer pal, who killed another playwright when he came out of the belly of the beast. Genet's murders are all fantasies. "I want to sing of murder only," proclaims our new Homer at the beginning of her work. But she only sings; she tells tales and avoids the dull acts of crime.

Fassbinder could not wait to get to the act: The murder of himself. He read Schopenhauer and kiddie porn. He made death his only act of will and boylove his only act of wish. Sure, out of this earthless male chaos he could make some remarkable movies.

In Querelle you don't have sailor boys, but you have men from the merchant marine, all cloaked in timeless blues and gold, performing magickal scenes in mirrors, which makes them appear to dance on top of the sea like ambisexual mermaids. Rich and tasty stuff, yes.

But in the final cut: Genet chooses life and Fassbinder chooses death. That is their artistic difference, which gets lost in translation from book to film. Fassbinder tacks on to the end of his film some forged statement implying that Jean Genet wants to die. No. Genet at 73 wants to stay alive--there is a lot of actor, a lot of Ronald Reagan, in Genet. The little bastard was born the same year as Reagan, and for I know, they will die in the same year. But the little bastard did learn early one truth he has always survived by: "Males are vulnerable for they 'always kill the thing they love'--only the female will survive!" And that's how Mother Genet gets away with her greatest crime: staying alive.

Too bad Fassbinder never learned that trick at the Lysee, when he came of age and decided to be a mother fucker, even if it killed him.

chapter thirty-two

WHY GAY MEN GO TO GAY BARS | 1983

Gay men go to bars, baths, and bookstores (to borrow a line from Robert Frost[41]) more for "grex than sex." They are looking for gregarious good fun and companionship. Generally, in the land of the bottom-line and Dynasty, we choose to look at ourselves in the hardest and most cynical mirror: "I know what you are here for--you want sex." That's the score; that's why gay men go to gay bars.

You cannot, however, reduce the sociology of gay bars to a single sex score. The most painful life experience for most gay men occurs right before "coming out," when you think you are the only gay person in the world. You feel dismembered and cut off from everyone. You feel so alone and isolated in your narcissistic nightmare that at times you feel like you are trapped in a suicidal black hole facing psychic death.

---

[41] "The ruling passion in man [is] a gregarious instinct to keep together by minding each other's business. Grex rather than sex."--Robert Frost.

When you first enter a gay bar or bookstore or bathhouse and discover that there really are other men like you--men who come in a variety of sizes, shapes and flavors--that there is a whole society of people like you out there, that you are not a freak of nature or the last pariah, there is no way to describe the joy of the discovery that you are in fact a social being: You belong to a group. To know you are a social being, to know you are not and never will be the only one, is a greater thrill and release than any momentary sexual blast.

Outsiders have an image that gay bars and "haunts" are filled with anonymous strangers, replicant clones eager to plug into each other and then split. Not so. Gay people are not anonymous but protononymous: We know each other by our first names and are eager and quick to learn them. In the military you can be known forever by your last name, but in the gay world your first name is your magic name. The network of first-name friendships extends everywhere: I know Michaels all over the world, from Alpha Michael to Omega Michael.

Can we talk? The main reason guys go to gay bars is to talk and have a social experience. They go to let their hair down as much as to let their cocks up. Wear a pink slip to work and you get a pink slip; wear a pink slip in a gay bar and someone might buy you a drink. On your regular job during the regular day, if you let one word slip, or don't laugh hard enough at a macho joke, you might find your career sidetracked. But in a gay bar you can talk like you feel and won't get cursed with voodoo death.

Even at baths and bookstores, which are supposed to be strictly scripted for anonymous sex, if you watch carefully you will see that the pattern is social--the same cluster of guys tend to gather like pigeons at the same spot almost at the same time every week. I know lots of "couples" who have been enjoying each other's "anonymous" company at the same movie house for the last 10 years. These "anonymous" guys in clusters know each other's first name, talk sports, gossip about being together last week, snicker over their imagined encounters, do a lot of looking at the other pigeons outside their group and a lot of false bragging about how they have been with those others, when in fact they seldom have exogenous sex, or venture beyond their home group of buddies. They are there more for grex than sex.

God, Mary, can we talk in our bars! Like proverbial housemothers and soap opera gossips, we dish it in and out. And those mumblers who just stand around and model, talk with their bodies--they have exhausted their vocal cords selling insurance or something like that in the day, so they let their bodies do their talking as they get their social feedback in the bar.

Irony of ironies: Gay men go to gay bars to have the straight experience of feeling like a square, a regular social being. We go to gay bars for straight talk.

Outsiders define us only by our sex, so naturally that's the only thing they think we do. But as insiders, we know that when we are in our bars sex is there for granted. That leaves us free to do all the other things, like play pool, dance, hold hands, talk baseball, horse play, drink, and be social.

Police raids on gay bars, in most cases, are so stupid. The police come in from the outside-- usually on an "anonymous tip." They are into "anonymous" investigations thinking we are into "anonymous" sex-- everyone is so "anonymous" it's like ghosts dealing with phantoms. No wonder most arrests in gay bars never make it to court: They are all "phantom" arrests.

An even more ridiculous game is when undercover leather cops come to undercover leather bars. The arresting officer is in drag, and the customer (who might be a bank teller or a social worker) is also in drag. The cops see the sacred symbols of the leather world on the wall, an icon leather figure drawn like a *Playboy* centerfold, a couple of guys wearing chains and wristbands and wow!--a pornographic movie begins to pop into their uninitiated heads.

Both undercover cops in Levi's and leathermen represent a small inside-outside minority group in our society. For some leathermen, every time they "smell" a policeman makes them think "police brutality." And some cops, every time they see two men in leather, think "fucking faggots." But if each could step out of their paranoia, they would see that each is a trained person. Arresting officers are trained not to use more force than is necessary. And leather-men are trained in their sexual games never to use more "force" than is erotically stimulating. They are both professionals at what they do. Too bad they cannot respect each other's training.

Unless there is a complaint from within, unless there is a real injured party, the police have no business coming into a gay bar on an "anonymous tip" chasing "anonymous" sex. That is why our mayor and police superintendent, if they really want to understand our "proclivities" and "eschew" false and phantom arrests, must learn what the function of a gay bar is. Gay bars function in the gay community just like churches function in the black community--as places of social sanctuary, where a minority group can be away from their oppressors and be their social selves. Just as more than religion goes on in a black church, so in a gay bar, if you watch closely, you will notice there is more grex than sex.

PART THREE

chapter thirty-three

AN EASY MARK IN A ROUGH TRADE | 1984

Danny Bridges[42] was buried on Aug. 25, in an unmarked grave. Friends of the family are now raising money to put his name on the headstone. By all accounts Danny suffered the fate of an easy mark.

Even in his burial it is no accident that he should have a problem getting his name on his marker. All his life Danny Bridges seemed to have problems with names. He said he didn't like the name "gay."

"I don't consider myself gay," he told a *Chicago Tribune* interviewer. "I did it [had sex with other men and boys] so I wouldn't starve to death."

He didn't like the names his friends called him in school. Fag. Sissy. Queer. Girl. Whore.

---

[42] Danny Bridges' dismembered body was found in a dumpster on the north side of Chicago. Larry Eyler was arrested, tried and convicted of the murder in 1986. Sentenced to death, Eyler later confessed to a series of murders from death row, where he died of AIDS before the sentence could be carried out. Damski's coverage of Eyler's trial begins on page 295.

Bitch. Above all, he didn't like the name describing the work he did: Male Prostitute.

"I really didn't like to have sex with other men," he said, "because it did make me feel cheap." He didn't much like the guys who saw him as an "easy mark," answered his signal and picked him up on the streets of Uptown: "Most of the men who picked me up were stupid middle class guys."

Daniel also got into trouble because he was willing to name names and tell all about the other men and boys he had been with. Danny was a key witness for the prosecution in the Joe's Juice Joint[43] case in April 1982, in which three men were found guilty of charges involving sex with minors. Danny's sister, Sharon, described him as a loner: "Daniel didn't have a lot to do with other kids. He didn't want to be bothered." A lot of other kids didn't want to be bothered with Daniel, either, because they were afraid they were afraid of what they heard about him: that he would give their names to the police. Danny lived under the mark of a tattletale.

While he was alive I knew Danny by name only. My sources were always telling me to watch out for Danny Bridges. I saw Danny in his shiny satin disco jacket many times on the streets going

---

[43] A non-alcoholic bar that catered to patrons under the legal drinking age.

about his business, but I got no impression of a person being there in that blank blond body. To me he was ghost-like. It was only after seeing the TV pictures of him, after his horrible murder and dismemberment, that I put together the person and the name.

Danny's family says no one knows the hurt they feel. They are right. I cannot feel their hurt. Life's hurts and penalties are passed out in individual doses. I have been in shock for days. I feel sad and would like to reach out to the family with sympathy; but they are right. Their hurt is theirs.

Danny had a horrible death--not just the murder and mutilation: the hacksaw and the pieces in the garbage bags in the dumpster--and not in the "homosexual acts" that the popular press insists on linking to the murder. No, the horror comes from the evil of the event. It was evil, pure and simple. The horror makes me, as well as a lot of other gay people, just sick. I live an open gay life. And what happened to Danny Bridges in no way represents what I call gay or life.

I will never forget the way Danny died. But I also hope his family and friends won't bury him twice and forget the way he lived. Every mother in America wants her son to grow up and be a doctor, so he can have "M.D." after his name. No mother wants her son to be a male prostitute and have the letters M. P. (which doesn't only mean Member of Parliament) written in graffiti after her son's name. The popular press--especially TV--is simply not able to handle a mother's fears about male prostitution. They approach the topic with so much prejudice--sexual and sexist: only females are supposed to be whores in our society--that they cannot render a judgment on the subject. They try to be so moral and macho about it that they only end up being hysterical and inaccurate.

This last week I walked the streets in Uptown where Danny worked. I listened to the way his fellow male prostitutes talked, and learned some startling simple facts. When you look up from the mean and dirty streets around Magnolia and Montrose (there are no green Magnolia trees in this urban Appalachia, and no mountain of roses as the street names imply), you see Lake Shore Towers to the east, where doctors live. Any kid coming out on those streets, even before he goes to any school, learns a fundamental lesson of American life: Rich is good, and poor is bad. And the American way is to hustle yourself from being bad and poor to the land of rich and good.

The chances for kids in Uptown of becoming real doctors and going to Northwestern Medical School are about the same as $1 winning $34 million on Lotto. So some kids find another way into the American hustle. They take up another profession, even older than medicine. To the rich, the good, the normal, male prostitution seems perverse and degenerate.

But actually, the professions of medicine and prostitution have a lot of similarities. In olden times they used to think all physicians were low-lifes, butchers, bloodsuckers. Leeches. Doctors and male prostitutes both have "clients" whom they like to keep in waiting rooms, whom they see for about 30 minutes, to whom they administer a little magic relief which the client could do for himself if he were in more control of his own body, rather than having a professional intervene. And for this dubious service they take a little money. "It's a swindle," says the client. But he always goes back.

Listen to the way "male whores" talk. When they make a score and come back with $80--enough money to pay for a room and food for three days--they feel "higher than God." They don't feel bad, or that they are bad. They feel good. They feel like they have done good. They have made it good. They have earned it the old-fashioned way.

Male prostitutes. if you listen to them, talk a lot like businessmen. They will say things like, "I am having a financial problem today," which means they need $5 for a meal. The normal people, the rich, the good can stay in their comfortable towers and sleep. And never know the harm they do to others. The bad, the poor, live up against it every waking moment of their life. The good, the rich, never have to live anywhere near it--they can sleep through it: all the harm they do.

When the bankers at Continental Illinois go broke, they call on Ronald Reagan and the U.S. government, the richest sugar daddies in the world, to bail them out. And their government sugar daddy lets them go back to the corridor at Continental they call "Sleepy Hollow"--and they still collect their gigantic salaries and guaranteed retirements. Yet when a male prostitute goes broke plying his free enterprise, there is no government sugar daddy to bail him out. When he calls his private sugar daddy, he will either be told, "Sorry. I am as broke as you are," or the daddy will pretend not to know him at all. So he will have to stay awake, go back on the streets, and try to hustle for his survival. In our society, when the poor and bad try to get something back from the rich and the good, it's called a crime. But when the good take from the poor, that's called supply-side economics.

Male prostitution is a rough trade. It was no business for an easy mark like Danny Bridges to be in. Charlotte Duggan, the upstairs neighbor of the Bridges family, told the Lerner *Booster*: "All I know is Danny was a generous boy, loving, kind-hearted and willing to give to everybody." She is right. But he was too willing to give to everybody. He gave his body to his girlfriend so she would say he wasn't "gay." He gave his body to other men and boys--some for money, some for love--so, as he said, he wouldn't "starve." He was so generous that he gave the names of some of the men and boys he had been with to the police. He was so kind-hearted that he would give any journalist or any professional counselor the story they wanted to hear. He was an easy mark.

He never learned the first lesson of street hustling. You have to stand out there and look like an "easy mark," so your client will notice you and try to pick you up. But once they pick you up, you are the doctor--you can't play easy mark anymore, you have to control the life-and-death situation.

Finally, as every novice male prostitute learns, the action you choose speaks louder than any words you say. You can say you are "gay" or "not gay"--"I do this, I don't do that"--but if you keep coming back for the same action, then that is what you want to do.

All kids, whether they are 9 or 29, when they go out of their mother's house, go out seeking what they want to be. Even before they have gone to school they know the old Shakespearean question: "To be or not to be." It seems to me, from the type of action Danny chose repeatedly through his life and the type of pose he chose as "easy mark," that he answered that old Shakespearean question in the negative. He wanted not to be. His death drive was stronger than his life force. That was the root of his evil, and all the counselors and all the police and all the teachers and social workers and journalists--yes, even all the gay men who reached out to protect him--they all got there too late.

chapter thirty-four

TOP MAN, DEAD MAN--A TRAGEDY | 1984

Everyone is calling Ben Wilson's murder a senseless crime.[44] What happened to Ben was so quick and horrible that we will never know why it happened. Detective Michael Bosco of the Pullman Area Police said. "This is a random, senseless shooting. It wasn't premeditated. It was just one of those things that happens in our streets."

I think this crime makes too much sense.

This kind of random violence happens too many times on our streets for us not to figure it out with some premeditation on our part.

Put boys and guns together, and add the stupid, macho idea that a guy has to make it to the top, quick and fast, in our society--by the time he is 16, or else he thinks he's a total failure, as good as a dead man--and you've got the simple elements of this kind of crime.

---

[44] Ben Wilson was a 17-year-old Chicago high school basketball star whose murder was front-page news.

Gun, young males, and the drive to be the top man are the threads that repeat over and over in our statistics. In six out of seven of these crimes. the weapon is a gun. In nine out of 10, it is male on male. And in the other one, it's male on female. The explosive element is not race, or poverty: it's young males, guns and dumb fantasies.

Without a gun, those two skinny little kids would have never challenged Ben, an awesome, muscular 6-foot-8 basketball hero. No kid has the right, reason, or authority to carry a gun on our streets.

We fill our boys' heads with pornographic fantasies of what it means to be a tough man. Get a gun, pick a fight, and you will either be top man or dead man. There is no middle ground: It's either your turf or your burial ground.

Girls don't do this kind of crime. Women know better. Only young males are not taught to control their aggression. They think they must be on top to survive. Ben Wilson used his male aggression to become a top man in basketball. His accused assailants tried basketball, music and school, but failed at each.

Omar Dixon, one of the accused, is the grandson of Chicago blues pioneer Willie Dixon. According to his grandmother, Omar was the only one in the family with "no singing talent. "

Bill Moore's mother was quoted as saying, "Don't say my boy was the devil." She portrays her son as a victim, too, of the dead-end streets.

We call these young males juvenile delinquents because we think they are youthful and rowdy. But we misname them. They are not juvenile: they are senile at 16. Their minds are as wasted and gone as though they were suffering from Alzheimer's disease. They hold the same resentment and bitterness toward life--and their lost dreams--as do bitter old people stuck away in a senior "citizens" warehouse. These kids are senile, old, ready to die--there is no "pro-life" left in them. "Blow me away, man!" Situation hopeless.

The difference, of course, is that we don't allow our senior citizens, once they have reached a state of total despair, to have guns in their nursing homes. Under the perversion of our Constitution, in which we insist that every top man "has a right to bear arms," we allow senile delinquents to carry guns. So not just in Council Wars, but also in gang wars, Chicago is twisting into "Beirut on the Lake."[45]

---

[45] "Council Wars" referred to the political infighting between Mayor Harold Washington, a black reform Democrat, and his opponents in the Chicago City Council, a struggle that led Chicago to be dubbed "Beirut on the Lake" in the media.

This male-on-male type of crime also carries a heavy homosexual undertone. "Punk" is a dirty, double-edged word on the streets. Allegedly, Wilson and his assailants tossed the word "punk" at each other, as well as "pop him" and "plug him." Punk comes from the Latin phrase saepe femina puncta, which means "a woman often punctured," and refers to a male whore. And when you've got a top man who wants to plug or pop a bottom man, you've got a good, old-fashioned case of sublime sodomy on your hands.

The crime here is that we never teach our young males anything clear or practical about their homosexual urges. We tell them it's a crime against nature and God. We pervert their minds away from male love because we would rather have them stand tall like cowboys and blow each other away, than get caught in a homosexual blow job. Better dead than gay. "Suck my bullets!"

Do all our streets have to be dead-end streets for males! Can't a boy become a man in our society without being something other than a gang warrior? Are we teaching our young males it's better to make war than love? Can't we give them something other than the lurid stories of martial arts? What about civilian arts? What about no guns? What about living past 16! Why not tell them they don't have to be a top man to survive?

chapter thirty-five

OEDIPUS' DADDY AT THE CROSSROADS | 1985

The old joke runs: "My mother made me a homosexual. If you are a good little boy, she can make you one, too." As the old story goes, your mother made you do it.

But, as any old crone like Mary Daly[46] knows, there is something terribly rotten and fishy about this argument. It blames the woman first, the mother, if the son turns out gay.

It is an odious argument, and it doesn't matter whether it is mouthed by men in a barber shop or by smooth, professional social-psychologists. They, who dispense this particular explanation, use it to hide their own latent homosexuality, but also to cover their fear of everything feminine. They become neurotic over men who act like women, almost in equal degree to the way they hate women who act like women.

Dr. Milton Rosenberg, by day, is a professor of social psychology at the University of Chicago, and, by night, a talk-show host on WGN 720. On most subjects he is polymath and sensitive, but whenever

---

[46] A radical feminist Catholic theologian.

homosexuality comes up he becomes stiff, orthodox, conventional. While interviewing Erik Lee Preminger--the only son of Gypsy Rose Lee, who didn't know until he was 17 that his father was Otto Preminger[47] --Dr. Rosenberg could not resist introjecting Freudian psycho-social theory.

"Since you were very close to your mother--almost like her husband--and since your father was always absent--close mother/absent father--why didn't you turn out homosexual?"

Erik added more material for Rosenberg's hypothesis by saying that the man most influential on him was his mother's tenant and factotum--who was a practicing homosexual. When Erik and the tenant would go to Paris together, they would each cruise different sides of the Left Bank. Erik for girls, the tenant for boys. But despite all this close mother-love and influential homosexuality in the household, Erik turned out a "flaming heterosexual" who had a live-in girlfriend at 17. The only thing his high-strung mother caused him to do was like other strong, intelligent and high-spirited women.

Strong mother/weak father, ever-present mother/ever-absent father as the etiology of homosexuality makes cute barber shop talk, but this easy formula

---

[47] Erik Preminger, author of the memoir *My G-String Mother: At Home and Backstage With Gypsy Rose Lee,* was the result of an affair between stripper Gypsy Rose Lee and filmmaker Otto Preminger while Lee was married to another man.

becomes a noxious notion when raised to scientific dogma. Dr. Freud's speculation that every gay son wants to blow away his "old man" and be his mother makes for intriguing episodes of Dynasty, but in no way reveals the Oedipus family in all its complexity.

In developing Oedipal theory, Freud (see E. Brooks Peters in *Christopher Street*, Issue 77) completely overlooked the fact that Laius, Oedipus' father, was homosexual. Some ancient sources even claim that Laius was the originator of "Theban pederasty," the inventor of man-boy love in ancient Greece.[48]

Oedipus, as we all know, was very close to his mother--in fact, he married her. But what we all conveniently forget is what his absent father Laius was doing when he was "absent." He was out with and after "the boys!" Laius liked boys better than women--better than his wife Jocasta. He preferred to sleep with his boy-lover Chrysippus. If he hadn't been drunk one night--if Jocasta hasn't gotten him drunk--he would have never slept with her the night he made little Oedipus.

Oedipus would have never "known" his father, even if his parents had kept him in their palace,

---

[48] In the ancient Greek city of Thebes, upper-class adolescent boys were mentored in relationships which were, depending on one's source, mostly sexual (Dover, 1978) or rarely sexual (Davidson, 2009). The practice reached its pinnacle in the fourth century B.C. with the establishment of the Sacred Band of Thebes, a battalion consisting of 150 pairs of male lovers.

because his father was always out with the other boys. By chance, they met at the Crossroads on the highway going to Thebes. By then, Oedipus was a handsome young stud. Laius, not knowing that this handsome young man was his son, began cruising Oedipus. He hit on Oedipus. Oedipus rejected his homosexual advance. Laius wouldn't take no for an answer, so Oedipus killed the old fag--nothing so strange, then or now!

According to another version of the ancient story, Oedipus found Laius with his young lover Chrysippus ("Golden Horse") at the Crossroads; Oedipus became immediately so aroused by the seductive young Chrysippus that he and his father began to quarrel over the youth's favors, and Oedipus killed his "father," the Sugar Daddy, so he could have the boy for himself.

Dr. Freud's Victorian eyes could not follow these homosexual trails. As they myth reveals, it is much easier for a son to learn how to be a faggot from his father--AWOL or not--than from his loving mother. You can love your mother to death, but it won't give you same-sex pleasure. But run into your father just once at the Crossroads--or wherever he goes to get his rocks off--and he can teach you how to be a faggot in the flesh.

What do "absent fathers" do when they go out AWOL from home? They go out with "the boys." They do sports and beer, cars and politics--and sometimes even overt sex. Or they go out pretending they are Don Juans chasing "the girls." But Don Juan was a veiled homosexual. Men play Don Juan and chase girls when they are too closeted to chase their real heart's desire: each other. If Big Daddy Don Juan wants a woman, he can stay at home with his wife. No, the Don Juan finds a woman too much for him to handle--he wants a boy like himself--but he will settle for a girl who will play like a boy. Someone he can trick. Someone he can treat like a faggot.

After a fear years of these nocturnal wanderings, Big Daddy Don Juan may get up his courage to go for a boy--as long as "he" looks like a girl. Roll with the Rolling Stones--Cross Over, Cross Dress, at the Crossroads. But the point is that whomever he chooses as his "extra," he will treat them, boy or girl, like a trick, like a rolling faggot.

That's how faggots are made: Following Big Daddy's footprints in the eternal sand. And if Daddy comes back home drunk, or impotent, he can always beat the Mommy--and continue blaming her if her son turns out like him.

So the next time a learned man tries to put you on and says, "Homosexuals are made by too much mother-love," tell him the story of Oedipus' Daddy at the Crossroads--and ask him if he wants to meet you there later.

chapter thirty-six

72 HOURS AMONG THE SUB-YUPPIES |1985

In college, after they have taken Econ 101, Future Yuppies often go on to take a course in "Money and Banking." For them this is an odd and theoretical experience. I'm sure, because unless they have a relative who owns a bank, they may never work in one: and as long as they have their personal Ivory Carved Credit Card they will never use filthy money.

There is another class of young urban people in our society that I call Sub-Yuppies. They would have been Yuppies if they had not dropped out of high school. They don't like waiting rooms, they went directly to life--they didn't want to wait in a dorm room for four more years. So they will never take "Money and Banking" in college: in fact, they will never do much banking because they live off of cash flow and they don't think it is wise to put your real name on paper. For them it's "Money and Money"--never any banking.

Steve, Joe, and Teddie are an example of this class of Sub-Yuppie. They always have cash, but they never do any banking. Cal Coolidge--Ronald Reagan's favorite president--used to say that "time is money."

For most of us, that means we fill out calendars all our lives, waiting for two-week paychecks.

Sub-Yuppies have an entirely different concept of Time and Money. In the last 18 months--calendar time--Steve, Joe, and Teddie have been, on and off, each other's roommate, lover, and friend. They have lived in seven different places in Chicago and in five different cities besides Chicago. For them, 72 hours can be a lifetime. They might say things like, "I'm in school now," or "I don't do coke anymore," or "I'm working now at the Water Tower," or "I've got this girl in Philadelphia I'm going to live with," or "I'm not really gay. I'm just living this way for now." Each of these statements is true, but only for 72 hours--for the lifetime in which it is spoken.

These guys are not runaways or throwaways. They visit home for holidays, or their mother might visit them for Christmas. They live in Lake Shore Drive apartments. They have VCRs and microwave ovens and they ride cabs even if they are just going to the post office. They like nice things, and they will pool their cash, so one of them can rent a nice apartment--even though they will probably not live together, except for various 72-hour intervals.

Some people imagine that they must "earn" their money from drugs or hustling. But when you study their habits closely, you will find they are not that organized, or that consistently in business. Sure, they will know a few "benefactors"--lawyers, doctors, accountants--in the community they can sometimes turn to for a loan. Benefactors are very convenient for coming up with money to party on, but not for basics like lights and food and phone and heat.

In their circle of friends there also is often a shadowy figure who is likely to be young, pretty and rich with enough bad habits that he doesn't mind sharing. Someone, perhaps, whose family has thrown him out with a prepaid inheritance, with an insurance settlement from an "accident." This type of shadow-friend often will think nothing or spending money in big chunks. Like putting out $50,000 in a year on airplane tickets. If your motto is that of the Motley Crue--"live fast, die young"--you really don't care about retirement or final expenses.

Each of these energetic Sub-Yuppies can generate and spend a thousand dollars in 72 hours. In the real world, there is no accounting for how the money comes--they can't even account for it themselves. You have to live their way for it to happen that way. Cash comes to cash, much like old money used to come to old money, or dust to dust.

If you are into the way of the Sub-Yuppies, things happen intensely and miraculously. And, as with other classes, you take care of your own. Between last Tuesday and Thursday, Steve, Joe and Teddie went through one of these miraculous money cycles. Teddie came back from Houston Tuesday night and Steve said he could stay with him a couple of days "rent free." Teddie then called Joe to say he was back in town and needed "a little help." Joe said "Not tonight, but Thursday. I could help with about $100."

Wednesday, Joe sold a couch and a mirror (which he never liked) for $100, which he intended to "loan" to Teddie on Thursday.

Wednesday night around midnight, Steve got arrested for "smiling in a hustler zone." Steve has a bad habit which his friends have warned him about: He smiles at people, as if he were still in his home town of Ames, Iowa.

This night, Steve smiled at an undercover cop. He got arrested for something like "prostitution" or "disorderly conduct." But his real crime was...smiling. In fact, the female officer putting him in lockup told him right out: "Hey, guy, if you don't wipe that smile off your face. you'll stay here till morning!" Then Steve's two cellmates informed him that he "owed" them his gold chain.

Steve was not liking his part in this real-life Hill Street Blues, so he called Joe and asked him to bring $100 in cash to bail him out. Joe hesitated and thought about it for an hour, and then decided he would take the $100 he had set aside for Teddie and bail Steve out.

Joe told Steve while they were leaving the station that he needed to be paid back in the morning (which is 4:00 in the afternoon, Sub-Yuppie Time). Steve said. "I have a check for $50 now." "No," Joe said. "I want it all in cash!"

The next morning--3:30 in the afternoon--Steve went to a friend and got his check cashed. Then he went back to Ted and said he needed $50 because he "needed it to get out of jail." The story was not clear to Ted, but he gave Steve $50 anyway, not thinking that he must be out of jail now, or he wouldn't be talking to him. Mere chronological details.

At 7:30, Steve handed $85 back to Joe saying it was "all he could raise right now." That was $100 less $15 "commission"--with the promise to pay back the rest by the 71st hour.

At 8:30, Teddie came to Joe's place and Joe gave him $100 so he would have a deposit that Teddie could give to two other friends who want him as a "roommate." During their conversation, both Ted and Joe confessed that they were "a little short" because they had helped to get Steve out of jail the night before.

Sub-Yuppies don't do double-entry book-keeping, so to Ted, Steve and Joe these interlocking transactions all seemed fair.

Praise be the Goddess of Cash Flow. Besides, in another 12 hours they would each be ready to try their next world, like new-born babes.

chapter thirty-seven

DRUGS, HABITS AND MORALS | 1985

I met a young man last summer who for the past seven years--almost a third of his life--has had a heroin habit. He sleeps little, eats little, and every few hours needs to find the stuff. He finds the stuff, nods off for a half hour, then gets up and goes out to find the stuff again. He says he needs the stuff to get going, just like the rest of us may need coffee or cigarettes.

It's not junk to him; it's medicine. "Don't you understand? If I don't get this garbage, I get sick and lose my balance. I need the stuff for health reasons. Don't you understand?"

No, I don't really understand. I have no habit. I take no drugs. And it sounds upside-down to me to say heroin can make you "healthy."

My friend lives in an upper-story lakefront apartment overlooking Belmont Harbor. His parents have furnished his place twice. Each time, I guess, they thought he was going to get married. Yet each time his furniture seems to disappear. Now he just lives there in four empty rooms with two baths, a bed, and a boom box on the floor.

He is not easy to talk to, because he pays no attention to anything being said.

He keeps getting up in the middle of a sentence to call his "lover-dealer." This guy is just his "lover," because they are good friends and never have sex. But he isn't a very good dealer, because supply never equals demand.

My friend likes tunes on his box. He seems to get inside them, and they've get inside him. When he tried to talk to his "lover-dealer" and listen to Jim Morrison's "Hitchhiker" at the same time, he got lost in a quadraphonic conversation, because he thought Morrison was talking to him and going to kill him.

My friend spikes his conversation with repeated interjections, saying, "See, that shows how I am honest." "You know I'm good." "You can trust me." "You see, I'm not a junkie!"

I didn't doubt his honesty. But "not a junkie"? That was like Nixon saying "I am not a crook."[49]

"You see," he said, "I am not a junkie, because I always pay for the stuff."

At the end of summer, my friend entered the Martha Washington Hospital for their drug abuse

[49] In November, 1973, President Nixon stated, "I am not a crook." Nine months later, he was the first United States President to resign the Office.

program. Before going in, he explained to me that for the past five years he had lost his romance for heroin. It was just garbage medicine for him now. The thrill was gone. He didn't get real rushes anymore. He just was taking the stuff to stay even with the game.

Some game.

I have thought a lot about my friend since, and how he thought he was "not a junkie." I have not known many people who took heroin three times a day. And I've always thought that was what a "junkie" was.

Then it occurred to me: how easily we confuse habits and morals. We think that because we have a "no habit" position we are free to take an absolute moral position. We don't do heroin, so death to all those who do!

We forget that we don't even get to moral first base until we accept the proposition that "I could be you, and you could be me." A priest can glibly condemn a sex habit, because he doesn't do sex. Or I can condemn a heroin habit, because I don't do the stuff. We don't realize that "not-doing-the-stuff" is just our habit too.

Habit is the way you do or don't do things.

You don't get to a moral position fighting habit and nonhabit. Habit keeps you at the brute level, both in morals and in thinking. You are not in a moral position until you can pop out of your skin and into another person's life. Moral ground is equal ground. And acting superior because you don't have your friend's habit is a bad ego habit, not a moral position.

From what I read, heroin has such a "divine rush" that you don't even want to try it once. If I did it once, maybe I too would end up living in a room with a bed and a boombox. Maybe I too would suffer long chills looking for a few seconds of warmth. Maybe I too would puke on myself in the morning and wonder why I am so sick.

My friend does not need my "superior" no habit advice. He does not need me to verbally puke on him. When he says he is "no junkie," he means he still has a moral self, a person beneath his habit. If I puke on his moral self, he will have nothing to come back to health and sanity with.

On the surface, it is a lot easier to live with no-habits. Then you don't have to pass any real moral tests, or trials like my friend's. You can just stand there and pass out gratuitous moral judgments. This superior stance does not put you in the moral realm; it puts you at zero, thinking you are number one--a delusion.

My friend the "no junkie"--I don't know what number he is. Or if his number is up. But he did teach me to be a little more careful in distinguishing between habits and morals.

chapter thirty-eight

THE PRESS TURNS THE SCREW | 1985

The press turns the screw, and TV turns up the heat. The press cooks up a story, and TV reheats it till it burns, and finally burns out. That's how news is made in America.

Since Rock Hudson's illness and death[50] became Page One news, the press has been turning up the screw on the so-called "AIDS story," and TV has been making it their burning issue.

Sex, drugs, death, mystery, fear, panic and Hollywood: AIDS has all the makings of a hot, hot story. A cooler head, like Dr. David J. Coynik, the medical columnist for *Gay Chicago* Magazine, has followed this "hot" story from its inception. But he hasn't been writing much about AIDS lately, because it's all been over-said before--and this overkill and "underskill" journalism only scares healthy people out of their ever-coping minds.

---

[50] After living the life of a closeted movie star, Rock Hudson died in 1985, shortly after announcing to the world he had AIDS.

"Most persons at risk of AIDS," Coynik reminds us, "will probably survive this epidemic as the number of presumably immune individuals grows in relation to the number of susceptible individuals."

As the press turns the screw, male homosexuals and IV drug users--the cliche "high-risk" group--are the ones first getting screwed and politically sodomized. The crime and sickness of homosexuality is still homosexuality in most news reporting. In *Newsweek* you don't get fag-bashing, you get waspish and genteel "gay-bashing." Their attitude echoes back to Narcissus and the Trials of Dear Oscar Wilde, where anybody who has ever assumed "the pose of a sodomite" is a diseased, degenerate sinner. As *Newsweek* tells us, "the breakage of the rectal lining through anal sex--that's probably how the vast majority of the cases have been transmitted so far."

Pose as a sodomite, "break your rectal lining," and Bingo you come down with AIDS. Since most people never assume such a pose--they reassure us--the risk of getting it, for most people, is remote. Death to all Sodomites! But you, John and Mary Puritan--not to worry--as long as you are missionary in the position you take in sex. Such is the good news from mainstream journalism.

The Big News Networks and their Local Happy Talkers are burning the AIDS story into our brains and bodies on a nightly basis--three times a day with their news hot flashes, they are breaking the cranial lining of our heads until the only thing we think is fear itself--so that now under the guise of information and fairness we--are being bombarded with AIDS news right and left.

It used to be all we had to worry about was the news on the right. Jerry Falwell[51] wants to quarantine us, and blast us into Hell. Paul Cameron[52]--who absolutely believes that the consummation of every homosexual delight is to "ingest fecal matter"--wants to smash us into potatoes and put us in camps in Idaho. And Pat Buchanan,[53] director of communications at the White House, states pontifically that since homosexual acts are acts against nature, AIDS is "the awful retribution nature is exacting from us."

These deluded father-worshippers on the right have never understood that Mother Nature

---

[51] Televangelist and anti-gay crusader known for co-founding the Moral Majority and Liberty University, Falwell died in 2007.

[52] Conservative psychologist and founder of the Family Research Institute, expelled by the American Psychological Association for non-cooperation with an ethics investigation.

[53] Conservative political commentator and former adviser to Presidents Richard Nixon, Gerald Ford and Ronald Reagan.

is one of us. She is as queer as us. Before we were dancing in discos, we were in Earth Mother Temples dancing on the Trivium with Hecate. If the pseudo-fathers and fakirs don't watch their words and mind their manners, Mother Nature will have her Three Sisters cut their strings--and that will be the end of their story. They will be dumped into the realm of "fecal matter."

More subtle and insidious is the press coverage on the mainstream left: CBS, the *New York Times*, *Newsweek*, and the Washington *Post*. CBS and the gothic *New York Times*[54] still dare not call us by our name: they dictatorially insist upon calling every gay and lesbian a "homosexual." *Newsweek* opines that the press has been "oversolicitous of high-risk groups." Thus, we should not be treated as though we have the same constitutional rights as every other American.

The Washington *Post*, *Newsweek's* half-brother, originated an opinion piece by Richard Restak, an establishment medicine man and neurologist--a piece later picked up and put screaming on the Sunday front page of Murdoch's Chicago *Sun-Times*[55]--which states flatly, "AIDS virus has no civil rights." Implying

---

[54] The *New York Times* began to use the word "gay" in 1987.

[55] In 1985, conservative media mogul Rupert Murdoch owned the Chicago *Sun-Times*.

that those who have ever been exposed to the AIDS virus also have no civil rights.

Forget the patients and their rights, the victims and their suffering, think only of the "common good." And since obviously homosexuals are by definition neither "common" nor "good"--segregate the sickies! Set up centers of "Contamination Control." Scare the holy nightmares out of the citizens of Clinton, Illinois, so they will vote for isolation camps, so this alien plague will never come to their town.

What scares me most about this turn of the screw in mainstream left journalism is that *Newsweek*, the *New York Times*, CBS, and the Washington *Post* were the voices of mild sanity opposing our policy in Vietnam. Now their voices are not with us anymore; they are sending signals that it is okay, in the name of sickness and health, to take civil rights away from homosexuals.

William S. Burroughs[56]--borrowing from Wittgenstein[57]--says: "Language is a virus." I would extend that statement and say: "Mainstream news is waste matter." Thus, I would urge readers to avoid ingesting too much "waste matter"; stick rather with voices like Dr. David Coynik, Dr. Ron Sable, Dr. Steven P. Brasch, Chet Kelly, Katie Sprutta, Dr. David Ostrow, and the weekly health news in the *New York Native*--for these are the voices nourishing us with clarity and health.

---

[56] American novelist, essayist and social critic primarily associated with the Beat Generation who died in 1987; associated with both the terms "junky" and "queer," respectively, the titles of his first and second novels

[57] Austrian-born Oxford University philosopher Ludwig Wittgenstein (1889-1951), perhaps better known for mid-20th century biographies which scandalized his sexual orientation than for altering philosophy's course twice: (1) his work on logical philosophy simultaneously solved its greatest problem and silenced its use in real life and (2) his introduction of "language games" democratized the role of philosopher as someone who "puzzles" *with* us rather than authoritatively directs "problems" *at* us.

chapter thirty-nine

BEING A SEXUAL BEING | 1986

Being a sexual being, I find it out of character to pull in my full-moon hornies and deny my being. Even in the face of AIDS and scary-death, it is not a good policy to shrivel up and deny your nature.

For some time now, my sexual mood and acts have modified: I'd rather flirt than fuck. Not for one moment will I stop my roving eye and cut myself off from the flowers: from looking, admiring, dreaming. In these times, we must all keep our roving eyes and sexuality open: we all need that fruitful nourishment and vitality rush to keep on going.

There are three traditional ways to express your sexual being: you can flaunt it, hide it, or simply live with it. Pier Paolo Pasolini flaunted his; Michel Foucault mainly hid his; and Jean Genet cunningly lived with his.

Pasolini, born in Pisces, had a predilection for "rough trade." At 53, he died in Scorpio, having traded all his oceanic talents for a life in the swamp.

Pasolini probably was the greatest talent to come out of post-war Italy: poet, auteur, painter, sculptor, political partisan, scandalous "faggot." He defied people right and left: he confounded both his Mother Church and Father Marx.

For his movie, *The Gospel According to St. Matthew*,[58] he had nuns across the world weeping and saying "Hail Marys." The Pope gave him a prize. Then the Pope realized who he was--that "Commie queer"--and took the prize back.

The Marxists found him an impossible contradiction too. He would go to their meetings and suck off the farm boys in the back of the meeting hall.

Pasolini actively loved Christ more than the Church Fathers, and tried to love the proletariat--especially, if they were young and male--one by one.

When he was a guest of the state of Israel he embarrassed his hosts by going out of his hotel every night to cruise young Arabs.

Pasolini oozed with homosexuality and flaunted it so that no one was surprised when, at

---

58 1964 Italian film *Il vangelo secondo Matteo.*

53, at Ostia, a seaside resort near Rome, he was bludgeoned (or assassinated) by a trick.[59]

Michel Foucault, along with Lacan, Derrida and Barthes, is one of the great postwar French thinkers and anthro-philosophers: an archeologist of the mind.

During his life everyone knew and whispered that Foucault was the "gay" one. He tried to make a "gay" living out of Goy Science. Graduate students across the continents speculated continually about how his "gayness" influenced his inverted thinking--and how being gay would help in getting, or not getting, a job or recommendation from him.

Foucault developed a style of life and prose that is so oblique, arrogant, and opaque, that he is almost impossible to follow. I get nauseated, or seasick, every time I try to read a chapter of his prose. It is full of blockage and subterfuge. Derrida is pure diarrhea: his shit flows. Foucault is all blockage; nothing flows. He squeezes and hides his thoughts until they get stuck in a dark hole.

Foucault died just as he lived: hidden. Now we, and his lover, learn that he died of AIDS.

---

[59] In 2005, 30 years after Pasolini's 1975 murder, former street hustler Giuseppe Pellosi, who had confessed to the killing, retracted his confession, claiming that Pasolini was assassinated by a group of anti-communists.

Writing in the New Yorker--is that where you want your lover and the world to learn these things?--George Steiner makes a cute hint about Foucault's life and death: "there is a terminal isolation and unresolved dark in Foucault's own consciousness."

His great contribution to ideas was his invention of the concept of "epistemological space." He wrote continually on death and sexuality, yet hid his own death and sexuality. His ideas have no space, no movement. They remain, much like his life, in isolation, the cause of snide intellectual jokes.

Jean Genet, at age 75, died a couple of weeks ago in bed, in his hotel room, which was as small as a prison cell, but as clean as a bourgeois mansion.

Genet outlived all his perversions, because they were never his in the first place. As a kid, when society called him a thief, he took up male prostitution so they could call him worse. But he never even tried to live up to his bad name and reputation. Nor did he try to live the life of a saint, just because Sartre wrote a thick tome calling him one[60].

Genet did a lot more flirting than fucking and sucking. If you invited him to your house, he

---

[60] *Saint Genet, Actor and Martyr,* by Jean-Paul Sartre, published 1952.

would steal something, or make a pass at your nephew, just to keep up a sense of friendly betrayal between you.

But Genet was always the playful moralist. His sexuality was so open and rock solid, he never hid it or flaunted it: like Ferdinand, he just smelled the flowers, and enjoyed all his flirtations to the point of imaginary murder. But, unlike Fassbinder, he was not a foolish realist; he did not try to experience his kamikaze fantasies; and so he died a natural French peasant's death: quietly in his own bed. Thank you.

chapter forty

THE YUPPIEFUCKATION OF WELLS STREET | 1986

At three in the afternoon, on Wednesday, May 21, two voyeuristic vice cops made another raid on Wells Street. They entered the Over 21 Bookstore, pulled seven guys out of their private movie booths, and arrested them for "public indecency." One guy was 29 and the rest were in their 40s and 60s. They also arrested the clerk on duty as a "keeper of a house of ill fame."

They then went down the alley to the Old Town Bookstore and arrested a 45-year-old tourist from Nevada, while he was watching a movie in his private booth. They charged him with "public indecency," and also arrested the clerk on duty for being a "keeper of a house of ill fame."

These stores and booths and movie machines are taxed and licensed by the city. If the city is going to license and tax these places, then they should also be arrested as a "co-conspirator," and the Mayor arrested as "the Madame of the house of ill fame."

Ever since the yuppies have come back to Wells Street, and the development of Cobbler Square, gay people who have lived, worked, and played on this street for more than 10 years have noticed a peculiar pattern to these arrests. No one goes to jail; but everyone arrested mysteriously seems to get their name, age, and place of employment put in the newspaper, or their picture on TV.

One man in this raid, after his boss read his name in the Chicago *Sun-Times*, had his job suspended.

The reporter for the Chicago *Sun-Times* justified the "full disclosure" of those arrested by saying: "You wouldn't want someone arrested in a place like that teaching children in public school, would you?" [One arrested was a teacher; the man suspended was a prison guard.]

The image is that these are sleaze joints for "faggots." Good people and good gays--yuppies--would never go to such a dirty place.

How soon we forget. Fifteen years ago police conducted these same kind of raids in gay bars. Then they were called "homosexual haunts," and a gay could get arrested and have his name in the *Chicago Tribune* the next morning, if he held another guy's hand, or danced with another guy.

Bookstores today, with their private booths, are less public, and no more sleazy than those old "homosexual haunts." The yuppies' sense of morality want us to betray these "faggots," and show what good gays we are. While they buy up our property, stores and businesses, and chase us to some other burned-out neighborhood.

The majority of those arrested on May 21 have already been given a legal pass for "insufficient information." The rest of the cases will probably also be waived.

One bookstore and their arrestees are thinking of bringing a class-action suit in Federal Court. And they should! Other such suits recently have met with some success.

They should also think of suing the *Sun-Times* and their reporter. For in this case the paper committed "cruel and unusual punishment." The people arrested are punished and punished: punished by the shock of arrest, and punished by public exposure in the newspaper.

Last summer when a bank executive was arrested for embezzling a large sum of money and the *Sun-Times* ran his story on the front page, they withheld his name, because it would do harm to his family.

Real criminals can have their names withheld: but a 60-year-old man pulled out of his private booth because he was playing with himself behind his shut door while watching a movie: his name is exposed to his boss, family and friends.

The real scandal on Wells Street is not, however, the raids and arrests, but the way "faggots" are being pushed out to "upgrade" the neighborhood. Mother Carol's place[61] was a "black" disco, where the gangs from Cabrini-Green[62] used to hang out. The "faggots" were let in to chase them back, and a lot of customers had to fight for their right just to go to Carol's. No one--especially the complaining lady who lived behind them--thought Carol's would outlast the snows of '79, and Mother Carol's death. Now they have even outlasted the Bistro and Paradise.[63] They were the first to bring a New York style disco with progressive music, lights, and videos to Chicago.

The Bijou Theatre[64] is unequalled in the country and internationally known as a video outlet. They have a staff and management team that is as clean and clever as the folks who run the Dove Bar Ice Cream Company. You pay--but

---

[61] Carol's Speakeasy, a popular Old Town gay disco in the 1970s and 1980s.

[62] Public housing project.

[63] Popular gay discos, now closed.

[64] The Bijou is a well-known gay adult movie theater.

the Bijou gives its customers an extraordinary experience.

The Glory Hole is a people's bar run as much by its customers as by its owners. Rosie Grabel, who calls herself the resident "fag hag," sees to it that all new customers--especially if they are young--get words about safe sex.

The Peeping Tom started out as a hippie garage and is now evolving into the Old Town Video Shop. Its bookstore features are dying out.

Ultra Ink not only puts out a model gay bar magazine, *Gay Chicago*, but they also do typesetting, printing and graphics for the merchants of Wells Street. They do the program for the Wells Street Arts and Craft Fair.

When the Yuppie Temple, Cobbler Square, was being built, pressure started coming on all the "faggot" businesses on Wells Street. There were rumors that the workers were getting blow jobs in the day time. So the police came at night and arrested the male go-go dancers at the Glory Hole. That's how police act on complaints on Wells Street. Think up a crime, then go and arrest a "faggot." That's how justice for these last two years has been done on Wells Street.

Once built, Cobbler Square invited Andy Warhol to come from New York to promote and entice "the right kind of gays" (Guppies) to move in and locate shops in their Yuppie Temple.

Now is the time for the "faggots" on Wells Street who have been there more than 10 years to hold on and fight back. They have been there working, living, playing and building up that street long before Cobbler Square and the friends of Andy Warhol ever heard of the place. The "faggots" are the ones who have made Wells Street once again a decent and livable place. And they deserve more than to get arrested and harassed by archaic laws and mores about "public indecency."

chapter forty-one

IT'S LIKE TENNIS | 1986

What is it like being gay?

When you are gay, you are always playing doubles, even when you think you are playing singles. This effect comes about from the queer structure of our society. Everyone is born a little homosexual, but everyone is raised, taught, and indoctrinated to be heterosexual. Most gay people come out of church and family as "trained and house-broken heterosexuals." It is not that we don't know how to do it that way; it's just that we prefer to do it our way.

We do it our way, not just because it is more pleasurable for us, but basically because it is more honest. And we too were taught by our heterosexually-oriented school, church, and family: above all be true and honest to yourself.

When you are fully and outrageously gay--willing to march in the Gay and Lesbian Pride Parade, to show yourself in all your colors--then naturally you will feel some clash and conflict between being born homosexual and raised heterosexual.

That's why we must live to some degree or other a double life. I am a very gay-identified man in Chicago, but still many of my students take me for heterosexual. I enjoy the mixture myself. For when you are gay, you don't have to be mixed up anymore--homosexual/ heterosexual, you are gay, nicely mixed together, thank you.

I enjoy it when I hear tales about our kind: when I hear that one of us dated Greta Garbo and then threw her over for a stable boy. Or: that Kate Smith[65] lived her last years with a live-in female companion.

God Bless America.

I can tell some tales, too, about the homo-hetero mixture.

Angelo was born the baby in a large Italian family in St. Louis. He had five older sisters, and three older brothers. Being the late-in-life arrival, he was doted and pampered by his mother and father and grandmother and brothers and sisters and uncles and aunts and a chorus of cousins.

---

[65] Popular American singer during World War II, famed for singing Irving Berlin's "God Bless America."

Angelo didn't have a life or personhood of his own. He existed in their eyes only, and he was to mirror their perfect expectations.

But Angelo had a body of his own, which he discovered all by himself. When he was nine or 10, he shocked the whole clan at a family gathering: he went up to the television set and kissed Dr. Kildare (Richard Chamberlain[66]) on the lips, and he said, "I luv you."

Why would Angelo do such a thing, they all asked. They pointed and laughed at him. Was he trying for more attention? "Boys don't kiss men on the lips."

If Angelo's family seemed confused by Angelo's act, his church was not. His church would teach Angelo, quite specifically, what was a natural and unnatural act.

Masturbation was an "unnatural act"; it could lead to homosexuality, or worse; and homosexuality was an unthinkable act.

In school, Angelo puzzled mightily over this concept of "unnatural act." The way he looked at the anatomy of his body, it seemed all too natural that his hand easily fit his cock when he was standing in front of a mirror, or in bed. It was

---

[66] Actor who identified himself as gay in 2003, at age 69. In an account of Damski's muse, Omega Michael Orsetti, after his 1991 death, Damski repeats this act, placing it within the biography of Orsetti.-JMV

harder for him to scratch his back than his balls. How can you not touch there? Your hand rests there naturally.

What is so unnatural about a hand job? Baseball players on television are always grabbing themselves there, after they have hit a double and land on second base. They rub it up and smile like they have done a good thing.

Angelo wanted to trust his teachers and parents. They said don't do it, and that's what the church says--so it must be right. Angelo wanted to please people. He was not a trouble maker.

After two years of junior college, he pleased his father by coming to work in his father's company. He pleased his mother by marrying the girl he had dated in high school; the woman he was supposed to be in love with.

To please his wife, they had four children: two girls and two boys.

When he hit 40, 40 hit back and he suffered a total breakdown. He had a "serious" drinking problem, but even more--a serious living problem. He did not know how to do anything that pleased Angelo.

After a couple years of therapy, and an amicable divorce, Angelo was free to try to be himself. He bought a van and went to Mexico. He had a few altered-states experiences. He went on the road to find himself, a career move he should have made 20 years earlier.

He met a young Mexican who wanted to come to the States. He would be Angelo's teacher in matters of pleasure, and Angelo his protector. Julio taught him how kissing lips in the flesh could be more satisfying than kissing TV scenes.

They moved to LA and set up housekeeping. But Angelo missed the Midwest: his roots and his heartland. So they set up housekeeping in Chicago, where they could be near his kids in St. Louis.

For several years Angelo pretended his family did not exist anymore. When his father died, he returned home and brought Julio with him. They treated Julio like he belonged in the servants' quarters.

Angelo had a few meals with his mother and his ex-wife; but they refused to understand the importance of Julio to Angelo. His kids, however, were warm, curious, and open. Angelo left St. Louis for the last time. He said, "Forget the family, but my kids are welcome to visit me anytime."

This year two of Angelo's kids are coming to be with him and Julio for a month.

Angelo and Julio plan to have them march with them in the Pride Parade so they can learn what Dad and his lover's life is like.

Angelo and Julio are happy now that they are out and gay. They have no great plans or ambitions. They want an ordinary life together. And Angelo wants a chance to recover some of the pleasures that he once thought were forbidden to him.

Like Angelo, I came to the Gay and Lesbian Pride Parade 10 years ago--a little late because it had already been going for six years.

Also, like Angelo, what I like most about being "gay" is the space. Gay is different from being homosexual. Everybody is a little of that. Gay is different. Gay gives you the space to sort things out.

I like my new landing space, my new ground; but I also remember my points of origin. After all, I too was raised a heterosexual. But I started to go physically "the other way" early in the fourth grade.

Tommy with his little hands and bee-bee eyes caught my fancy in the fourth grade. I already knew enough about making movies that all the cowboys, like Alan Ladd and Audie Murphy, were real short in real life. Tommy was real short in real life, and I wanted him for my cowboy.

Tommy used to fight them off at the pass, and make the way safe for me to walk to school. He was neat, even though he would wear dirty clothes to school. I had to have clean clothes everyday.

Our family went to Aspen, Colorado for the summer. I rode horses and learned how to do it from the big cowboys. And they got me a gen-u-INE cowboy hat. I loved that hat so, I slept with it every night on the train home.

As soon as I got back to school, I continued my habit with Tommy. I was already giving him all my allowance. So I gave him my prize possession, my gen-u-INE cowboy's cowboy hat.

I told my parents that it had fallen off my head at Playland, and that I had lost it. I wanted Tommy to wear it (which he did), and I wanted to hug him while he had it on (which he never did).

Tommy was a bit bewildered by all my affection and gifts. He took everything I gave him, but never gave anything back. Tommy, for me, was a great initiation to the rituals of love and marriage.[67]

---

67 "True" Damski fans will recognize Tommy from "Fat Head!," which begins on page 129; even as a repeated anecdote, it demonstrates Damski's ability to weave biographical details into a narrative with little actual repetition-JMV

In the seventh grade, Joey B. had an uncontrollable crush on me. His family owned a bank. So when he spent his allowance on me, we had some trips. He gave me (I still have it in my library in Seattle) *The Portable Mark Twain*. Inside the cover, in red ink, he inscribed it to me. He also drew a heart with our initials in it, just like boys draw hearts on trees with their girlfriends' initials.

Joey was a sweetie. But I really didn't love him that much. This time around I got to play Tommy's revenge.

My real ardent flame in the seventh grade was Doug Smith. He knew the ropes. He had been in seventh grade the year before we got there, and he was repeating the experience.

Girls flocked around Doug as though he were the star of *Room 222*. He was a great athlete. More exciting for me, however, he picked me up to be his sex partner. He quickly taught me that masturbation could be more than a minimalist art.

Our school had compulsory gym for all boys. It was a good policy, because when we were in the Chapel feeling each other up, we weren't allowed to wear our sexy clothes.

But gym clothes are sexy no matter what you wear. Doug and I used to dress and undress together. We shared a locker. When we both signed up for basketball, I was thrilled and he was cagey. We seldom every made it to basketball practice.

Doug was always taking me down to the wrestling room for a private session of tumbling jack. Doug was pure sex. He never sent me a heart inscribed in red ink.

We did it in the gym, in the Chapel, on the bus, in his dorm room, in his home room, and at my house. We were lucky that our parents were such important people in the community because they were always out of town on business, and that left a lot of time for Doug and I to do our business.

Tommy was the first in our class out of high school to get married. Marriage seems a very important thing to Tommy, because he has tried it several times since.

Joey B. today is president of his family's bank in Astoria, Oregon. After missing out on me, Joey hasn't missed many tricks since. He probably was the first of our class to come out "gay."

He once told me at a reunion that he loves his double life. Astoria is not far from San Francisco, when you have the company plane. He enjoys all the excitement of making business deals. Then he likes to go to his ranch-home and invite a few friends over to watch him play host, where he plays a smart-mouthed woman in a dress and boa. He loves his double life because he can be "Edgar Rivers" by day and "Joan Rivers" by night.

Doug married Patty, the girl I took to the Governor's Inaugural Ball in 1956. They have five children. I am still close to Patty, but not close anymore to Doug. We stopped our "wrestling" after each of us went to college.

Doug, after all, is a confirmed married man. I just savor the thought that I was taught how to do all these homosexual acts, which still give me such pleasure, by a heterosexual partner. It would seem so unnatural to have learned them from anyone else.

PART FOUR

chapter forty-two

LARRY EYLER: TOP MOUSE | 1986

[68]All through his brief six-day trial for the torture, murder, and dismemberment of 16-year-old Danny Bridges,[69] Larry Eyler sat at the defense table quiet as a mouse. Each time he entered the court, he came in like a timid mouse. You had no sense of his faint presence, until the Judge would stand and say: "And Larry Eyler is here."

Each day Larry wore mousy colors: a beige short-sleeved shirt, brown tie, and tan slacks.

His most dramatic gesture through the trial was curling a ball-point pen in the mousy fingers of his right hand. Or glancing down with his dull colorless eyes at a piece of blank paper.

I guess he was hoping to disprove Asst. State's Attorney Mark Rakoczy's contention that Eyler

---

[68] This column is the first of five columns published by Damski on the Larry Eyler trial; they have been collected here in the same order of original publication.

[69] Danny Bridges was murdered in August, 1984; Damski's column about him can be found on page 235.

"was the most dangerous person that ever set foot in this building."

The most emotion I ever say him give was when he stared back hard at his ex "lover" John, while John added a corroborating human voice to the mountain of inanimate objects that linked Eyler to Bridges.

Each day Eyler looked squeaky clean: his hair short-cut and slicked back, leaving a very uncreative hairline in front. Eyler's skin color too had a brownish yellow pallor. The young jury--seven women and five men, each about Eyler's age of 33--all glowed in contrast to Eyler and suburban health.

When he walked into court the bailiff did not call out: "Lawrence W. Eyler is here." It was always the less formal "Larry Eyler." Who cares?

When John Wayne Gacy, that monstrous clown, used to stride into court everyone gave pause, because he was JOHN WAYNE GACY. He came in with three names. He was a man of top rank in any crowd--an ex-Democratic precinct Captain--and then the Top Cat on death row. Larry Eyler's life has been a series of games of cat and mouse. Larry always wanted to be a Top Cat, but has never managed to get any higher than being the Top Mouse in a stray cat's game.

I had the decided feeling that Eyler's trial was over before Eyler's formal trial began. Larry's game had already played out. This was the mouse who liked to restrain and tie up cats; then stab them. This was the mouse who always insisted on playing "top." This was the guy for whom sex had become a homicidal blood sport.

Now the State had finally caught him and kept him in a mouse house for two years, and he seemed unusually pleased. He has yet to speak up or say anything interesting in his defense. He likes being a caught mouse.

We are always told "you can't get away with murder." But murder in real life is probably one of the easiest crimes to get away with. Especially when, like for Eyler, it becomes your line of work.

In jail, Eyler seems relieved, because he doesn't have to go out and "work" anymore. He likes it that way. He timidly accepts bondage from the State, when he never accepted bondage, even in play, from anyone else. The mouse has no will of his own left.

David Schippers, Eyler's defense attorney, must have also known that the trial was over before the trial was over. The first thing he told the jury in summation was: "I'm not going to talk very long."

The second thing he told them: "I have no evidence. And neither do they [the state]."

The prosecutors in six days had brought in 181 separate pieces of physical evidence. It took grocery carts to haul in all the evidence each day. They had: plastic garbage bags similar to what Eyler used to carry out the eight cut-up pieces of Danny Bridges' body; they had pictures of Danny Bridges' cut-up torso; Eyler's blood-stained gym shoes; Eyler's "blood-soaked" Levi's, size 32/32; Danny Bridges' Duke University T-shirt found in Eyler's apartment; Eyler's green goggles he used while painting over the blood-splattered walls; and they had the blood-stained mattress taken from Larry's bed.

This was insurmountable physical evidence, which Schippers could not make disappear in a magical phrase. He ended his summation by quoting from Daniel Webster, and Thomas More from the movie A Man for All Seasons.

These days it is hard to defend even real innocent people, when the national mood in our country is "vengeance is ours."

Prosecutor Rakoczy easily knocked out Schippers' argument in rebuttal. "I don't know Who this Thomas More fellow is (the crowd and jury laughed at his witless vulgarity)...but here is the blood-stained mattress." He indignantly threw it down on the floor and said in easy-to-follow irony: "now, I know what happened:

Danny Bridges killed himself, and he dismembered himself!"

Through the trial I sat with Austine Bridges on the mother's side of the courtroom. I was a prejudiced onlooker. My sources on the street told me more than what was brought up in the trial. But gay people are reluctant to cooperate with the cops and judges, when they know that they are going to be put on trial, too, for being a "homosexual."

I knew from my sources that Danny Bridges had played cat and mouse with Eyler on several occasions before his death-night in August. Bridges was not an innocent victim. He was a hustler, a punk, and a smooth manipulator of adults. He gave adults what they wanted to hear, and took from them what he wanted to have: sex and money.

At this trial, I was on the mother's side more for J. J. Johnson, 25, the gentle poet, gentle teddy-bear.70 He was last seen before he supposedly got into Eyler's little red truck--wearing his Cub Scout uniform. His decomposed body was found on Eyler's blood trails, abandoned alongside an Indiana highway.

---

[70] J. J. Johnson was killed December 25, 1982. When *GayLife* initially reported on his disappearance, it ignited a growing realization that a serial killer was at large.

Since the outcome of the trial was never really in doubt in my opinion--the mouse was getting what he deserved--I concentrated on two other points. (1) How much was Eyler on trial and thought guilty because he was a "homosexual"? (2) Since the U.S. Supreme Court has once again resurrected the slur at "homosexual sodomy,"[71] can a "homosexual" get a fair and unprejudiced trial in this land?

The Eyler trial was, in my opinion, grossly prejudicial against "homosexuals." The defense attorney--who seemed at times to be sabotaging his own case with redundant homosexual slurs--was the worst offender.

I came back from the trial feeling even if by chance Eyler had been innocent within the range of reasonable doubt, the homosexual slurs would have made him seem to the jury guilty again. An innocent "homosexual" has about as much chance of proving his innocence in our modern liberal courts as a "faggot" used to have at the inquisition.

---

[71] In its 1986 decision, *Bowers v. Hardwick*, the U.S. Supreme Court upheld the constitutionality of a Georgia law that criminalized oral and anal sex between consenting adults; the decision explicitly rejected the "fundamental right upon homosexuals to engage in sodomy." In 2003, the Supreme Court overruled its own decision in *Bowers* when it struck down a Texas sodomy law in *Lawrence v. Texas*.

Like many in the gay community, I wanted to avoid the Eyler case as much as possible. I know the difference between homicidal and homosexual; but the public mind does not.

But I came to realize that Eyler cannot be so easily denied and dismissed by us. Unlike Gacy, an outsider from us, Eyler was an insider clone. His little mousy body in black vest was a regular in our bars. The little mouse used to hide in our crowd, at the Gold Coast on 501 N. Clark, and the Redoubt at 65 W. Illinois, and Little Jim's in the morning.[72]

So the second point I was looking out for were clues that could warn you to keep away from the Eyler type, so that you don't go home with a homicidal mouse who wants to play top.

[72] Three well known gay pickup bars.

chapter forty-three

WHAT DO SISSIES WANT? | 1986

Don Eric[73] took me to breakfast at 11:00 Monday night, because I had to be down at City Hall the next morning at 6 to observe the proceedings.[74] I was telling Don that we would probably get between 12 and 16 votes. Any more would be real good, and 20 or more would be tantamount to victory. I left Don around midnight to get a few hours sleep. I put in for a 5:30 a.m. wake-up call.

Around 1 a.m. I got an emergency call. "Hi. I met you a couple of years ago at the Golden Nugget, and you gave me your number. I've got a problem. I'm in trouble. And I need your help. My Dad--I mean my step-father--and I were arguing over the gay rights bill and he got violent. He hit me and kicked me out of the house. He said, 'No fag will live in my house!'

---

[73] Columnist for *Gay Chicago Magazine.*

[74] A long-pending proposed gay rights ordinance was up for a vote before the 50-member City Council, needing 26 votes to pass. It was defeated during the Eyler trial. Damski's column began with apologizing for interrupting his Eyler analysis: "Just as events interrupt life, so news interrupts commentary."

They live in one of those neighborhoods where the alderman thinks 'there are no homosexuals.'

"I have nowhere to go--can I stay with you. I know you don't know me too well, but can I come to your place."

"Come on over."

While I waited for him, I thought about the story of Sodom that I had just written about. How the issue there too was sanctuary. How the town's people, the real "sodomites," refused sanctuary and kicked out God's angels, because they thought they were "fairies." This kid's step-father was behaving like a true sodomite.

I took the young man in for the night. I determined first that he had been hit in the face, but he was more wounded in the heart. His step-father has been on-and-off- the-wagon three times, and when he gets out of control, he uses his "fag" step-son as a punching bag. The kid has tried to make a private accommodation with his step-father for the sake of his mother and sisters.

While the kid was telling me his story, I had my radio on to WBBM and they kept updating the gay rights story at City Hall. "Linda Leslie, spokesperson, was predicting the bill was three short of passing." People always seem so baffled about "who are these sissies that want special rights?" Why are they the only ones today crying about rights? Perhaps we are the only ones still crying about rights, because we are the only ones still left out of legal protection for job and home.

Who are we? The numbers are confusing, but you can pretty well say there is one of us in every family. Chicago the city of families and neighborhoods has one in every family. And this night, on the eve of our City Hall vote, I was being hospitable and entertaining one "fag" who had been kicked out of his own house and family by his "sodomite" step-father.

I stayed with the kid until noon the next day, when I got him back in touch with his mother. This "interruption" meant that I arrived at City Hall, even for a press person, too late for a seat.

No matter. The halls were filled with us and talk about us: Two young men came out of the License Bureau and rode the elevator with me.

"What do these sissies want?"

"I don't know."

"Rights?"

"They've got good jobs don't they?"

"Yes. But I think they are worried about Reagan. He's pressing hard on their ass about AIDS. He wants to fire them for AIDS."

Lesbians and gays are often the great ellipsis: even when they talk about us, they leave us or our name out of the conversation. I overheard two grey-haired ladies, regular Council watchers, who had gotten there too late for seats:

"You know what they are doing in there, don't you."

"Yeah."

"You know what's going on in there?"

"Yeah."

"You know who's in there, don't you?"

"Yeah."

"You know what they are talking about, don't you?"

"Yeah. And I wish there were seats so we could see them."

Three men, impeccably dressed, were carrying the *Foreign Affairs* journal, and they looked like they should be going to a State Department hearing. "I tell you it's a private matter. What they do in their bedroom is no one's business."

One woman standing there had on more crosses than Billy Idol's mother. She smiled and handed me a paper "Anti-Homosexual Teachers in School."

I asked her if she belonged to "the Cult-of-the-Month Club," because I had seen her in a pro-Contra demonstration about a month ago.

We "outsiders" in the hall took a biblical consolation knowing the last would be first at something. When the vote was over and our friends and supporters came out of the "operating room" singing "We Shall Overcome," we saw them first. I could not hold back my tears. I ran up to hug Sarah Craig, Kit Duffy, Frank Kellas, Eddie Dugan, Alderman Hansen and anyone else I knew.

I felt that we too had been slapped down by a bunch of step-fathers. But since we belong to the same neighborhood and the same family, we are not going to leave home.

We are going to stay here in our town and fight for our town. The day of the fag-bashing sodomite has passed. For when you strike one of us, you strike one of your own. For there is one of us in every family. We are going to be "homosexual teachers" like you have never seen before. We are going to send a few of these bigoted step-fathers, including the Cardinal,[75] to counseling.

They will quickly learn what we sissies want.[76] It's really very simple: we just want to feel safe on our job and in our home like you do.

---

[75] Cardinal Joseph Bernardin, archbishop of Chicago, had opposed the gay rights bill.

[76] In wake of this defeat, a community organization called Gay and Lesbian Town Meeting was established. Under the leadership of activists Rick Garcia, Arthur Johnston, Laurie Dittman and Jon-Henri Damski--the so-called "Gang of Four"--Town Meeting spearheaded a campaign to pass a revised gay-inclusive Human Rights Ordinance. The campaign was victorious, and the City Council passed the ordinance in 1988.

chapter forty-four

"HOMOSEXUAL" MEANS "GUILTY AS SIN" | 1986

[77]Larry Eyler's janitor has a dog named "George"--a 14-pound German shepherd. Every time Larry went to the dumpster outside his building carrying a heavy garbage bag, the dog snarled and showed his teeth. The janitor asked Eyler what he had in those bags, and Larry told him: "I'm just getting rid of some shit I had around the apartment."

I knew I was at a modern trial, with modern English, when Prosecutor Rakoczy said right out in his opening statement: "Ladies and gentlemen, the evidence will show the shit he was referring to was the dismembered body parts of Danny Bridges."

I also knew I was watching a modern liberal trial, because Judge Joseph J. Urso kept referring to the head of the jury as the "Foreperson."

But I also knew that when the authorities in Indiana and Lake County (Illinois) had caught Eyler more than two years ago, they had badly botched

---

[77] Damski resumes his five-part series with this second installment.

the case. They seemed more anxious to try Eyler for his "homosexual acts" than for his acts of murder.

Dr. David S. Dennis, coroner of Newton County (Indiana), told the *Chicago Tribune*: what we have here is a "homosexual killer." "I think we are dealing with a systematic, ritualistic, and homosexual type killing here." The trousers of each victim were pulled down around his ankles "suggesting homosexual activity."

Lake County Sheriff Robert "Mickey" Babcox held a press conference to announce they had Eyler's handcuffs, blood-stained hunting knife, rope, and hiking boots. The sheriff assumed that all this "homosexual paraphernalia" pointed directly to a "homosexual type killer." Their case was solid.

The sheriff went on to conclude: Eyler "was a homosexual with a hate of himself for being homosexual." The sheriff never explained why Eyler didn't just kill himself, since he hated himself so much for being a homosexual.

Circuit Court Judge William D. Block was not moved by all this press speculation that Eyler was a "self- hating homosexual killer." He ruled that Eyler had been detained illegally, and that all the evidence seized without probable cause was inadmissible.

Judge Urso, obviously aware of how Eyler's case had been mishandled earlier, seemed at first very circumspect" about the kind of evidence he would allow in this trial.

The judge admitted in evidence: Eyler's plain black leather vest, his black hiking boots, his Levi's, his cut offs, his gym shoes--all things he was probably wearing on the night of the crime. He also let in Eyler's painterly green goggles--which look like glasses you would buy at an Andy Warhol hardware store--because it would be shown that Eyler wore them while painting over the blood-spattered walls in his apartment.

The judge also let in some books and videos found in Eyler's apartment. He cautioned that the jury could examine the titles but not read or watch them.

Of the 35 photographs of Eyler found in his kitchen and bedroom, the judge admitted only those that showed Eyler clothed, so the jury could get an idea of Eyler's size and shape before becoming so thin and mousy from being in jail for two years.

The judge did not allow photographs of Eyler standing only in a jock-strap, or just in his leather vest with no pants on.

He did not allow in evidence a pink dildo found in Eyler's apartment; a large jar of petroleum jelly; or a "black (sic) women's negligee." Nor did he allow a butt plug, or a string of Ben-Wa-Wa anal beads, also found in Eyler's apartment.

The judge at first seemed to realize that Eyler was on trial for murder, not for being a homosexual.

All this extraneous paraphernalia found in Eyler's apartment, unless it was physically connected to the crime, was kept from the jury.

But after being very careful about the physical evidence, the judge seemed to pay no heed to the verbal evidence: the "homosexual slurs" that fell off the tongues of both the prosecutor and defense. In the Larry Eyler trial we were treated to more descriptions of "homosexual acts" than you get commercials on a bad TV show.

Defense attorney Schippers opened by saying "We freely admit that our client is a homosexual-- that is not in dispute."

The prosecutors picked up on the term, and the judge never objected. Almost every other sentence in the trial was "homosexual" this and "homosexual" that. We heard about John, Larry's "homosexual lover," "homosexual boy friend," how they carried on a "homosexual affair," and had "homosexual intercourse."

How they both carried on "homosexual affairs" with other men: Dave, Ray, and Mike; and how Eyler went to all the "homosexual leather-Levi's" bars in Chicago looking for other "homosexual men."

We heard about Danny Bridges, the "male prostitute," who quickly became the "homosexual prostitute," and who performed "homosexual acts" for money; who hopped into any man's car going down Montrose and would offer to have "homosexual sex" with them.

We also got to hear, in detail, about the great sex scene between John and Larry, after Eyler had left Danny Bridges' body parts bagged and ready for hiding back at his place. Larry came to John's house sometime after 4:30 a.m. John had already put a blanket down on the kitchen floor so they could have sex immediately after Larry got there.

Larry seemed unusually preoccupied this time. He was out of dress code: he had his boots on, but no sox; his cut-offs, but no underwear. He did not seem up to the performance this time.

On cross examination Schippers got John to confess that for this one time "Larry did not ejaculate semen."

At 5:35 a.m. John's mother-in-law's alarm clock went off. They had to cut short their "homosexual intercourse"; interrupt their "homosexual lovemaking"; and Larry would have to wait another night until he could see his "homosexual boy friend"; and John could be with his "homosexual lover."

Dr. Robert D. Little, chairman of the department of library science at Indiana State University at Terre Haute, was Eyler's "Platonic lover," Socratic Mentor and diffident Sugar Daddy. For seven years while Eyler was a "student," Professor Little gave Larry room-and-board and expense money.

Without any instruction, I am sure, the jury got the point: "homosexuals" were on trial here.

In final summation, Schippers told the jury: "you know about homosexuals. They are all vain, immature. They are like teenagers; and they are all insanely jealous of one another." "We all know their sex is weird." "Bridges, a homosexual prostitute, went with all kinds of men, and there is no evidence to link him with Eyler that night."

He could have gone with one of those other "jealous homosexuals," like Professor Little, who was also staying at Eyler's house.

"John the lover is good-looking--but strange"; he is also a "homosexual," and does weird sex. How can you trust his testimony? He is just a jealous ex-lover testifying against his "ex-lover" Larry.

Even in a modern liberal trial, when you are a "homosexual," you are already as guilty as sin, no matter what other charge you are on trial for. And once you admit in open court that you are a "homosexual," you are as guilty as sin, so how can you prove your innocence of any crime?

In a modern liberal trial, you can say "shit" and the jury will not be offended; but you cannot say "gay," for fear the judge, the jury, and the whole court will take offense at your childlike honesty and innocence.

chapter forty-five

JOHN THE "LOVER," JOHN THE JOHN | 1986

[78]Larry Eyler, unlike John Wayne Gacy, actually had a "homosexual lover." Over a period of three years, Larry both lived with and apart from John Dobrovolskis and his wife Sarah. On the night of Eyler's arrest for the Bridges murder John was sleeping with Larry. The police took them both into custody, and John was kept in seclusion at the police station and in a hotel room for four days of questioning. But John was never charged with anything, and he became the chief witness for the State on Eyler's behavior the weekend of the crime.

John Dobrovolskis is a tall, good looking blonde, in his late 20s, with flowing hair and a full mustache. In press and media accounts John is often called "Larry Eyler's homosexual boyfriend." But "boy" is not the word for John. He is very manly looking both in attitude and presence. He was a married man when Larry came from Indiana to Chicago to live with John

---

[78] The third of five columns about the 1986 Eyler trial.

and his wife. The Monday he testified against Larry would have been the day of his seventh wedding anniversary. Sarah divorced John a year and a half ago over his "affair" with Eyler.

Entering the court, wearing a blue blazer, grey slacks, and soft maroon tie, John walked directly to the witness chair without looking at Larry. It was clear by the tone of John's voice, and by his angered stares at Larry, that John now knows exactly how he was used and betrayed. He wasn't Larry's "lover"; he had been just another one of Larry's "tricks," his regular weekend "John."

John does not want any part of Larry anymore. When Prosecutor Rakoczy started to hand him Eyler's painterly green goggles, and asked him to try them on, John jumped back in horror in his chair.

John and Sarah Dobrovolskis gave Eyler a place to stay when he first came to Chicago and for three years, while Eyler's name was linked to crimes in Chicago and Indiana, John and Sarah gave him an alibi, cover, and protection.

John or Sarah would offer themselves for interviews, and tell how Larry was a devout Catholic: How he always wanted to be a priest. How clutching his rosary and Bible he still went regularly to Mass. Larry was their nice friend and their little church mouse.

The public and many reporters were all taken in by the sincerity of John and Sarah. How could Eyler be this "self-hating homosexual" when he seemed to get along so well with this straight couple?

Their landlords liked them because they usually paid their rent. But one landlady said of three of them living together, "Boy, that was a strange situation." She could not understand why John and Larry always went out together at night--leaving Sarah behind--and why they never went to the neighborhood bars because Larry was introducing John to the scene: they were going downtown to the Gold Coast and Redoubt[79] and returning early morning to watch porn and have a "nightcap" at Little Jim's.[80] Larry was taking John on the fast track.

John was extremely vulnerable to Larry's experienced ploys. John wasn't just coming out, he was coming out of a marriage. Married couples when they go to a bar are expected to stay together for the night. Larry used that expectation to keep John on hold in the bars, while he went off to "party" on his own. He insisted that John wait until he got back. Yet Larry demanded that he be free to go off and cruise on his own.

---

[79] The Gold Coast and Redoubt were leather bars.

[80] Gay bar on Halsted.

John was Larry's "John": he had to do or try to do everything the way Larry wanted it. Larry had more demands for John than desires. When Larry got a place of his own, he was always keeping John away. "Don't come over now, Dave's here--and you know how Dave doesn't like you." "This is a weeknight, I've got to work tomorrow." "This is the weekend, I've got house guests."

To please Larry, John even tried a couple of scenes of bondage, which were very distasteful to him. Some sport. Larry could tie him up, but he could not tie Larry up. Some trust. In Larry, John had a one-way lover, but he was too new to the scene to know that one-way lovers should be just all-night lovers.

Meanwhile, John kept telling friends and the police that all the stuff in the papers about Larry was untrue. "Larry is a nice guy--and I can't understand why they are picking on Larry all the time."

Larry must have enjoyed having this cat on the string, playing chaser-chasee. One Saturday night John went looking for Larry and found him at the Gold Coast at 5025 N. Clark. Larry did not like it that John had found him while he was busy. Larry said he had to take a piss, went to the back garden of the bar, jumped over the wall and left John there waiting for him.

After an hour, John went to Larry's house. He peered through the window and saw--how Larry was "busy." Larry was having sex with a "long-haired, tattooed, dirty street person."

During the week that Danny Bridges was mutilated and murdered, John had tried all week to set up a date with Larry. Larry broke their date twice. When John called on the weekend Larry said, "I've got house guests and you can't come over."

Finally at 4:30 a.m. Monday they had their famous tryst in John's kitchen with the blanket on the floor. Their sex was doubly unsatisfying because Larry didn't seem up to it and because John's mother-in-law's alarm clock went off and rudely interrupted their scene.

On Tuesday night John finally begged and got Larry's permission to come over to Larry's. When he got there something was odd: everything was immaculate, everything had been straightened up, and the walls were freshly painted. John wondered why Larry had painted the walls in the bedroom when he had just painted them a couple of months earlier. Usually Larry left his place a mess and it was John's duty to clean it up.

John went to the kitchen to make himself some macaroni. He noticed the sink was plugged. He went to the closet to get the plunger just as Larry came in. "No, no, don't bother about the sink--I'll get the landlord to fix it in the morning."

John already had the plunger in his hand and was loosening up the sink drain. Up came "white pieces of chicken fat, black gravelly material, and some swirling pink stuff."

Larry went over and gave John a big hug. "Oh, you've saved me all this trouble. How can I thank you. I had burnt some chicken soup and it got stuck in my sink." After dinner they watched Porky's II on the VCR and went to bed. The police came early in the morning and arrested them both in bed.

Later John told the police, "1 didn't believe you at first, but I believe you now, man!"

When defense attorney Schippers asked John, "Why did Eyler let you go--set you free--when he had you tied up in those bondage situations?" John made another off-the-record remark: "I guess I was the lucky one who got away."

John seems today much more emotionally upset than Larry--almost like he has had to relive the horror of crimes he never committed. Coming out as a married man and having Eyler as his first partner did not make him a very lucky "John." But facing it all in a trial and giving cool and brave testimony gives John a luckier future.

chapter forty-six

HOMOSEXUAL *MANQUE*[81] | 1986

[82]No matter how rigorously you examine the life and acts of Larry Eyler, you are still going to come up short with something missing.

The police and the medical examiners ran through Eyler's apartment like hungry hunting dogs sniffing every inch of the place for blood. But still, they came up with one glaring piece missing.

They used a new technique: they sprayed his living room bedroom and bathroom walls with Luminol, a chemical which interacts with blood to cause a dark green glow. They found blood and enzyme samples on the bedroom, bath and living room walls; they found blood stains on the bed cover; on the dining room red-cushioned chair; human tissue under the bathroom radiator. And blood specks under the bathroom threshold. They found traces of human skin in a drain in a tub in the laundry room. They found blood stains on a T-

---

[81] French for someone who might have become something, but did not.

[82] Fourth of five in the series.

shirt and Levi's; they found hair similar to Bridges' type, and little specks of green acrylic fibers matching Larry's green painter goggles. And yet there was still something missing. The crime lab ran oral and anal tests on Danny Bridges for spermatozoa and came up negative. They found no sperm or cum in Eyler's apartment.

After a frustrating and quarrelsome weekend with his house guest Dave, and after keeping his "lover" John at bay for a week, Eyler supposedly, according to the prosecutor, dashed out of his house, jumped into his little red truck, drove straight down Clark to Hubbard to find himself a "male prostitute," who would give him some homosexual action. He found Danny Bridges and took him home.

Usually, when homosexual men pick up homosexual prostitutes, they have one thing upper most on their mind: they want to share a cum shot, shoot sperm, and get their rocks off.

But not Eyler. Not that night. He seemed to lack obvious homosexual desire. He didn't want to get his rocks off, he wanted to cut someone's head off. Eyler lacks normal homosexual desires; he is not homosexual; he is a homosexual manque. He is not into homosexual acts, he is into homicidal acts.

As a loverboy, Larry was not a very good lover either. From John's testimony we learn that each time they placed the blanket on the floor, they had "good sex" which I take to mean they "ejaculated semen" together--and they did it once or twice a week, but that's about all they did.

Eyler was a lover manque as well. His relationship with John was not based on desire, but on demand, John did not excite his heart. The test was how many of Larry's demands could John meet. Larry just wanted a cat on command over whom he could play Top Mouse.

Larry Eyler wasn't a leather man either. He hung around the Levi's-leather bars and the leather crowd, but he never caught on to the look and feel of leather. Mouse-brown --the color he wore everyday at the his trial--is his natural color. He didn't really fit or measure up in black leather: he was just a brown-leather person in a black leather world.

Nor did he understand the leather sex scene, where threat is only an illusion, and acts are just "acts" designed to stimulate the imagination. Eyler's acts left nothing to the imagination. Someone spurned one of his demands and he executed them.

The reporters, the judge, the prosecutor, the court-watchers, everyone seemed to agree with the defense attorney: "Larry Eyler is a homosexual--that fact is not in dispute in this case."

Eyler's homosexuality, however, is the first fact that you have to throw into question, if you want to begin to understand Larry and his behavior. Sure he is a creepy mouse who committed gross and violent acts. But how much of a "homosexual" is he? Very little.

Eyler's acts are so haywire and off balance that they cannot be explained by labeling him a "homosexual." Homosexual desire is at the root of what he lacked most. Homosexual men like the feel and taste of flesh; they do not like to shop and chop: pick up hunky bodies and dispose of them on the highway like stolen cars.

The sheriff who first apprehended Eyler in Indiana kept insisting that Larry was a "self-hating homosexual," who killed because he hated his homosexuality. If that were true why didn't he just off himself and be done with it all?

The sheriff also asserted that Eyler "appeared to derive sexual satisfaction from the slayings." Danny Bridges may have danced around Eyler's apartment that night like a Mick Jagger clone, but I don't think either he or Larry derived any sexual satisfaction from their experience together. According to the lab tests, neither of them dropped sperm or had an orgasm.

One reporter speculates that Eyler "killed when other young-men reminded him of what he hated in himself: his homosexuality." But Larry was habitually going to gay bars, where he must have seen many young men there who reminded him of his homosexuality. If he killed for that reason, why didn't he enter those bars like Rambo with his Uzi blazing?

"Homosexual" does not explain the core of Larry Eyler. Homosexual lust and homosexual desire were very weak in him. He did not desire young men in a homosexual way, nor did he seem to satisfy his demands in a homosexual way.

Something early in his life must have choked off his homosexual desire. As a boy, he often told people he wanted to be a priest. As a senior in high school, he contemplated running off to Canada to join a monastery. During the last two years, while the police hounded him in Chicago and Indiana, he told a reporter that he "attended daily Roman Catholic mass." While in jail in Indiana he sat quietly in his cell with his Bible and rosary in his hand.

Eyler's desires, early in his life, got criss-crossed over what he wanted to be: he was too much a homosexual to be a priest, and too much a priest to be a homosexual.

Touch any aspect of Larry Eyler's world or scene and you will come up with something missing, something he lacked or wanted to be but wasn't. Larry is the perfect example of the homosexual manque.

chapter forty-seven

DEATH SENTENCE | 1986

[83]Having convicted Larry Eyler beyond all reasonable doubt of the aggravated kidnapping, torture, murder and dismemberment of Danny Bridges, the court reconvened Sept. 30 for a two-day hearing to determine the fate of Larry Eyler. The prosecution called four witnesses, tricks and pick-ups, guys who had actually been with Larry Eyler sexually and lived to tell about it. They told about the wild side of Larry Eyler.

The defense called his priest, his mother, his step-father, his sister and a co-worker from a social agency in Indiana--people, who could testify about the domestic side of Larry Eyler.

Instead of asking for another jury, Eyler chose to have his death sentence hearing before his trial Judge Urso. The Judge loosened the formalities of legal testimony, and let each witness speak in their own words: tricks talked like tricks, and his mother pleaded as a mother. The Judge obviously wanted to discover if there was any reason at all

---

[83] Last in five-part series on 1986 Larry Eyler murder trial.

that Larry Eyler should live: or any reason why he should not die.

The witnesses for the prosecution spoke first. Craig Long, an ex-Marine, testified that when he was 19 he was attacked by Larry Eyler in Terre Haute, Ind. Pointing to his rib cage he said, "He stabbed me right here---I have a scar right here."

In court Long had trouble, however, in pointing out Larry Eyler. On his first try he identified Eyler as a TV reporter sitting in the jury box. On his second chance he stood up in the witness chair and pointed at Larry Eyler sitting at the defense table.

Long told the Judge that Eyler had picked him up hitchhiking, drove him to a wooded area where Larry tried to tie him up and handcuffed him. He flipped backward out of Larry's truck, and Larry chased him through the woods and stabbed him.

At the time of the attack, eight years ago, Eyler told his lawyers it was "an accident, the knife slipped while he was cutting the ropes around Long's legs." Eyler claimed he intended no harm and had actually come back to the scene and given the paramedics the keys to the handcuffs.

Eyler paid $2,500 for medical expenses, and Long dropped the charges.

Another young man from Indiana testified that when he was 14, Eyler picked him up in his red truck and "gave him a beer and a black pill." Two days later he woke up in a hospital room dehydrated and weak.

Eyler's lawyer's pointed out the boy had not been sexually touched, and he was found with all his clothes on in a wooded area outside a bowling alley near his home.

Tom Starcher, 32, a light-delivery person from West Virginia, told of the night five or six years ago when he was cruising and hustling at Monument Circle in Indianapolis. Tom jumped into Eyler's red truck and they bargained for sex. They first asked each other "if they were police officers," and then Tom agreed to go with Larry "for $20."

Eyler said "he was into S & M, but would respect Tom's limits."

Eyler told him they were going to Greencastle 40 miles away because he was staying there at his sister's place. They stopped at a country and western bar along the way and each had a beer.

When they arrived at Eyler's sister's place, they started "making out" in the front of the truck. Eyler got nervous and went into the house to make sure his teenage nephew was not watching them. He came back and they shared a rum and coke. They got undressed in the back of the truck on a blanket. Tom immediately got aroused and climaxed. While he was coming down, Eyler quickly handcuffed his hands behind his back, put a gag in his mouth, and put a strip of bandage across his eyes. He told Tom: "This will last for 60 minutes." He pounded on Tom's chest punched him with a blunt instrument, and made an inch cut in his chest and let the blood drip. He kept telling Tom the time: "You have 45 minutes, you have 35 minutes, you have 20 minutes, etc..."

Eyler seemed more interested in torture than in sex. He picked up a 12-gauge shot gun and toyed with Tom. Tom did not resist or make any aggressive moves. "Kill me now...If you are going to."

When the 60 minutes were up, Eyler said he would release him. He stood over Tom and ejaculated semen into Tom's wounds, which smarted and stung, and cursed: "You bitch you slut, you whore."

Then he drove Tom back to Indianapolis and said: "Let's be friends."

"NO WAY, man--you are bad news!" Tom did not think his wounds were deep enough to go to a hospital. He put alcohol on them and called the Speedway police to make a formal complaint. Since it was early in the morning, he only reached the police answering service.

After hearing in graphic detail about these sexual encounters with Larry Eyler, the testimony of his priest, his mother--though brave and full of tears--his step-father, sister and co-worker all seemed too lame and beside the point. Domestically Larry is a good little mouse, and he could stay in jail forever. They were not pleading for anything more than a life in state bondage.

The prosecution saw through his "life-in-prisonment" argument and ended their case by telling the Judge: "If you give Eyler life imprisonment, you are really setting him free. He and his kind prey on the young, the frail, and the weak--don't let him be free to roam the general male population in prison. In prison, Eyler will be free to pursue his lust."

David Schippers for the defense strongly objected to this line of argument. "No one is 'free' in prison!" The defense begged mercy, "Do not put Larry Eyler to death on circumstantial evidence alone." Schippers again reminded the Judge that "neither of us will ever understand their bizarre lifestyle and its bizarre sex. Why, Judge, they have S & M bars--if you go into them and their back rooms--that have more bondage equipment, torture racks, ligatures and handcuffs than Torquemada and the Spanish Inquisition." His remarks drew muffled snickers from the crowd.

The Judge asked Eyler if he had any final words to tell the court. As Larry stood to speak, all of us listened attentively, for these would be his first public words in over two years: "I want to thank Officer..." and then he named his jailers. And I want to thank my lawyers, especially David Schippers, for taking on this unpopular cause." Larry is enthralled by his captors.

On Friday, Oct. 3, Judge Urso made his decision public. He called Eyler and his lawyers to stand in front of him. The judge's words were firm, because he had written them out. But his voice was shaking:

"Mr. Eyler, you are an evil person. You deserve to die.

"I have heard the snickers in this court room when the acts you did with young men were described. You think you can get away with it just because they are weaker, smaller, younger than you--just because they have a lifestyle not generally accepted in society. But you are wrong.

"I find no mitigating factors or facts in this case. I find it unbelievable that you could walk away from the bleeding, bloody body parts of Danny Bridges and go and carry on a sexual relationship on a blanket on the kitchen floor...you deserve to die by fatal injection. Mr. Eyler, I pray to God that he will have mercy on your soul."[84]

---

[84] Larry Eyler appeared before Judge Urso again six years later; a second series on Eyler and Danny Bridges begins at Chapter 57, page 407.

PART FIVE

chapter forty-eight

BOY WITH BOOM BOX | 1989

I like summer, because men and boys show more of themselves than they do in other seasons.

I saw a guy strutting up Diversey with a boom box. He was totally into what he was doing. He was carrying what seemed like a 50-pound bucket of sound, and youthfully absorbed and oblivious to the fact that all around him there were senior citizens marching along out of breath and struggling to carry home a five-pound bag of groceries.

He was a wave of sound, churning up the street. You could hear him half a block away, and still catch the reverberation of his sound as he passed out of sight two blocks ahead.

His look, motion, and purpose were ambiguous. He could have been coming from the Rocks.[85] Or he could have been going to see a female friend. He wore his cap backwards like a catcher. Or like a gang-banger.

---

[85] Belmont Rocks, a popular gay sunbathing spot on the Chicago lakefront.

For pants, he had on black jeans cut off and hanging loose. They could easily convert to swim trunks. He had no shirt on. His skin was dark. But you couldn't tell if it was from tan or dirt. Or some inborn racial mixture.

He had a T-shirt draped over his left shoulder, in case he had to go inside one of those "no shirt, no shoes, no service" places. But he seemed to prefer the outdoors. He had that "take me out to the ball game...and I don't care if I ever get back" drift about him.

He didn't seem to care much for shoes either. He must have gotten-up and planted his bare feet into some dirty high-top Reebok's, with laces untied and flopping out of the sides.

I admit that guys with untied laces puzzle me. They often look like they could rob you, but I never can figure how they expect to make their getaway in loose shoes. I guess untied laces are a sign of freedom. But I don't get the hang of it. I have to tie my shoes in order to walk. But like the boy with the boom box, these guys move and their shoes follow them, magically stuck to their feet. I always think that if my shoes aren't tied, they'll fall off when I walk.

This guy was a wave of sound; he blew everything and everyone out of his way, like debris in his wake.

To some he must have been an intrusion, an annoyance. He was not strolling in bourgeois privacy with headphones. He was six feet tall, and bent over carrying a whole fucking radio studio with him.

No one voiced a real objection (or one you could hear over his noise box). He came on like a natural force, and to object you might as well have cursed the wind. Sure, there are laws and ordinances against this kind of sonic attack. But it happens so quickly and is over so fast, who can enforce them?

His music, to my taste, was awful. I couldn't identify with it. It sounded like flat house music without any foundation. He may have had his box dialed in between stations, for all I could tell. After it was over, and he had passed, I realized that the music didn't matter. Just as it was with Jimi Hendrix; the music didn't matter, Hendrix could play "Three Blind Mice" or "The Star Spangled Banner" and no one cared about the tune. What mattered was the sound, the instrument, and the effect. Same with this guy and his boom box.

Years ago, I had a running argument with Herbert Marcuse, a guru of the '60s.[86] He was against loud radios and boom boxes, They offended his trained classical ear. He had, besides his earned, advanced degrees in philosophy, an honorary doctorate in music from the New England Conservatory of Music.

I joked with the good professor and said, "If you ever become Sheriff of San Diego County, there will be no outdoor radio playing on the La Jolla beaches." Marcuse had enough of Lenin and the philosopher-king in him to be willing to sacrifice some youthful indiscretions. Lenin gave up Beethoven for his revolution, and Marcuse was willing to give up his ban on loud radio playing for his reason and revolution.

I could not cross that line then or now. Too often I have watched while the logical dictator in me wanted to censor someone else's behavior. I would prefer to put away the authoritarian in me. Then there has always been a faggot part of me that knows what I'm after when I see a boy with a box. Most people are unwilling to admit any desire to get the boy, so they play superior and clean, and pretend they are after the loud box.

---

[86] Herbert Marcuse, 1898-1979, was a philosopher, political theorist, and sociologist known for his works *Eros and Civilization* and *One-Dimensional Man.* He taught at Brandeis University from 1958-1965; Damski attended Brandeis on a Woodrow Wilson Fellowship in 1959-1960.

They want to take the box from the boy because it disturbs them. They will not acknowledge that it could also be that the boy, nearly naked and totally free, is making their flesh crawl more than the music.

To go after the box, when unconsciously you want to get at the boy, is perverse. To make a fuss over the music, when you really resent the boy having what you want--a free body--is unfair revenge.

In the past when I saw a boy with a boom box, I usually thought it was dumb and he was dumb. They "do the right thing" and strangle the guy with a boom box in Spike Lee's movie, don't they?[87]

But this summer, this guy and his box were different. They were a perfect match. His motion, his walk, his sound, and his body were all together. Actors train years to achieve that effect. His attitude was perfect. Rather than personally censor him, I'll let the "ordinance of Time" (as Anaximander said) do that. For how many summers in a row can a guy walk up Diversey with 50 pounds of sound in his hands and get away with it?

---

[87] Spike Lee's 1989 film, *Do the Right Thing*, focused on racial tensions in Bedford-Stuyvesant, a Brooklyn neighborhood.

chapter forty-nine

*F**RISK* | 1991

Frisk, the title of Dennis Cooper's new novel, should really be spelled F**RISK, because the book is fuckin' risky.

Steve Abbott on his "Hippie Histromap" in *HOMOCORE* #7 puts novelist-poet Cooper in the rank of "20th Century Hard." With Frisk, due out in May, I think Dennis has finally made it into the circle of Hell designated as "Ultra Hard."

Cooper can't win. Mainstream critics hate him because he is gay. And gay critics hate him because he is "antigay," fixated on characters and themes about homosex murders. Cooper represents post-punk snuff rock, brought to life and death in literature. Dennis is kind of a refined, high cultured G. G. Allin, a hairy, tattooed aggro-punk singer who was justifiably murdered in prison a few months ago.

Cooper writes in the tradition of Genet and Burroughs for fans of Sonic Youth. "Gay" is too straight for him; he thinks "gay literature" is a useless term. "Most gay people are not interested in my work at all," he told Kathryn Hixson in an interview in the current *THING* (number 4). "There are some weirdo gay people who are interested."

Dennis works on the "margins where everything great always happens." His last novel, *Closer*, I liked because it's the real thing. I loaned it to a couple of garage-band male groupies, who had been classified as "functional illiterates" in school, and they devoured the book like a new drug.

Cooper gets inside boys of the '80s, Reagan's children, better than any writer I know. He reproduces their skeleton souls and despairing razor-cut prose. His work "squeezes the shit out of American pretense." His characters aren't dumb dumb, like most of our leaders; they are smart dumb. They know they live in the twilight zone, the dead zone, the already-at-the-end zone of the American dream.

Ecstasy for them is a drug, not a promise. They are the last American scream before all turns to black. In *Closer*, the body parts of John, David, George, Cliff, Alex, Philip, and Steve seemed to get splattered all over the book. I wasn't sure, at the end, who came out alive. I wasn't even sure if I, as a reader came through with all my body parts intact. Cooper's candy-like words get inside you like poison. Not easy to get rid of. These are not cute Zubro-type[88] mysteries, where you stand outside the circle, omniscient, and know the answer. In a Cooper novel, you are the circle, the target, the victim. And nothing you know, or will ever know, helps.

In Frisk, I felt totally framed. I don't like being the bad guy. I kept saying to myself: "why is a pixie like me reading this stuff?" But I went on and got frisked. I wanted to read about frisky boys. Instead I ended up in Amsterdam snuffing out a 10-or-11-year-old "after I licked, his asshole clean, inside, out." Left four or five (I lost the body count) other Dutch boys swinging from a windmill. In movies I close my eyes during those parts. In this book, I just read faster and hoped I'd get out alive.

128 pages is not *War and Peace*. But because Dennis is every inch a poet, I read the first 89 pages in chill and ecstasy. But snuffin' a 10 year-old in the name of sex was just too much. I puked! Came back wobbly a few days later and finished the book. Dennis the lead character and Dennis the author--how stuck to each other they are--told me "it was only a book." "Get used to it!" Dennis didn't really do what he said he did, he was only writing it in a book. And I was only reading it in a book. Ain't "gay lit" grand?

---

[88] Chicago-based gay mystery writer Mark David Zubro.

I'm not totally naive. Anyone who has been in the urban-gay scene for long probably knows someone who was murdered. Maybe even a murderer. I have written on Gacy and Eyler and have known several of their victims. Our lesbian and gay center in Chicago, after all, named after Frank M. Rodde, a hustler/murder victim.[89]

If I can suffer through Gera-Lind Kolarik's book about Eyler, *Freed to Kill*, the dumbest piece of amateur journalism and made-up fiction I have ever read (even though she got lucky and fingered the real murderer at the end), then I should prize Cooper's work; it is super-intelligent, and a masterpiece of fiction which is probably the most realistic account of a homo-psycho wished-to-be-freed to kill guy that I could ever imagine reading.

The sexual hunts of snuffer-snuffee, I and the apparent subsequent fake murders complete with gags, shit and smell, is not what disturbed me. In *Closer*, the people were equals or equivalents. If they weren't close to me in morality, they were at least equal to each other in their amorality. I can even accept Cooper's sharp insight that cruising is a form of secondary murder: where bodies objectify and eliminate one another like bad shit.

---

[89] The Center on Halsted replaced the Rodde Center in June, 2007.

What disturbs me in *Frisk*, however, is more a feminist argument: these aren't mock murders; they are rape scenes. The older, smarter, bigger guys pick on the little guy. The crime is more disgusting than murder; it's an ugly power-over crime, fags bashing fags in the name of love. It's horrible. Puke!

To get the bad taste out of my system, I read some earlier poems of Cooper, which he wrote between the ages of 16 and 25, and which now are reissued under the title *IDOLS* (which I prefer to spell as I-DOLLS). These sexy, sweet boys of Pasadena belong in "gay literature" alongside A. E. Housman's Shropshire lads. There are poems about John Kennedy, Jr. looking for sex in the Red Light District in Amsterdam, and Peter Frampton finger-fucking himself in a mirror, plus the memories of boys Dennis wanted in high school. They read like a gentle series of Bill Sawicki[90] drawings. The cul-de-sac of death and splat enters the world of these Hockney swimmers only on the edge.

As Dennis grew, he went to the edge himself, and like a kid in Tom Petty's song, went over in a "free fall." He has taken a great risk. He has abandoned his frisky boys, this much more risky business. Cooper is dropping without a parachute, while sending these notes to us. He is

[90] A gay Chicago artist.

beyond our judgmental probings; all he can do is fall. And all we can do is watch him splatter.

chapter fifty

DAHMER BE DAMNED! | 1991

[91] I really resent Jeffrey Lionel Dahmer. His twisted brain. His sordid and diabolical murders. His hatred of queers and blacks. His luring the most vulnerable in our community, young guys who want to be Prince, and taking them home to his slaughterhouse.

I resent his sickness. A guy who craves sex with dead body parts, rather than bodies whole. A guy who has no gay or sexual identity, but was quite willing to make the whole gay community the fall guy for his crimes.

I really resent Dahmer piling up more deaths in our community, at a time when we don't need more deaths. Read the gay papers of Milwaukee and Chicago for any two-week period, you will find more deaths than Dahmer caused. AIDS is the serial killer no one has a chance of locking up. Last

---

[91] Written after the arrest of Jeffrey Dahmer, who preyed on gay men in Milwaukee and Chicago. In 1992, Dahmer was convicted of 15 counts of murder and sentenced to life in prison; he was beaten to death in prison by a fellow inmate in 1994.

week John Schmid[92]; this week Michael K.[93] My eyes are dry, my tears are spent. I don't want to see any more faces of dead young men staring at me from a newspaper page.

I really resent Dahmer taking kids from our Skid Row and putting them on his death row. I resent his cunning plan to commit murders in states where he will never have to sit on death row. Where he can sit in secure accommodations and be a media star for the rest of his "natural" life.

I really resent that he may never even face a death penalty. When so many of my friends have faced the death sentence of AIDS, from which there is no appeal. PWAs are lucky if they live two to five. But John Gacy has been on death row for 13 years, from the time Dahmer committed his first murder and disposed of the body of Stevie Hicks, 18, Gacy-style, in the crawl space of his divorced parents' home.

I really resent Dahmer blotting out the real connections between the lesbian and gay communities of Milwaukee and Chicago. Milwaukee has always been a leader in gay living. In bars, softball, and intellectual commentary, Milwaukee has often shown the way for Chicago. They had the first major gay and lesbian softball

---

[92] *Gay Chicago* writer who died of AIDS.

[93] Well-known gay bartender who died of AIDS.

leagues, the historic Wreck Room Classic on Memorial Day, and one of the first national Gay World Series. Their bars have a long tradition of being together, male and female, young and senior, beer and food. Bars like Roscoe's and Sidetrack in Chicago have their architectural roots in Milwaukee bars like Bob Schmidt's M & M Club. The WreckRoom, Club 219, Phoenix, and C'est La Vie have always been popular for Chicagoans to visit. Gay Political Union (GPU) was a gay and lesbian magazine of distinguished commentary in the '70s. Milwaukee has been a model for Chicago, things that start there are often copied here on a larger scale.

And Chicago has influenced Milwaukee. Ron Geiman's *InStep* magazine is an offspring of *Gay Chicago*, with Ralph Paul as godfather and Erin Criss as midwife. The real story about Milwaukee and Chicago is not Dahmer's sordid tale, but how these two sub-cultures have helped each other grow and develop into strong centers of lesbian and gay activism.

But what I really resent is how Dahmer has come out of nowhere to dominate the news. How he has skillfully intruded into our psyches and stolen our attention. We fault the three police officers in Milwaukee for taking Dahmer's word for it when he held the 14-year-old Laotian kid captive and said they were just "homosexual lovers having a spat." But now Dahmer is up to his same tricks, except he is holding the whole police department and all the media in his hands. He controls the news. We are supposed to trace out his story, follow his clues, take his word for it. We are still under the spell of this cunning cannibal.

As upset as I am about Dahmer--like many others, I haven't slept well lately--I must say the news coverage in the main has been better than the Gacy murders and Eyler trial; it shows the advancement of our community.

I can still feel the personal horror from the day John Wayne Gacy was arrested in 1978. In all accounts he was portrayed as the "homosexual murderer, who had committed homosexual murders of 33 young men and boys." Yet his victims were not identified as homosexual. The media took pictures of stores and bars on Broadway, where Gacy cruised, and called them "homosexual haunts." Any single male walking those streets was smeared with the same brush as Gacy.

But we too were silent lambs then. *GayLife* did not cover the story. I wrote a couple of columns for *Gay Chicago*, but very much on the defensive: how we are not Gacy. Larry Bush, a gay writer from New York, covered the trial for the *Village Voice*. Gacy has always denied being "gay," but we gay men suffered in silence for his crimes.

For the hunt and capture and trial of Larry Eyler, our community was more open. *GayLife*, with reporters like Paul Cotton, took the lead on the story, kept the community informed, and was helpful in shaping the stories of the Chicago downtown media.

For Dahmer, thus far, the media has been sensitive and informative. For years people like Al Wardell, Paul Varnell, Tracy Baim, and Bill Williams have been teaching and training straight reporters about our issues. Those years of quiet discussion paid off this time. I was particularly happy that reporters, both in print and on TV, have avoided saying anything like "homosexual murder." As one reporter told Vernon Huls, "We've covered ACT UP demonstrations, we know better!"

There have been several stories covering lesbian and gay reaction from the point of view of the community. Lambda Rights Network of Milwaukee as well as the Illinois Gay and Lesbian Task Force have continually been quoted in news stories. The word is out: "sensitivity training for police stinks!" Our society has to take gay kids and runaways more seriously when they make noise. Follow up their complaints before these kids end up as skulls in some bugger's refrigerator.

As far as I'm concerned, Dahmer should not be the center of attention--Dahmer, be damned. Rather, we should center our attention on how we teach young gay men who want to be Prince how to handle their sexuality.

NOTHING PERSONAL

chapter fifty-one

Before Dahmer, the one word that best described living in Milwaukee was the old German word: *Gemutlichkeit*. Meaning, living in Milwaukee was good and easy--comfortable, cozy, homey, friendly, easy-going. Their gingerbread houses, beer steins, and friendly neighborhoods--where you didn't lock your doors--was an urban heaven. This was the home town of the Fonz; the city where Laverne and Shirley worked and lived.

It's popular now to think that Dahmer changed all that. Even more than his heinous crimes, he exposed the sleepy hollow of Milwaukee to be more like Hansel and Gretel from hell. David Schultz, who was once budget director for Chicago Mayor Harold Washington and now is a county official in Milwaukee, says that "for years we looked down our noses at Chicago, we didn't have their urban problems. But now we do!"

When Milwaukee Mayor John O. Norquist spoke at the candlelight vigil for the Dahmer victims, he did not say "gay and lesbian." He is supposed to be a "reform" mayor, but for him, minorities are still people who have no name and count for little.

Even Gerald Boyle, Dahmer's defense lawyer, still has a very cozy relationship with the police department. For eight years he served as the lawyer to the police officers union. No wonder, on the Chicago Tonight[94] show, he tried to protect the police in regard to the "incident" with the "14-year old boy." According to Boyle, when they left the boy with Dahmer they "intended no harm." Their intentions were good. In fact, Boyle still would give the Milwaukee police a grade of "A" or "A-plus."

The cops wanted to link this couple to Dahmer just because one of them happened to work where Dahmer worked and because they were openly gay.

I have uncovered, however, a story where the Milwaukee police definitely score another "F." The night after Dahmer was arrested, Milwaukee cops invaded the home of a gay couple, who had been lovers for 15 years, and intimidated, incarcerated, and terrorized this couple for the next 24 hours. One of the gay guys happened to work first shift at the same chocolate factory where Dahmer worked third shift. The

---

[94] News show on Chicago's public television network, WTTW.

Milwaukee cops wanted to link this couple to Dahmer, just because one of them happened to work where Dahmer worked and because they were openly gay. The cops were willing to ignore the U.S. Constitution, the restrictions on search and seizure, and totally abuse their police power; just so they could play God and cowboy, round up a couple of fags and tie them to Dahmer.

This is a case of gestapo tactics used in *Gemutlichkeit* Milwaukee. 'Til now their story has not received much attention in the mainstream media. Ron Geiman, Editor of Milwaukee's gay magazine *InStep*, broke the story in the August 1-4 issue. I will paraphrase Geiman's account:

On Tuesday July 23, at 10: 15 p.m., the night after Dahmer's arrest, five Milwaukee police officers and two Milwaukee police detectives barged into the gay couple's home. They had no search warrant, and no probable cause to be there. They pushed the shocked couple aside and began rifling and confiscating their personal property. They took video tapes, photos, phone numbers, address books, and other items of a personal nature. They did not explain why they were there.

When the lovers objected, the police began to threaten them verbally and physically. They were treated like they were already convicted felons with no rights. One lover tried to pick up their phone and make a call for help. A couple of officers slammed the phone back on the receiver.

The cops then took the couple and their seized property downtown to central lockup for "questioning." They were told point blank by the detectives "if you don't cooperate we can do it another way." The implication was that the cops would get physical, if they didn't talk.

But talk about what? They tried to piece together why they were in lockup. What had they done? One of the lovers did work first shift where Dahmer worked third. Sometimes he saw Dahmer when they were checking in and out. But he didn't know Dahmer. He didn't know "Dahmer was a homosexual, or did things with gay men."

The police were trying to prove a "conspiracy." All gays who worked where Dahmer worked were linked to his crimes. With no cause or evidence shown. Guilty for being gay. What a perversion! For Dahmer himself is not really "gay." As Dr. Helen Morrison, nationally known forensic psychologist, says, "Dahmer has no sexual identity."

While the couple were in lockup, the cops threatened to reveal their names and lifestyle to their employers. And they would tell their family, too! How uninformed these uniformed brutes are! Wisconsin is the first gay rights state in the union. No gay man living in Wisconsin should have his job threatened because of his sexual orientation. The cops were making illegal threats.

The Milwaukee couple have been devastated by their night in the Milwaukee lockup. They want to remain anonymous, but have retained a lawyer to seek recourse against the cops for their night of illegal terror.

It's a chilling case, because it reminds me all too well of how cops have treated gays. They assume we are felons without any rights. That they can enter our private homes like cowboys and play God with our lives. They assume we feel so guilty about being same-sex lovers that we will never complain when they abuse our constitutional rights. And the media will never hear our story or cries for help.

chapter fifty-two

THE BAR WAS BEAUTIFUL | 1991

The Author entered the Unabridged Bookstore[95] in the same manner that he writes, with swift, sure steps. There he was in front of me, a romantic figure, like an impish pirate, talking to the clerks in his unaffected British accent. Dark black hair, neat goatee, extended mutton chops, a face that belongs in a Van Dyck painting.

The Author was dressed in American gay men's bar drag of the 1970s: black shirt, black boots, black leather belt, light-blue jeans, black hankie in the left rear pocket.

The Author's name is Neil Bartlett. But just as the characters in his first, and outstandingly successful novel, *Ready to Catch Him Should He Fall*, are known only by their quasi-anonymous generic names--Boy, Mother, The Older Man (affectionately called "O"), and the Father--so I will call Bartlett the Author.

---

[95] General interest independent bookstore in New Town neighborhood with a large LGBTQ clientele.

One of the points of his books is how "we gay men" know each other well by the in-group names we assign to each other in our bars, and we can be familiar and intimate with each other using these names over a long period of time; yet there are layers of surprise about our lives before, and even our lives now. If we tried to explain it all talking in the bars, or in the bedroom, we would get nothing on. What makes us interesting to each other is our mystery. From the first eye-contact to the last scene, we seem always to be guessing about each other and always discovering a fact we didn't know before.

Just the other day, "my Boy" surprised me. We have been seeing each other on the side for five years. Suddenly he gets up and says: "I've got to go see my Boy in Glenview." What Boy? My Boy had never told me about his Boy in Glenview. Was this some kid he had produced when he used to date real girls in high school? A boy he fathered to prove his straightness? Or a boyfriend Boy? A new conquest? The Author is skilled at capturing this ambiguous state of gay knowing. His books read naturally as a mystery, because our lives and loves play out like mysteries.

The Author is very popular with everyone. Already before he got to town, Unabridged had sold 60 copies at$19.95. This puts him in line with Armistead Maupin in sales. Forty people were sitting in chairs, in front of an empty table with flowers, waiting for the slightly delayed Author to come and read to them. The guys at Unabridged, Chris, Owen and Ed, each liked the book very much, and they have very different tastes. Kyle and Cyndie were about to read it and knew they would like it, too.

In music I prefer heavy metal, and in books, heavy mental. This Author is light mental, and romantic. I wasn't sure I was going to like his novel, but I did. Some critics like Camille Paglia would see dark shadows lurking behind Boy Apollo and Mother. But I found the book totally light. It is as plain as English food, and his books are made up out of notebooks. Nothing hidden underneath. Some of the lines in this book he wrote, or collected, or copied when he was 17. He is just a damn good collector, observer and storyteller about gay men and their lives, particularly of "those times," the Golden Age of Disco in the pre-AIDS '70s.

As he sat down to read, the Author reminded us that the novel is dedicated to his two grandmothers, Dorothy May Bartlett and Edna May Aston. His title for the novel comes from the ritual he goes through when he holds the arm of one of his grandmother as she crosses the road. He is "ready to catch her if she falls." That's his definition of "unqualified love."

The Author told us that he knows different people will read his book differently. He expects that. But everyone should find in it "something beautiful, and something to bring a tear." Now, I won't give the story away--that's for you to find out on your own--but like any good story, it gets deeper as it goes on and you will feel very involved at the end. Personally, I didn't find the boy that "beautiful"--not my type. Nor did I cry at their wedding, as many do, or when one of the main character dies.

What I found most beautiful was the Bar. The Bar was beautiful. It reminded me a lot of Buddies and Bucks. Chicken Shit Bingo would play well at the Bar. On its most festive nights, it is like Carol's. A touch of Jamie's and the Ten-O-Two Club were there, too. The Bar acts as the Mother of us all, our safe haven from the dangerous streets where gratuitous violence keeps interrupting the story in the book, as it does in the real lives on the streets in Chicago. The Bar is our peculiar and personal theater, where we act out our various roles on cue. These are the scripts of our lives revealed here.

The Author constructs the scenes in the Bar, just as if he were a VJDJ. He keeps I coming down from the booth asking us in the Bar if we like the show, or want to see something different. The most intimate relationship in the book is between Author and reader, not Boy and O.

After his reading, he told us he had been in "a bar on Halsted" (Sidetrack), where he had seen the best and most artful videos. He liked the way the VJ

(Pepe Peña) had cut up Faye Dunaway and made "a gay artifact" out of the coat-hanger scene from *Mommie Dearest*. That's what the Author does in his book. He slices, cuts and edits bar scenes for us. He shows our gay life back to us in disco light.

The Author made me cry not tears of sadness, but tears of joy. His celebration of ordinary gay men going about their ordinary gay lives caught my heart. In a footnote, in his portrait of Oscar Wilde, *Who Was That Man?* (1989)--another most excellent read--the Author puzzles over why the audience watching Larry Kramer's play *The Normal Heart* always cries at his recitation of famous men who were gay, from Plato to Proust. That's all well and fine. But as he tells us, "I belong to a culture that includes the very best Disco music, 1972 to 1978...hundreds of pornographers and drag artists, all my friends and lovers, and all the gay politicians in London."

These are the people he likes to celebrate in his stories. Even though he does have some 60 famous men, gay ghosts, hover around Boy and O's marriage bed, watching them consummate their pleasure and pain. The major theme of his books is how homosexuals learned to flower as gay men from 1880-1980. *Ready To Catch Him Should He Fall* is a delight. Not just a book you take home, but a book you will want to go to bed with.

chapter fifty-three

PAGING THROUGH PAGLIA | 1991

Camille Paglia is the ultimate anachronism of our time: for she has dared to write a "great book" when universities are decentering and throwing out the Great Books for being the politically incorrect manuscripts of Dead White European Males. Paglia's *Sexual Personae* is a cannon inside the Western canon, a book that explodes in its very own greatness. Page through Paglia and on any page you will likely find more ideas than in whole books by most of her contemporaries. She is intense.

I read a few lines from Paglia to Al, my friend the cab driver, and he wisely refused to take my bait and analyze them. He just said, "Well, that's her poetry." The lines were: "Female genitals are lurid in color, vagrant in contour and architecturally incoherent. Male genitals, on the other hand, though they risk ludicrousness by their rubbery indecisiveness, have a rational mathematical design, a syntax."

Here are some more lines from Paglia that tingle up your nose:

"Sexuality is a murky realm of contradiction and ambivalence. It cannot always be understood by social models, which feminism, as an heir of 19th-century utilitarianism, insists on imposing on it."

"All the genres of philosophy, science, high art, athletics, and politics were invented by men."

"Not a shred of evidence supports the existence of matriarchy anywhere in the world at any time."

"As history, the idea of matriarchy is spurious, but as metaphor, it is poetically resonant."

"We are hierarchical animals. Sweep one hierarchy away, and another will take its place." (Think of the USSR today.) "Nature rewards energy and aggression."

"Sex is daemonic [not demonic], and ghost-ridden. Like art, sex is fraught with symbols.... Adult sex is always representation, ritualistic acting out of vanished realities."

"Human beings are not nature's favorites."

"In Western culture, there are no non-exploitative relationships."

"Children are monsters of unbridled egotism and will."

"Female sex smells of marine life; male sex of shit."

"Male sexuality is inherently manic-depressive. Estrogen tranquilizes, but androgen agitates. Men are in a constant state of sexual anxiety, living on the pins and needles of their hormones."

"Male urination really is a kind of accomplishment, an act of transcendence. A woman merely waters the ground she stands on....A male dog marking every bush on the block is a graffiti artist, leaving his rude signature with each lift of the leg. Women, like female dogs, [sic--does she mean bitches?] are earthbound squatters."

". . . at sports events and rock concerts, [female physiology] will force 50 women to wait in line for admission to the sequestered cells of a toilet. Meanwhile their male friends zip in and out [in every sense]...While the modem male homosexual has sought ecstasy in the squalor of public toilets, for women perhaps the least erotic place on Earth."

"Fortunately, male homosexuals of every social class have preserved the cult of masculine."

"Woman's body is a secret. Woman is literally the occult, which means 'the hidden.' "

"Woman is veiled. Woman is chthonian [earth cult]. Man is projection [sky cult]. Man's genital visibility is a source of his scientific desire for external testing, validation, proof. By this method he hopes to solve the ultimate mystery story, his birth by chthonian woman."

"Sex crimes are always male, never female, because such crimes are conceptualizing assaults on the unreachable omnipotence of woman and nature." (Dahmer?)

"Every woman's body contains a cell of archaic night, where all knowing must stop. This is the profound meaning behind striptease, a sacred dance of pagan origins, which, like prostitution, Christianity has never been able to stamp out. Erotic dancing by males [see Lucky Horseshoe Lounge[96]] cannot be comparable, for a nude woman carries off the stage a final concealment, that chthonian darkness from which we come."

"Rape is a model of natural [?] aggression that can be controlled only by the social contract. Modem feminism's most naive formulation is its assertion that rape is a crime of violence but not of sex, that it is merely power masquerading as sex. But sex is power, and all power is inherently aggressive. Rape is male power fighting female power."

"Female sex smells of marine life; male sex of shit."

"History's most glaring error has been its assertion that Judeo-Christianity defeated paganism."

---

[96] Gay bar noted for its scantily clad male dancers.

"Promiscuity in men may cheapen love but sharpen thought. Promiscuity in women is illness, a leakage of identity." (Double standard anyone?)

"Masculinity must fight off effeminacy by day. Woman and nature stand over ready to reduce the male to boy an infant."

"Male aggression and lust are the energizing factors in culture."

"The first medical reports on the disease killing male homosexuals indicated men most at risk were those with a thousand partners over their lifetime. Incredulity. Who could such people be? Why, it turned out, everyone one knew. Serious, kind, literate men, not bums or thugs."

"The beautiful boy is homosexuality's greatest contribution to Western culture."

"I always think of the nipple-piercing pins in sado-masochistic sex shops."

"In the Renaissance as now, a pretty boy with a long, fine head of hair has a drop-dead androgynous allure."

"The gods give latitude but no civil rights. In nature we are convicted without appeal."

chapter fifty-four

TALE TOLD BY AN IDIOT | 1991

I couldn't get any of my hustlers to go and see *My Own Private Idaho*,[97] Gus Van Sant's voyeuristic tale about their scene, even if it featured two most excellent dudes, River Phoenix[98] and Keanu Reeves, playing the role of hustlers on the streets of Seattle and Portland, didn't seem to grab them.

On the night of an advance premier showing at Broadway and Belmont, I offered two free passes to a couple of hustlers. They sniffed and turned up their noses, like I had just offered them a can of bad-smelling dog food.

"Thanks, man. But can you do us a little favor?" They wanted some quick money, not free tickets.

"We've got a problem. See that guy over there? He just offered us $400 to put something big up his ass. He said he would pay us with a

---

[97] 1991 film.

[98] Actor River Phoenix died of a drug overdose in 1993.

check. And we don't know if his check is any good."

"Doesn't seem right to me either," I said. "In your line of work, I wouldn't even accept Master Charge."

My hustlers' instincts were right. *Idaho* is not a film for them, like *Streetwise*, or *Christianna F.* It is a dense, thick, rich movie, containing at least three stories in one. The story of a couple of street hustlers, one of whom happens to be the son of the mayor of Portland, and the other of whom happens to be gay. A soap about Mikie's search for mother and home. And a Shakespearean interlude full of Falstaffian rebels and counter-culture losers.

Savvy critics like David Kehr, Albert Williams, and Michael Bronski praise Idaho as an artful art film. Many critics and viewers are riveted to River Phoenix's performance as a boy "with a fucked-up face," "a connoisseur of roads." He is like a James Dean of the '90s, and probably deserves a second Oscar nomination for *Idaho.*

Our crowd has been dutiful in attending the movie, especially after *Newsweek* told us that Van Sant is "openly gay." I myself have become a "potato-head," and with a few other friends have seen it several times. I appreciate Van Sant's Northwest setting and mood. When I ran the streets of Seattle and Portland, the joke always was, after the big earthquake, Seattle and Portland would be ghost towns and Idaho a coast town. The Northwest is the home of the last settlers, and the home of the least settled. No one quite feels at home there. Natives, like the weather, remain gray on the outside, and threatening on the inside.

Van Sant captures this locale, and the interior of these interior people very well. His humor is eccentric, his style distorting and off-putting, very private views full of the unexpected. Idiot in Greek means "private person." That's why, to borrow a phrase from Shakespeare, this movie is "a tale told by an idiot."

Talking to our crowd as they go in and out, I sense that few get, or like, the movie as a whole. Some of the audience in the first 30 minutes seem to fall into a narcoleptic haze, and miss everything that happens. Several are thrown off by the Shakespeare parts, the royal language of queens used to say "fuck you." They miss Van Sant's music of words, visual puns and humor. To me, the made-up Shakespearean lines were no more annoying than running over a speed bump in one of Seattle's exclusive districts, such as Broadmore or The Highlands.

Most everyone, however, likes some part or the film. I think that's enough, because Van Sant took so many risks in this production that he was going inevitably to lose most of his audience some of the time. The film is too private, too much his own Idaho to please all the people all the time. Yet, nearly everyone likes the fireside scene between Phoenix and Reeves. Not since F.D.R. have we had such a famous fireside chat. I can't think of where else in a major film we have one male teen idol say to another: "I want to kiss you, man. I love you."

Others like the psychologically rich scene between Mike and his Brother/Father figure in their trailer home. But I like the little takes just as well. The opening sequence where Mike gets a blow job, and seems to enjoy it more than the money. While being sucked, Mike sees, in his narcoleptic dream, his home fall and splatter on the highway. For me that gives new meaning to the phrase: "coming from a broken home."

Several people complained that the just "didn't get it!" Others told me they squirmed in their seats. They didn't think the sex was very "gay positive." Van Sant's movie is dense and hard to get. He does not direct us to an easy answer. Take the ending, where Mike is picked up for the last time on the highway. Who picks him up? I was baffled. Scott, a waiter at Ann Sather,[99] said, "Well, that's easy. Mike is back in a narcoleptic dream, and he is carried off once again by Scott,

---

[99] Popular neighborhood restaurant.

his mother substitute." Todd, another friend, said, "No, the Brother/Father figure comes back to pick him up." Boyd gives another answer: "They're wrong, that's wishful thinking. Mike is picked up by an anybody, a stranger. This is also a clever device if Van Sant wants to make a sequel, Idaho II."

Van Sant is gay and coy at the same time, and his work hides as much as it shows. He offers interiors inside interiors. You can get lost in his private Idaho. But the film is obviously more gay positive than *Midnight Cowboy* of 20 years ago. Gus tells an idiot's tale, he has the nerve not to communicate and leave us baffled. He is more interested in showing private lives than sex lives. When he shows the private fantasies of Johns acted out, we don't squirm over their sex as much as we are embarrassed by them showing us their private human parts. No one wants to identify with a John. Yet each of us is a John, a private person.

Just as the Brother/Father figure paints his "normal neighbors" with fucked-up faces, and they give him the money, but never take the pictures home with them, so Van Sant has painted a private picture with fucked-up faces, that no one really wants to take home with them.

And irony of ironies, he has "America the Beautiful" played on a saw, repeated throughout the soundtrack, while he has the nerve to show us all these Americans who aren't very beautiful. Idaho is not a movie for hustlers; rather, it is a movie for Johns who are comfortable with their private human parts.

chapter fifty-five

TEEN SEX AND THE PERVERT | 1992

Teens, kids born between 1973 and 1980, are having sex as usual, like they have never heard of the word safe. Teens are getting AIDS in rapidly increasing numbers. When you calculate the often long incubation period for full-blown AIDS, teen AIDS is even more shocking.

Nearly one-fifth of all U.S. cases of AIDS occur among people in their early 20s. People who were probably having sex in their early teens. AIDS is the sixth-leading cause of death among kids ages 15 to 24. This new information was released by the U.S. House Select Committee on Children, Youth and Families, a panel led by Rep. Patricia Schroeder (D-Colo.). They concluded that "the number of teens who have AIDS increased by more than 70 percent in the last two years."

Teens having sex is not unhealthy or immoral or unusual. Every current study confirms that, despite the threat of AIDS, teens are still having lots of sex, believing it is physically unhealthy and sick not to. The Carnegie Council on Adolescent Development, at the same time as the Congressional study, reported that "teen sex is on the increase in two categories: 10- to 14-, and 15- to -19-year-olds." High risk behaviors are also on the increase for these age groups. "The American suicide rate tripled among 10- to 14-year-olds, and doubled among 15- to 19-year-olds from 1968-1985." From other studies we know that the suicide rate is three times higher among gay teens.

The Carnegie Council concluded that "adolescence in America is a kind of battlefield." Our kids are dying out there, and there is no Desert Storm rescue team coming to save them. "A quarter of our teens are at high risk, engaging in life-threatening activities." There are many gay men, mostly closeted, teachers and counselors, and school administrators trying to save kids in the battlefield. I know of many doing heroic work in the inner city. Guys who know Spanish as well as English teaching science classes, taking their kids to museums, and giving extra time on weekends. Gay teachers in the ghettos and the suburbs, who seem to have a special gift for working with teens.

But, I also know that a lot of these teachers and counselors are scared. Many leave teaching for safer professions, because they fear, if their gay identity surfaces, they may get entrapped in a sexual scandal. I know of a teacher in the West suburbs who parties in our bars on the weekend, but "degays" his car when he goes back home on Sunday. He makes sure there are no gay papers or gay bar matchbooks in his car. He is afraid he will get stopped on the highway, and somehow be "found out." An ad for a 900 number may be seen as "porn" by an arresting officer. The word could get out at his school, and he would lose his effectiveness as a teacher and role model.

I know another gym teacher afraid to come out. Kids at his school already write misspelled graffiti: "Fuck You Cisses!" He knows there would not be a lot of tolerance for his "gayness," among some of the functional illiterates in his classes. And teaching in a Cook County school, as yet, he has no protection of a Human Rights Ordinance.[100]

I know a senior counselor, who went into "private practice" because the strain was too much. "I love kids, and love working with them, but the risk was too great. I counsel adults now."

Gay men, even though they possess special the skills and awareness, and have a knack for working well with teens, stay off the battlefield. A wrong gesture, a show of affection, a pat on the butt could lead to a charge of sexual harassment. "You pervert!" Gay men in sensitive positions are

---

[100] Cook County passed a gay-inclusive human rights ordinance in 1993.

easy fall guys for charges of pedophilia. "Corrupting the morals of a minor." The same charge they threw against Socrates and Oscar Wilde. No matter how advanced our human rights laws become, gay men still live under the threat of the ancient sodomy codes.

Consider the recent case of Edward I. Savitz, the 50-year-old insurance executive in Philadelphia, who had his life totally ruined in a weekend of charges. The District Attorney late on a Friday afternoon, just as most AIDS service agencies were shutting down for the weekend, announced two serious charges against Savitz, and at the same time the Sex Crimes Division of the Philadelphia Police Department, which had been working on the Savitz case for six months. Despite laws of confidentiality, the D.A. let the media know Savitz has "full-blown AIDS." She also revealed that Savitz may have had "contact" with hundreds of teens, causing full-blown AIDS hysteria to flood the TV channels of Philly.

Lurid details from Savitz's life became instant news. He supposedly paid money ($30-$40) to kids for their dirty socks, and gave them a clean pair. He bought dirty underwear. Sometimes even their shit, which he placed in plastic bags. Some journalists compared Savitz to Jeffrey Dahmer, over-looking that, weird as it may be, to keep some guy's shit in your refrigerator is significantly different from keeping a guy's body parts in your freezer.

By Sunday the sex crime investigators had collected 312 bags of dirty socks and underwear from Savitz's home. Over 5,000 photos of boys in different states of undress. And several bags of shit. Savitz was beaten and robbed by his fellow arrestees in the van going to lockup. Taunted and jeered by his fellow mates in jail. Stripped naked of his AIDS confidentiality rights, and slapped with a $20-million bail bond, which his lawyer called "a ransom fee."

Oddly enough, only the *New York Times* seemed to give out less than hysterical reports. "Medical experts say that Mr. Savitz' activities apparently bore little or no risk of transmitting the virus...Oral sex is not likely to cause AIDS." "Mr. Savitz's lawyer denied that Mr. Savitz had anal sex with any teenagers, but said his client admitted involving them in sexual fantasies."

On the following Wednesday, Savitz was formally charged with two counts: "involuntary deviate sexual intercourse with a 15-year-old minor." Intercourse in this instance means: "Mr. Savitz performed oral sex on a minor." Second charge: involving a second 15-year-old, "corrupting the morals of a minor." Both these boys were fully-clothed when the police entered Savitz's home, and there is some suspicion that these boys were already cooperating with the police, and that's why they were there.

Mr. Savitz--a high school valedictorian--and, as a teenager, "the kid most likely someday to be a U.S. Supreme Court Justice"--has been convicted of being "a pervert" before he has had one day in court. What keeps many gay guys from going into professions to help teens is this fear of the "sodomy code," the idea that if you commit a minor act with a minor, like holding his hand, taking his picture, you could be charged with a "sex crime," and ranked in the public mind with the stigma of a serial killer.

chapter fifty-six

REPEATING OUR HISTORY | 1992

When you are gay and lesbian, you are not just on a fast track, you're on a fast cycle. Every 90 days, we seem to repeat our history. A major organization lets go its director and a couple of staffers. Activists are at each other's throat over lobbying strategies in the county and the state. Queer styles clash with gay styles. Blood spills, letters flow, and we have more speeches about the sin of infighting.

In the name of "unity" we bash each other, and get our best licks in at activists we don't like. Activism is a worrisome occupation. Being on the "cutting-edge" is often self-cutting. We enter activism because we each have set ideas and strong wills. Conflict is the name of the game. But instead of indicating the "end of our movement," it may more accurately be a sign of a community growing and thriving. For whenever our movement has flourished, there have been fierce rivalries and competitive agendas.

To get out of the trap of these immediate encounters, I have been reading a book on "the youth movement, the gay movement and male bonding before Hitler's rise in Germany." *Homosexuality and Male Bonding in Pre-Nazi Germany* contains the transcripts from *Der Eigne* (1860-1930), "the first gay journal in the world." It is edited by Harry Oosterhuis, Ph.D.,and Hubert Kennedy, Ph.D.

Der Eigne, in queer English, refers to "the do your own thing" crowd. They celebrated their sexual Eros, nude bodies, and proclaimed men loving boys as a very healthy thing.

"You can't be a good pedagogue, without first being a good pederast." The classroom is an erotic environment, and good teaching stimulates your desires. Gay teachers make great teachers, even for heterosexuals.

The *Eigne* crowd, ironically, were also square in their sexual morality. "Manly friendship" was the key to their world. They knew of, but didn't approve of, men who went down to Friedrichstrasse to pick up hustlers. They advocated friendship in the style of poets and philosophers like Goethe. They believed that "civilization is the possibility of living out our drives and strengths."

Adolph Brand was their leader and edited their magazine. He was also a brilliant activist in the struggle to get rid of paragraph 175 from the penal code: "Unnatural lewdness that is committed between persons of the male sex or by persons with animals is to be punished by prison." Calling yourself a "175er" became a code name for being gay. On the average 400 or 500 men and young men were sent to prison a year and lost all their civil rights.

Brand and his followers formed a *Gemeinschaft*, a "community of men loving men." They helped each other to express their Eros, circulated literature and ideas about homosexuality, and came to the aid of members who were blackmailed. They spent a lot of their time trying to repeal 175. They embraced no fancy or "scientific" explanations of why they were "homosexual." In fact, they didn't like that medical term, and fought and separated from a rival camp, led by the sexologist Magnus Hirschfeld, who founded the Scientific-Humanitarian Committee and an institute to study sexual behavior.

Hirschfeld was the inventor of the notion of "the third sex." Male homosexuals, he argued, were really "womanly souls trapped inside a male body." He practically invented the popular use of the term and concept homosexual, and often testified at trials to declare whether the defendant was, or was not, "a true homosexual."

Brand's followers found Hirschfeld's "scientific views" insulting. They were not "women." They were robust men loving masculine men. They didn't like elaborate explanations for their "feelings." Too much emphasis on the medical made them seem like "abnormal case studies." The "scientific" approach to homosexuality put too much power in the hands of the physician. They liked to gossip about Hirschfeld himself. They called him "Auntie Magnesia," because in his "private" life, he was a transvestite. Wherever our movement thrives, there also flourishes the politics of queens.

Brand was prosecuted, and later put in jail, for a charge of "pornography." He published pictures of naked men in his magazine. Hirschfeld refused to come to Brand's defense at his trial. He didn't think the issues of Der Eigne were of much "scientific'" importance.

When Hitler came to power, one of his first acts was to destroy Hirschfeld's institute and burn many original gay documents and manuscripts. All because Hirschfeld was both Jewish and "queer." He fled to Paris and died on his 67th birthday in 1935 in Nice, a broken man.

Brand, the great advocate of man-boy love, escaped Hitler's clutches. For he was also married to a nurse. He wasn't Jewish, and the Nazis treated him as a "normal family-man." If you read between the lines of his bio, you can also detect that Brand had a couple of "Platonic affairs" with German officers, who protected "their friend." Brand and his wife, however, died in their home in 1945, destroyed by bombs from American planes.

Just as the rival leaders, so the rival camps, the common and the scientific, had different criss-crossed fates. Both camps broke up into sets that fought over all the issues of the day. Some activists wanted to try "outing." They argued that if the general public only knew the "truth" about Alfred Krupp, the industrialist, members of parliament, and several members of the royal family--then they would quickly win their rights. "Outing" was tried in a few instances, but in the main fell on deaf ears, because what made these targets different, was not their homosexuality, but their money and power. A star outed is still a star.

Several of the activists didn't want to have anything to do with women. They were Gynophobic supermen. But other activists argued quite convincingly that the freedom of male culture was tied up in supporting the women's movement. None are free 'til all are free.

German sociologists of the day invented a critical distinction in terms: They said there were two kinds of groups, which often overlap, *Gemeinschaft* (a community) and *Gesellschaft* (a society). (They would make perfect names for a gay leather bar and a gay drag bar.) The difference in queer English is a *Gemeinschaft* "is a group of people you can fuck with." A *Gesellschaft* is a "group of people who will fuck you over." In all our community struggles, as we keep repeating our history, I think we should aim for the first, rather than the second type of groups.

chapter fifty-seven

MR. HAMILTON AND THE PUNK | 1992

Your first sexual experience? All I recall are clusters of early sexual experience--teen and pre-teen. Sex has always been a yes and yes experience for me. There was nothing in my youth that caused me to lose my innocence. Innocence is not something I lost 40 years ago, but something I keep finding and redefining every time I have what I imagine to be a sexual encounter.

Sex, for me, has always been an art, and I approach it like an artist. I still imagine my best time to be the next one. I had no single first experience and my next one will have an element of first about it, too.

But I do remember a cluster of experiences, at Funston Field in the Marina District in San Francisco, where I lived during the summers when I was 13, 14 and 15. I would get up in the morning, go out and play with my mates 'til I was tired, come home, gulp down a dinner, go to bed, sleep and get ready to do it all over again.

My mates in those days fell into classes. Kids my own age, like Fred, the punk in a leather jacket. We played hardball and went fooling around together, heavy petting and to movies together and talked kid's stuff. He was a little older, about ready to enter Galileo High; and when we danced, he knew how to lead.

My other mates were old men, veterans of World War I. They were in their 70s and above. Calculating today, I figure some of them must have been Civil War babies, most of them born in the 1880s. They were sharp putters in golf. Funston Field had two large putting greens, where these old men played competed with each other from dawn 'til dusk. Sometimes even under the lights at night. They were tough. But I, too, had a passion for golf, had worked in a pro-shop, so they let me into their circle.

Most of them wore white shirts and ties. All of them wore straw hats. Many smoked cigars. They all emphasized the "gentleman" aspect of the game. They called each other "mister." A Mister Hamilton took a special liking to me, gave me pointers and psychological support, because golf is such a mental game.

In between rounds, or during breaks, Mr. Hamilton and I would sit on a bench and talk. He knew about history and business, because he had lived one and had done the other. A diamond merchant, he had been all over the world. I was charmed by him, and his wide reading and knowledge. He had even met Dr. Carl Jung, studied myths and archetypes in one of Jung's seminars, and was a cool guy. Tall, usually in a blue suit, tie with stick pin, dapper straw hat, but with an old man's gnarly hands with tobacco stains on the fingers.

On the park bench one day, he talked "a little funny." He seemed fascinated by the story of Florence Chadwick, who on Aug. 8, 1950, broke the world's record for swimming the English channel--and then swam the channel the next year in the opposite direction, thus becoming the first woman to swim the channel in both directions. Her picture was on the front of all the newspapers. When I went to a movie with Fred, during the newsreel, they showed Chadwick climbing out of the water triumphant. Her bathing suit was so tight that Fred and I jabbed each other in the ribs. For in our teen eyes, we thought we had seen "a naked woman."

Mr. Hamilton had a fixed eye on that "naked woman," too. She was born in San Diego and he saw her in person when she swam off Catalina Island. He said they greased her whole body before she got into the water. He asked me if I would like to come to his apartment and see a picture of Florence Chadwick on his wall. I got the strong idea that Mr. Hamilton liked to grease up bodies. And would have liked to do mine.

I declined his offer. My mother had nine brothers. One uncle was abducted, and another (I was never clear whether it was the same one) liked to wear dresses around the lumber camp in Everett, Wash. We were cautioned not to go off with old men like Mr. Hamilton, for fear of being abducted.

But my second summer, I did go home with Mr. Hamilton. After all, I was already greasing my pole and pounding my pud into my pillow as often as I could get away with it in my own bedroom. Fred and I were pulling each other's pole. So what Mr. Hamilton had in mind didn't seem so frightening or far-fetched to me. In fact, I found his offer exciting and I wanted to go with him.

Yes, we did shower together. And he greased my pole and gave me full back rubs. He also taught me how men can please men and kept the discussion on a natural basis. He taught me not to be afraid of my own body and its parts. He respected social limits and never went very far with me. Not only did he relieve my teen urges, he relieved me of the fear of sex and old men. He pleased me so that I never had any idea--'til years later--that he got pleasure from it, too.

When we were done, I now realize he went into the bathroom and finished himself off. At the time, I just thought he was a kind old man who was willing to do all the work to please me.

I was also carrying on with Fred, the punk, every time I could hitch a ride with him on his bike from the ballfield. Fred was foxy and playful. Audie Murphy eyes and large lips. I would lick him and his jacket, for I acquired a taste for him on his jacket, and his jacket smell on him. One night I remember he stayed over and slept on the floor. I slept in my bed on his jacket.

Not fully conscious what I was doing those summers, I was dating a 79-year-old man and a 17-year-old punk. I was experiencing cross-generational affection. These two types have constituted my affinity groups ever since. They are the reason I have had success in teaching senior citizens and cruising punks.

I did not tell my mother about my trips to Mr. Hamilton's house. They met each other once at Funston Field, and she thought he was a "nice gentleman." And he was! I did hear her and my stepfather talking loudly one night to the effect that it wasn't "healthy" for me to be hanging around all those "old men."

But those old men were my friends, mates, and buddies just as much as my contemporaries like Fred. The long-standing guilt and Puritan tradition of our country makes everyone suspect old men of being dirty child molesters. Oprah Winfrey and her specials are scaring kids shitless about sex in the Age of AIDS. I'm just here to say not every old man is a molester, and not every one's sexual history is filled with horror stories.

PART SIX

chapter fifty-eight

TRIAL OF A FALL GUY? | 1992

Larry Eyler, suspected serial killer, entered court on Thursday, Sept. 24th, in penitentiary drag--in green inmate jump suit, looking like he belonged in a Notre Dame cheering section--with chained and cuffed feet and hands. Personally, he didn't want to be there. He prefers to remain laid back in his cozy pad on Death Row. But Cook County Circuit Court Judge Joseph Urso--the trial judge who originally sentenced Eyler on Oct. 3, 1986,[101] to death for the dismemberment and murder of Danny Bridges, 16, a fast-track hustler and snitch from Uptown--ordered Eyler be present at this evidentiary hearing, his trial for a new trial.

Eyler, who is compulsively good at taking orders from his superiors, submissively complied with the judge's wishes.

---

101 Damski's five-part series on the 1986 trial begins on page 303. The 1992 hearings have also yielded five parts, of which this is the first.

Kathleen T. Zellner, the tall, brash and aggressively inspired attorney for Eyler's petition for a new trial, requested that his handcuffs and leg irons be removed. Judge Urso, who works hard at being sensitive and fair, so ordered. Several sheriff deputies scrambled around the room for chairs, as the judge told them "this will take a while."

Star journalists and Eyler groupies were already in court eager to watch the proceedings. Gera-Lind Kolarik, author of the book about Eyler, Freed to Kill, came directly from a Geraldo show to witness the hearings. Major TV reporters dropped by for sound bites. Sarah Dobrovolskis and her sister attended a couple of sessions. Sarah was the wife of John Dobrovolskis, Eyler's lover and a former Mr. Broadway Limited.[102] John, at the original trial, gave damaging testimony for the prosecution against Larry. In the courtroom, then, John and Larry stared at each other intensely, and if looks alone could kill, one of them could have been dead on the spot. But John died two years ago of AIDS, and Sarah and her sister smile friendly and wan at Larry. The only time Larry broke his submissive and serious pose, sitting next to Zellner at the petitioner's table, was to flash a happy wave at Sarah and her sister.

---

[102] A popular gay disco in New Town, since closed.

At the end of Thursday's hearing, Eyler again approached the bench with his lawyer and asked to go back to Pontiac. He was afraid the accommodations at Cook County jail would be unsuitable for him, and he needed his medication. Judge Urso ordered him to stay in custody in Cook County jail throughout the hearings, and also ordered that his medicine be provided. One guard said at Cook County, "he would have a simple cell with a mattress on the floor." Nothing fancy.

One guy from Indiana, a relative of one of the victims of Eyler, whispered into my ear: "If he gets a new trial, he loses. He will be put off Death Row and placed in the general population. There, the gangs who rule will get him. A lot of people want to fuck, rape, torture and kill him." Eyler is everybody's potential fall guy. He can't win for winning. My impression is that Larry hasn't changed his nature. He is a compliant mouse in any cat's game. In many ways he personally doesn't want to be there, doesn't personally want to fight for a new trial. Passive and accepting, he doesn't even seem fired up to get revenge on his sugar daddy, Dr. Robert David Little, the professor of library science at Indiana State University, who Eyler says killed Danny Bridges. Eyler claims he only cut up the body the next morning.

Kathleen Zellner and her associates are the ones fighting for a new trial to get at the truth. Zellner, with her long black hair and severe face, stalks the court like Prince Valiant and looks like she has slain dragons before breakfast. She, not passive Eyler, is the one demanding a fair fight, that justice be done.

The murder of Danny Bridges happened early Sunday morning Aug. 19/20, 1984. Zellner and her associates have gone back to the old haunts, and searched out anyone who is still around. She has uncovered more facts about the original crime and the participants than did Eyler's original defense attorney David P. Schippers, or the original prosecutors, Assistant State's Attorneys. Mark Rakoczy and Richard Stock. But the trail is cold and the footprints covered over.

Most of my original sources are dead and gone. The whole scene is dead and gone. Gordon's, a fancy restaurant for elite clientele, has replaced Jumbo Jerry's, the all-night chili stand for night crawlers from Hell. The New Flight at 420 N. Clark, the internationally famous hustler bar, where stars like Tony Perkins used to drop by when they were in town, is now a straight yuppie bar called Boss, and as you walk in you face a huge mural of "the Boss," former mayor Richard J. Daley.

Zellner and her team are raising two narrow issues. She claims that the defense attorney was under a "conflict of interest," because he and his firm were receiving payments for fees from Sugar Daddy Little, a guy who paid for Larry's apartment and was there the weekend Bridges was murdered in that same apartment. But Schippers, without objection, let Little be the surprise lead-off witness against Larry for the prosecution.

Zellner further argues that the Chicago Police Department and the State's Attorney office withheld crucial information about Bridges from the defense--namely, that Danny was a police informant. Also that Danny was into "bondage," and it should have been no surprise that he had "ligature marks" on his hands when he was murdered.

My notes and recollection from interviews with people around the scene at the time corroborate many of Zellner's points. I talked to guys that Danny himself cruised for bondage-style sex, guys Danny voluntarily went home with.

The weakest part of the police and prosecution story on Eyler has always been that Larry is a "pedophile," a "chicken hawk." Bridges was not Eyler's type. Ironically, Eyler was more Bridges' type, the kind of guy Danny cruised for pleasure. Knowing some of the guys that Dr. Little has hit on, I would say that Bridges was more Little's type than Eyler's.

Secondly, the idea that Eyler came swooping down to Hubbard and Clark in his red truck and picked up Danny Bridges, as though he were a little altar boy from the suburbs--a one time deal--has never made sense to me. Danny Bridges knew Eyler from the scene, and from the continual publicity of our running Eyler's picture in *GayLife* as a man to watch out for.

Danny told one of his cuddly roommates, "I know Larry (Eyler) and I can handle him!" The two of them had been seen together "as an item" in the coffee shop at the corner of Clark and Illinois.

Knowing their respective tastes, it is easier for me to conceive that Bridges would seek out Eyler, not the other way around. If Eyler got caught up with Danny Bridges, he was either doing it for someone else, or couldn't stop Bridges' advances. In other words, a situation where Eyler was the patsy or fall guy.

chapter fifty-nine

OMEN CHILD | 1992

[103]Connie Fletcher writes books about the police told from the cop's point of view. She uncritically takes what they tell her and writes it down. Pure cop bull! But she does accurately get into the minds of cops and their thinking.

In her book, What Cops Know, in the chapter on "Sex Crimes," she gets one cop from the youth division of the Special Investigative Unit of the Chicago Police to say just what he thinks happened between Larry Eyler and Danny Bridges: "Here's a perfect example of what can happen to sexually victimized kids--Danny, a 12-year-old kid, who was murdered and hacked into pieces and tossed out into the garbage by a pedophile named Larry."

On Aug. 20, 1984, when Danny Bridges was murdered, he was not "a child," not a "twelve-year-old kid" as this cop wants you to believe, but a few weeks short of his 17th birthday on Oct

---

[103] Second of five in a follow-up to Damski's 1986 series on Eyler.

11.[104] Already, Danny had been on the streets, out of the control of his out-of-control dysfunctional family for eight years. Danny was no kid; he was an Omen child fending for himself, in business for himself, choosing pleasures for himself.

Larry Eyler was not a pedophile. He tended to cruise gays in their mid-20s and older, mesomorphs, with beards and hair on their chest. He preferred to date men, not boys. Ironically, it was Danny Bridges who used to hang out in front of Little Jim's, or the old Gold Coast on N. Clark, and used to follow leather men home--not for money, not for love, but his own pleasure.

The prosecutors of Larry Eyler have always based their information on the cop's story. Throughout the original trial, the assistant state's attorneys kept saying Danny Bridges was a child, 15- and 14-years-old. Sixteen would have technically made him a "consenting adult" and blown the pedophile/child molester stereotype of Eyler. Even Judge Joseph Urso, in sentencing Eyler to death, followed the police line: "The senseless and barbaric aggravated kidnapping and murder of a 15-year-old boy..."

During the recent hearing for a new trial, a mother and father sat next to me one day waiting

---

[104] Reports about Bridges' age varied with time and distance from his actual murder, when it was listed as being 16.

for their son's case to come before Judge Urso. When Assistant State's Attorney Timothy Joyce described the murder of Danny Bridges in terms of being "a child," the mother looked at Eyler and leaned over to me and asked: "How could he kill and cut up a baby?"

Danny could play sweet boy, cuddle with an old man, take his money and hit the police station the next day telling on that man. Danny was no baby. He would dye his hair yellow straw, twitch-his bunny-nose, give you his pick-me-up eyes and jostle through Joe's Juice Joint in his satin disco jacket like he was playing Tom Sawyer in a rock opera by Rush. But he had another side to him too. He could change back to his natural brunette color and act more like a moody punk in a neo-fascist club in Pink Floyd's *The Wall*. Danny played a wide field: He could act like he wanted to take a day off with Ferris Bueller; but when he followed his heart's desire, he really wanted a night out with Claus Von Bulow.

When I wrote my original piece about Danny for *GayLife*, after his murder in August 1984, I had the blond Danny in mind. I called him "an easy mark in a rough trade," a hustler who had gotten into a scene over his own head. Gera-Lind Kolarik basically followed the "easy mark" theme in her book, where Danny comes out a hollow boy, used and abused by chicken hawks, journalists, cops, counselors, family and priests.

It was only after I saw another picture of the brunette Danny, checked with other sources who knew him, that I put together another side. He was no "Sweet Cheeks." In 1982, he was the star witness for the cops in their bust on Joe's Juice Joint. He was the cop's best witness for nailing men on sex crimes. Little "Tom Sawyer" had over a 90-percent conviction rate.

Danny was the best kid the cops had and used. Typical procedure was to catch a kid in a small infraction on drugs or minor theft. Threaten to send the kid away. But if he cooperated in trying to get a guy on a sex crime, let the kid go free. That was Danny's work.

A revealing passage in Connie Fletcher's book shows the method of the cops: "Proactive is the only way to go in uncovering this most secretive, virulent crime, says one SIU investigator. 'Our opinion is that you should go out and find the crime. What better way to prove the crime than get it in progress or to follow somebody home and have him go to bed with a kid? My opinion, it's the only way to do it.'"

The cops were pimping Danny, having him go home with men so they could, catch them both in bed. Arrest the man and let Danny testify against him. Many believe that the cops were trying to set up Eyler with Danny Bridges. If they could get Eyler on a "sex crime," they could revoke his then-pending bond in Lake County and send him back to jail.

Personally, I don't believe the cops actually pulled off this set-up. The real Danny Bridges worked for no man but himself. He took aid and money from cops, journalists, good hearts, chicken hawks, sex weirdoes, girlfriends, family, friends--he was a total hustler. He used the system and everyone in it as much as they used him. Think of what a power trip he was on. No one at school gave him much recognition. Teachers called him "slow." The other kids called him "queer" and "fag." But out on the streets, he was the main man. He could get big men busted, just on his word alone. He could get on national TV, just to tell his story, in the way he knew the producers wanted him to say it.

When Danny told his roommate, "I know Larry (Eyler), and I can handle him," he was boasting about himself. He was a top guy in his world; he had cops, journalists and well-connected professional men all willing to kiss his ass for his favors. With all his clout, I am sure, Eyler didn't scare him. He must have thought he had Eyler by the balls. Word from him could send Larry back to jail. At the Juice Joint bust he was Star '82.[105] Why wouldn't he also think he could be Star '84, and a media darling, in an Eyler bust?

The legacy of Danny Bridges is that he left a lot of people feeling guilty and pointing fingers at each other. The guy who did a national TV show about him and male prostitution had a nervous breakdown and went into retirement. The cops who brought him back from High Point, N.C., to do some more for them, have always felt a little guilty for his murder. Journalists who used him for their stories feel a little like the men who used his body for their pleasure: soiled.

Someday, we may get wise enough to recognize that kids have minds and bodies and lives of their own. Danny didn't learn or take orders from us. He was a wild child all on his own. He learned social dating from Iron Maiden, sex scenes from Judas Priest and Black Sabbath. His sense of justice did not come from a court but from Metallica. Danny made his choices, and what happened to him was much more his doing than ours.

---

[105] Star '82 alludes to Bob Fosse's film, *Star '80,* starring Mariel Hemingway as ill-fated Playboy playmate Dorothy Stratten.

chapter sixty

THE CASE THAT WOULD NOT CLOSE | 1992

[106]By 10:30 a.m., the jury box in Judge Joseph Urso's court was filled with major media, TV reporters and TV sketch artists. This was the big day when Judge Urso would rule on whether Larry Eyler should get a new trial for the murder of Danny Bridges. At 11:07, the judge returned to the bench and put the court in session. "Where is Larry Eyler? I ordered that he be here for the hearings!" Timothy Joyce, assistant state's attorney, made an excuse for Eyler's absence, and Kathleen T. Zellner, Eyler's lawyer, agreed with Joyce that Larry did not have to be present for the ruling. Urso seemed displeased, adjourned court until noon, when he said he would make his decision.

Reporters returned to the jury box around noon and waited for the judge. He didn't come back until nearly 1:30. Waiting there, we all thought this would be "a high noon decision." One reporter correctly assessed the situation:

---

[106] Third of five Damski columns on Eyler in 1992.

"Urso can't win on this. As the trial judge, he either goes against his original work and calls for a new trial, or covers things over and looks bad."

There had already been several dramatic moments and flash points in this hearing. The time Timothy Joyce demolished Zellner's expert witness on conflict of interest, a professor from Northwestern. Under Joyce's forceful cross-examination, the professor learned that a courtroom is not like a class room. When Joyce finished, the professor was left muttering and sputtering in the witness chair, and Joyce returned triumphant to his table proudly holding his pen in his mouth, looking like a happy dog who had just found a tasty bone.

David Schippers, the original trial lawyer for Eyler, gave a smooth and rehearsed performance defending himself against the charge of conflict of interest. But during Zellner's cross examination he lost his liberal cool, and became a very hostile witness. He admitted he had hung up on her on the phone and had called her a name ("bitch"). On the stand, Schippers was arrogant, did not treat Zellner as a fellow attorney, but acted towards her as though she were in fact the bad dog-name he had called her.

In the last day of testimony, Zellner called a surprise rebuttal witness, DeJon Karlae, a former gay bartender who worked at Take One the night

Bridges was killed. Karlae said he served Dr. Robert Little that night in the bar, and Little was there till midnight. That contradicts Little's sworn testimony at the original trial when he said he went back home to Indiana that night around 10:30.

More fireworks were expected at Urso's ruling. But he returned to court very business like at 1:30 and deflated Zellner's balloon. "I find no prosecution misconduct, and no conflict of interest." The bid for a new trial was denied. He spoke in a flat, matter-of-fact tone. Perhaps he thought by adopting that tone, no one would notice that he too was covering his own ass and spinning a new fiction.

Urso argued that the prosecution really didn't have to tell the defense that Danny Bridges had been a police informant, and had previously engaged in bondage sex. Urso said "the prosecutors were not obliged to do the work of the defense."

On the issue of conflict of interest, Urso started out by saying he found this "troublesome." Then, in his argument, he went on to praise "the defense team." Eyler received "exceptional representation in this case." Schippers did" a masterful job." Eyler continually requested that he wanted Schippers to be his lawyer. Eyler had "competent lawyers."

Well, if this was such a masterful trial, why did it end with everyone believing in the wrong facts and interpretation of Bridges and Eyler? The court never did get the victim's age right. They still call him 15. Still follow the police story that he was "a child," instead of a nearly-17-year-old, who on the streets had participated in adult sexual behaviors for several years.

And if Eyler got the best of all possible defenses, than why didn't Schippers ever bring to the court a psychological profile of his client?

At the time of Eyler's hearing for the death sentence, Schippers contacted Dr. Lyle Rossiter, "one of only 250 board-certified forensic psychiatrists in the United States," but never followed through to have his client receive a complete psychiatric assessment.

Zellner in 1990 recontacted Dr. Rossiter and he come up with the following profile which she submitted to the court. Larry Eyler "had a childlike dependency upon others for security and a striking intolerance of being alone." With Dr. Robert Little, the professor of Library Science, he "maintained a non-sexual, childlike and intensely dependent relationship with an indulgent and fatherly older male with whom he lived for many years... The most pathological aspect of this relationship was demonstrated by

Mr. Eyler's surrender to the older man's perverse demand for destructive and violent action... "

Rossiter found a clinical study done on Eyler at age 10. Even at that young age, after his dysfunctional family had experienced a couple of separations, Eyler believed that "he was only a pawn under the control of dominant others."

Everything about Eyler's profile screams out that he is a co-dependent serial killer. He does not and cannot act alone. This is the profile of a guy who committed acts of murder in a team. As we know, even with Eyler in jail, young gay men with cut-off torsos are still being found along the highways of Indiana, Ohio, Michigan and Kentucky that fit the pattern of Eyler's former teammates in murder.

Judge Urso showed a lot of courage to open up these proceedings and have a hearing for new trial in the first place. Trial judges and former assistant state's attorneys generally do not overrule their own work. Most court watchers did not expect Urso, in effect, to rule against himself. That's why Zellner immediately had asked for an appeal, which should come up before the Illinois Supreme Court in about a year.

But even in Urso's flat ruling there are some glaring contradictions. The prosecutors didn't err, the defense should have investigated and known more about Danny Bridges' lifestyle. Yet, the brilliant defense team didn't even dig very deep into their client Eyler's profile, let alone Danny Bridges.

Of course Larry thought Schippers was a good lawyer for him. Just as with Dr. Little, Eyler assumed a "childlike dependency" on Schippers. The cruel and weird irony of this case is that Eyler, the supposed "child molester," behaves in and out of court more like a child himself, while Bridges, the child-victim, showed a definite ability to play in adult games, which brought him media attention, police "protection" and sexual pleasures.

On the eve of Halloween, Judge Urso may have put a temporary lid on this case, but, in real fact, this is a case that will not stay closed.

chapter sixty-one

COURT CASES, TOO, ARE CIRCUMSTANTIAL | 1992

[107] After covering Larry Eyler's 1986 trial for the murder of Danny Bridges and his hearing for a new trial these last few weeks, I have learned that trials, too, like murders, are circumstantial. They happen at a point in time, and all the players--judge, lawyers, reporters--are influenced by the current attitudes of political and social life.

In 1986, Eyler was a gay man tried as a "homosexual." I don't recall that the word "gay" ever came up in reference to him. He said nothing in his defense. His own defense team filled the courtroom with homosexual slurs. They actively pursued "the weird defense": "Our client is a homosexual; homosexuals do weird and crazy things,but my client didn't murder."

Even at the hearing in 1992, Tom Allen, partner from the old defense team, when asked on the witness stand about "the defense plan," kept referring to Bridges, Eyler and possible murder accomplice Dr. Robert David Little as

---

[107] Fourth of five in the 1992 Damski series on Eyler.

"these people" and "them"--"they do strange activities," "crazy stuff."

I wrote at the time that I thought the nearly all suburban jury would find these homosexual slurs condemning in themselves. They implied that Larry was "as guilty as sin," even before the jury considered the circumstances of the murder.

Many reporters got the wrong idea and described Eyler's acts as "homosexual murder." This is a prejudicial stereotype. When non-gays murder, we don't call it "heterosexual murder." When one African-American murders another, we don't say "Black Murder." If the participants in this case were nearly all Catholic, surely no one would say this was a "Catholic murder."

John Conroy wrote a fine piece on "The Return of Larry Eyler" for *Chicago Reader* on July 31, 1992. But his lead sentence ends with a long series of "gruesome homosexual murders." Many readers were so disgusted at that point by his misconception, they stopped reading his article.

In 1986, the state's attorney's office and the Criminal Court Building were not free and open spaces for gay people. Our orientation was hush, we were called "homosexual." And in the main, except for a few loud drag queens and activists, we behaved in court silently, like good little homosexuals. State's Attorney Richard M. Daley had opened his office and reached out through

Kathy Osterman, his liaison to us. But it was on a quiet, personal and family basis.

The prosecution team at the original trial did not start the homosexual slander until the defense team brought it up. Judge Joseph Urso was obviously on unfamiliar ground. He tried his best to be fair, excluded some potential prejudicial items from evidence: photographs of Eyler standing only in a jock strap, or just in a leather vest with no pants on. He didn't allow in evidence a pink dildo found in Eyler's apartment, a butt plug or a string of anal beads.

But the prosecution and the judge stood passive as David Schippers, Larry's lawyer, smeared and ruined Larry's reputation in front of the jury. Nobody objected when he said things like "these people consent to allow themselves to be bound, hands and sometimes feet, for some sexual gratification, which frankly is beyond my imagination...The homosexuals we are dealing with (Larry and Dr. Little) are vain. They are selfish. You can see through their testimony that each person seems to be more selfish than the other. They are emotional, immature. Indeed, their emotional immaturity ranks in the low teenagers and--probably most important--they are virtually insanely jealous.'"

With your advocate, your defense attorney, saying this kind of drivel about you, who needs a prosecutor?

In graphic detail, Schippers allowed the story of Larry having sex with his "homosexual lover" on a blanket in the kitchen of the lover's mother's house, just after Larry supposedly killed and cut up Danny Bridges. That detailed "homosexual encounter" surely stayed vividly in the minds of the jury, and Judge Urso referred to it in his sentencing. Larry Eyler was on trial as much for his gay porn-star role as for murder.

In 1986, I too came to the trial with prejudice. In my gut, I thought Larry Eyler was responsible for the murder of my friend J. J. Johnson,[108] the poet-leatherman who used to stand on the front float of the Gay Parade in just a G-string. From 1982, at *GayLife* under editor-in-chief Albert Williams, Paul Cotton,[109] Ron Ehemann[110] and I tried for two years to track down the killer in our community. We wanted to catch the guy who was offing our friends in cold blood. When Eyler was finally caught the second

---

[108] J. J. Johnson was killed December 25, 1982. When *GayLife* initially reported on his disappearance, it ignited a growing realization that a serial killer was at large.

[109] A *GayLife* reporter.

[110] *GayLife* legal columnist.

time, I was pleased. I came to court wishing he would get his justice, and he would soon be gone.

Many of us in the gay community had the same mind about Eyler as the police and the state's attorney. We wanted this dirt bag off the streets. But during the trials, as I reported then, I could not easily connect Eyler to Danny Bridges. Something didn't fit. Even then I had my doubts that he actually killed Danny. And I was certain, if they had got together, it was no "aggravated kidnapping." Danny was not the kind of kid Larry would have to force against his will to come home with him.

Seeing Larry Eyler in court recently, looking like Major Dad, my animus towards him has lessened. Also, knowing that there have been other "Eyler type" murders since Larry has been locked up makes me more suspicious that Eyler, as he implied in his confession to a murder in Indiana, did not act alone.

John Conroy in his Reader article wonders why the gay press and leaders are not as interested in these continuing murders. Why are they no longer front page news? Simply because The Virus is now the real serial killer in our community. Every week more bodies pile up killed by The Virus, than Eyler and his teammates have done.

The search for the killers is somewhat out of our minds and hands. Kathleen T. Zellner, Eyler's current attorney, is, around the court, often accused of "shooting blanks." What a sexist remark! Ironically, even though she is technically Eyler's lawyer, she is doing some of the state's work. She is bringing in witnesses who say, "Little did it." She is trying to continue the prosecution side of the case, while the prosecutors are content to stay within the old facts and keep a lid on it.

State's Attorney Jack O'Malley, under the circumstances, with an election coming up, could not have "made a deal" or "bargained with Eyler," a convicted murderer. The circumstances did not allow him to open up the case. Judge Urso went about as far as he could in holding the hearing.

As Zellner told me outside the hearing room, "The murder happened in my client's apartment, and he has admitted he cut up the body. We are not talking about an innocent man here. And he will never get out of prison." What we are talking about is going beyond 1986, when homosexuals were just "those crazy people who do bizarre acts," to 1992, when more queer bodies are found along the highway, and nobody, except a couple of female reporters in Indiana and Zellner seem upset about it.

chapter sixty-two

THE (IN)CREDIBLE WITNESS | 1992

[111]On the last day of testimony, Kathleen T. Zellner, Larry Eyler's lawyer, called DeJon Karlae, 32, to the stand as a surprise rebuttal witness. Karlae as a gay youth was a survivor of the streets who became a popular bartender at Take One and Touche's. Currently, Karlae is executive director of Windy City Angels, a non-profit organization for "the express purpose of providing assistance for children afflicted with the AIDS virus."

DeJon appeared distraught and nervous. Zellner quickly got to her point and asked if he knew Dr. Robert David Little. "Yes," DeJon answered. "In 1976 I met him at Bughouse Square. He was a customer of mine." DeJon explained that at the time he was "a male prostitute." Little patronized him several times; the scenes got heavier and "eventually I let him tie me up and have sex," DeJon said.

---

[111] Fifth in a series of five 1992 columns on the Eyler hearings.

Zellner then asked DeJon about events on the night Danny Bridges was murdered in August 1984. DeJon related that on that very night, Larry and "Dr. Bob" (as he called him) came into his bar, Take One, after dinner. Larry left after one drink. "Bob stayed until around midnight," DeJon testified. This statement contradicts Little's alibi, when he swore under oath at the original trial that he left for Indiana around 10:30 p.m.

From 1976 through 1984, Little continued to be "a customer" of DeJon's. In November 1984, Little rented a room at the Surf Hotel for them. He tied DeJon up for sex, then "stabbed me four times. Once on the wrist, once on the chest, and two times on the buttocks. After he stabbed me, he told me that he had killed Danny Bridges. And if I ever told anyone about this, he would kill me too!"

While telling his story, DeJon was in tears, like a rape victim retelling a night of horror. DeJon offered to show the judge his scars. Later, Zellner brought DeJon in front of the judge, and he showed him the marks on his wrist and chest, turned, and the judge said, "That's enough."

Timothy Joyce, assistant state's attorney, rose up and in a loud voice showered a series of point-blank questions at DeJon that seemed to leave him hopelessly drowning.

"Answer yes or no. You were a prostitute?"

"Yes."

"You performed sex acts for money?"

"Yes."

"When you were arrested for soliciting, did you use an alias?"

"Well, yes, because I was a minor."

Then Joyce launched into a series of tacky questions about DeJon's personal life. "Where do you live? Who do you live with? You say you had a stroke. What other health problems do you have? You say you contacted people in the state's attorney's office about your story. Who did you talk to?" DeJon couldn't remember their names. "Did you talk to Dick Daley? Jack O'Malley?"

DeJon was crushed. He left the courtroom wobbly, like he had been knocked down in a prize fight. The state moved that DeJon's testimony be stricken. Judge Urso contemplated a few minutes, then agreed. Zellner told reporters later she expected DeJon's testimony to be thrown out, because it didn't pertain to the narrow issues in this hearing. But she was glad Judge Urso let DeJon tell his story under oath and be cross examined, because she can use this information at a new trial, or, maybe someday, against Little.

As the reporters and lawyers were walking out of the Criminal Courts Building, I noticed an ambulance outside with its red light flashing. It seems DeJon had fainted after the ordeal and was taken away in an ambulance.

Gera-Lind Kolarik,[112] standing with me in front of the ambulance, verified DeJon's story that he did go the state's attorney. He met them at Belmont and Western; she went with him, but was not in the room with them when he told his story.

During the next 10 days, I went around our community asking people if they knew DeJon Karlae. I found that he is a well-liked and popular member of our community. People who worked with him in the bars, or whom he worked for as a cook at Crazy Mary's, all had good words for him. He would not make up a whole story. He is a charmer, and will sometimes try to present his tale in the best possible light, but he does not make up lies about people. If he says, "Little attacked me," he is not lying.

Last week I sat down at Mike's on Broadway with DeJon and his roommate and had a private interview. First point: "I did not testify to help Eyler." As he said on the stand, while the prosecutor looked perplexed,"I'm scared. I am

---

[112] A reporter who wrote an account of the Larry Eyler case called *Freed to Kill*.

worried about the others who may go through what I have, and worse."

A part of DeJon doesn't want to tell his story to anyone. Not even his roommate. He's embarrassed. Frightened. And no one sees his story in context. They just say, "Oh, a male prostitute," and stigmatize him like he is the whore of Babylon.

In 1974, DeJon came to Bughouse Square when he was 14 as a runaway from his middle-class mulatto family. They didn't want him to be gay. He entered the world in the only way available to him to be openly gay: He joined Horizons Youth Group and hung out on the streets. Bartenders like Angelo at the Gold Coast and drag queens like Trigger watched over and protected him.

"Sure I hustled. But do you know what $50 meant to me then? It meant I paid my $40 room rent at a hotel on Dearborn for a week. It meant I had a place of my own. It meant I was supporting myself. And it meant I could be gay like I wanted to be.

"My folks saw a picture of me in the gay parade and hauled me home. But I went back to the streets because that's where my friends were and where I could be openly gay.

"Sure I went with Dr. Bob. He was nice. He paid well. Very well. No hassles. It was easy stuff in the beginning; then he asked me to do S&M scenes with him, but he paid me even more money for them. When having sex with him, I would fantasize I was with some of the guys in leather I would see coming in and out of the Gold Coast.

"When I got back from California in the summer of 1983, Angelo introduced me to Larry Eyler. We dated several times. Not sex for money. He had just been let off a murder charge in Lake County, and like a lot of guys in the bars, I thought be was some kind of gay hero. He fought the system and won. Yes, we dated.

"I feel embarrassed about it all now. And I wouldn't say anything, but others out there have been with Little too. Other guys have experienced what I went through and even worse. Someone has to come forward and tell the truth."

DeJon's roommate interjected, "I hope you don't screw him in your column. The press likes to smear him, because he was a prostitute. He's telling the truth. I know when he went to the state's attorney; they can look it up. It was that same night Little got acquitted for murder in Indiana."

When I put DeJon's life in its gay context, with the way many kids came out in the early '70s, his story seems credible to me. He is truly a victim-witness who deserves the respect of the courts.[113]

---

113 Larry Eyler's attempts to gain a new trial in 1992 failed. He died in 1994 while in prison, of AIDS; his appeal attorney, Kathleen Zellner, upon his death, released information from Eyler indicating he had murdered 21 young men between the ages of 16 and 27 in Indiana and Illinois. Eyler also offered to cooperate with authorities in apprehending an unnamed accomplice who had participated in four of the murders, according to Zellner.

PART SEVEN

chapter sixty-three

HISTORIAN OF HOMOSEXUAL DESIRE | 1993

Boyd McDonald, homosexual historian and cool inventor of books about male-on-male sex, died this September of lung cancer in his SRO in New York. He was 68. I never knew him personally, but he has always been a hero of mine. I used to read his stuff undercover and under the covers, but now read him in public as a dominant force in queer literature.

In the back of his book Flesh (1982), he writes his own bio. He was born in 1925 in South Dakota; was a high school dropout; was drafted into the Army; graduated from Harvard; and settled in New York. He took "a hack writing job" as a film critic for Time, and wrote for Forbes as well as company manuals for IBM. In 1979 he started the magazine *S.T.H.* (Straight to Hell), *The Manhattan Review of Unnatural Acts,* later re-named *The New York Review of Cocksucking.*

Guys would send him raw material about their sex lives and specific acts done and desired--in the Army, in parks, on ships, bridges, highways, anywhere and everywhere--and Boyd would edit and publish them in books with titles like *Meat, Flesh, Smut, Wads, Juice, Sex, Cream, Raunch* and *Lewd.* It was not unusual for his books to sell 50,000 copies or more. Stores like Unabridged helped pay their rent with them.

Respectable gays would look at them, read them and toss them away. Respectable gay critics and literati would toss McDonald away, too, as an "obsessed sex maniac." But like masturbation, guys could not resist picking up his books. For they tell true homo experiences, and don't talk down to you. The guys in the books are not idols or porn stars; they have bodies and lives like yours. In Boyd's books, the reader and the writer, the storyteller and the author are on the same level. His works have direct appeal and will remain popular for years to come.

In the early days of gay journalism, Boyd's stories and columns appeared in most all of our rags. Then gay journalism turned respectable and dropped him. Only the magnificent *Guide* out of Boston continued to publish him regularly until his death. Bill Andriette conducted an interview with Boyd in his hotel room and the *Guide* ran it in their memorial issue of November 1993.

Because Boyd spoke for himself much better than I can interpret or re-invent him, here are some excerpts from that last interview:

"I consider my books history, not pornography. It's very serious work. A lot of people in the gay press just put it down as being jack-off, but I don't write for that. I consider these books the true history of homosexual desire and experience.

"Gay is abstract. Homosexuality is very specific, like in my books. Randy Shilts[114] is a nice guy--too nice--he writes for acceptance; his books are not the true record of homosexual desire. This book by him about gays in the military, *Conduct Unbecoming*, is written in what I would call a U.S. Department of Agriculture Crop Bulletin style, or an Associated Press style. It's absolutely without feeling, passion, heat, lust or specifics about sex. But there is a tremendous amount of information in it. It's like, 'A soldier had homosexual sex with a sailor'--that's as much as they are going to tell you. Shilts is an extremely chaste writer in public--tremendous purity--but in private I imagine he is different.

"My books tell what the soldier and sailor do! In the language of the guys themselves: 'He blew me. I liked it very much, and want to see him again. I get a hardon just thinking of him.'"

---

114 A journalist and author of *And the Band Played On* and *The Mayor of Castro Street*, Shilts died of complications from AIDS in 1994.

Most of the material in Boyd's books, oddly enough, is about man-to-man sex before 1968, before gay liberation and the movement for rights and respectability.

They are the tales of guys out in the sexual woods in the 1940s, '50s and '60s. They constitute the most honest and accurate sociology and literature for any future studies about us in what Boyd calls "the golden age of homosexuality":

"Before gay liberation men were having sex with each other, but didn't think of it as homosexuality. And if you would have accused them of being homosexual, they would have been outraged. As a matter of fact, that a sailor or soldier was having sex with some civilian didn't mean anything. It started to mean something very clearly around 1968.

"My work is an alternative to the gay liberation movement and to the gay press. The gay press has to be sexless because they are public. And in order to be publicly gay they have to be closet homosexuals. My books are all about homosexuality rather than gayness.

"If you are going to be to be a lobbyist or lawyer running a fund-raising campaign, you cannot be sexual. It is a necessity that the whole gay liberation movement had to give up sex in order to go public as gay. They had to give up homosexuality in public, but they still are secretly homosexual."

Boyd knew that he was arrogant and obsessive in his point of view. He enjoyed himself and his ways. His "homo act" was done with style, done on purpose. Like he wiped his ass, he wiped away the artificial. "It's an obsession for me. It's monomania. You have to be fantastically, confidently arrogant to do this because in general we live in a sex negative culture."

He believed, and I agree, that his crowd, once you got over the adolescent smirk, was decent, honest and sensitive. Guys out in the field looking for and having man-to-man sex, in a peculiarly homo way, do also look out for each other. Anonymous sex involves a lot of surprising tenderness. And men are often going after the soft tenderness as much as the hard sex.

The guys to worry about are the prudes who hate sex and hate themselves, and want to force it and enforce it. The authoritarian types. "Gays in park get arrested by cop." An old story, and Boyd clearly knew that in all cases the bad guy is the cop. Even if you are out there "getting nothing" but arrested, you are better off than the cop, because you are not denying your homosexual desire. Sexual desire leads properly to caring, not criminal acts.

As Boyd summed it up: "Even if he (the homo) is unsuccessful sexually picking up people in the park, just wanting to is pleasanter than anything the cop has in his life. It's like the old Cunard slogan, 'Getting there is half the fun.' Well, in homosexuality it frequently is unsuccessful, but just wanting it is fun. Having a kind of brain that can have those desires, it gives you some interest in life."

Peace, Boyd. Love ya.

chapter sixty-four

CONSENTING CHILDREN | 1993

I have never much cared for or about Michael Jackson[115], Tiny Elvis, King of Pop. He is not Elvis, not gay, not black, not male, not an adult, not a child, not innocent, not guilty. Talk about Mr. Mixed Signals. His crime is that he is the great signal crosser, not a true transgender soul. He is a straight boy toy whom the whole world thinks is a sissy--and for that the world will never, never forgive him.

He looks bad and dangerous to kids in his act, and he calls his tours by those names. But is he really bad or dangerous? He is a thriller to Liz Taylor and a lot of other kids across the globe. But most kids put him away from their minds when they put away their toys and other childish things.

---

[115] In 1993, several months after singer Michael Jackson had given a 90-minute interview to TV host Oprah Winfrey, Jackson was accused of child sexual abuse by a 13-year-old boy. The case never came to trial; in 1994, the boy and his family settled out of court for a reported $22 million. In 2005, Jackson was charged with child sexual abuse involving a different youth, but was acquitted. Jackson died at age 50 in 2009.

Kathy O'Malley, perceptive *Inc.* columnist for the *Chicago Tribune*, puts her finger on the problem: "Michael Jackson makes us feel uncomfortable, a 35-year-old man in bed with 11-year-olds. How gross, how disgusting!"

So he makes us feel uncomfortable. Is it fair for us to shove our discomfort on him and make him the scapegoat of our fears? In the public mind, and probably in the mind of his family and handlers, Jackson is guilty of being a sissy, and he will never, never clear himself of that charge.

When I watched Oprah Winfrey's smarmy interview, I wanted to scream out to Michael: "Get real!" Why are there only boy statues in your living room? How can you still pretend to be dating Brooke Shields--a fact she denied the next day? Why do Oprah and Liz go along with this charade? Can't they tell their friend Michael, "Gay is OK?" Oprah and Liz are very good at promoting gay causes when it solidifies their core audience, but neither has shown much willingness to help a gay child when he or she is a close member of the family.

Oprah has conducted vigilante-style mob justice programs against child abuse, like Zeus dispensing justice and punishments before she hears the case. I was not surprised by her silence and failure to go immediately to Michael's side when the charge that he allegedly "fellated a 13-

year-old boy" came out in the media. Oprah seems to prefer Michael's heterosexual fantasies of dating older women. And she sends out chilling messages that she considers child sex the most horrible crime in the world.

With her views, did she ever expect Michael to open up to her? With Liz Taylor playing the role of Big Momma to Michael, how was he going to talk freely to his most trusted confidantes? Most of his lawyers and flack catchers, PR hacks and handlers treat him as a sissy child and a very sacred cash cow. They aren't likely to talk on the level with him.

His father abused and terrorized him as a child. His mother withdrew. His siblings kept up their rivalries. So Michael's only friends were kids of his psychological age: 11 to 13. In the blind eyes of the law, Michael is 35 years old and (if found guilty) will have to pay the penalties the law assesses when a 35-year-old takes a 13-year-old to bed.

But is there anyone who doesn't also believe that Michael is a 13-year-old too?

He cries out for help. He's stuck. He was his family's money-making machine. They were careless toward his feelings as a teen. He felt isolated. Reached out to touch other boys his age. Couldn't touch them. But now he can. He wants to repair the damage of his soul when he lost touch at 13.

Our society is not very sane in the way we handle child sexuality. Freud was never able to resolve the problem of how real or imaginary child sex play is. A mother today goes into court, shoots and kills the accused molester of her son and becomes an instant national hero. Parents in a lush Chicago suburb don't want their kids taught from a text which says: "It is impossible to masturbate too much."

When I was a child, I played with neighborhood boys and girls, doctor and nurse and other games of body/ sexual experimentation. As an early teen, a lot of us boys played look/see/feel/touch together, in bedrooms, in showers, at camp, at slumber parties and in dark movie houses. That's what 13-year-old boys do growing up.

Michael never grew up, and he is still doing it. Child's play. Sex between consenting children. The problem is: Michael is no longer a child by age and circumstance, but still a child in actuality.

Big lawyers, big investigators and media hot types will make a feeding frenzy out of this case. Sad. Few will be there to talk to Michael and befriend him on the level. Few will talk to the other kid. Each of them will become expendable pieces in an adult war game.

O'Malley is right. We adults are all uncomfortable with this subject. In our frustration, we will turn and punish Michael or punish his "cosmic" friend. All parties involved will seem to us guilty, no matter what the facts are. Cock sucking equals rape, hand touching equals murder, kissing equals sin, masturbation equals sodomy. We freak out. And then call the parties involved freaks.

Our expectations of behavior are way off too. When we arrest an adult in a sex case, such as the guys who were in a circle jerk in one of our leather bars and recently arrested, we and the law treat them like children. We belittle them and what they were doing, and we send them to their rooms without dinner.

But when we investigate children, such as Michael and his friend, we assume the adults in age all have the power and faculties of an adult. We assume that Michael was mature enough to know exactly what he was doing, and all the consequences of what he was doing. We don't see him as a consenting child too.

It's an easy game for us. We can always be right in saying Jackson is the adult in the case, and therefore the responsible and guilty one. We take no responsibility for never teaching Michael about the real world. For letting him live in Never-Never Land. For thinking how swift and cute a boy toy he is when he grabs his crotch on stage. But if he grabbed his crotch in front of a friend in his private bedroom, then to hell with Michael. That should be the end of his pee-wee and his career.

If he did the dirty deed, he is guilty. We are not responsible. Even though we are the ones, in our mind, who have the final judgment and power to say what is and is not dirty.[116]

---

[116] The Damski fan might compare the ending of this to "Drugs, Morals and Habits" at pages 262-263. His refusal to condemn out-of-hand, one hopes, evidences his resolute commitment to the idea underscored on page 5.--JMV

chapter sixty-five

UNCLAIMED KIDS | 1994

John/Jack Wayne Gacy is dead.[117] The double nature of his life remained even in his final minutes; state authorities had to perform a double lethal injection, one to put Jack to sleep, and one to kill John. He has been put out of our misery. And justly so. We don't have Gacy around anymore to lie to us.

His Jack and John story had grown old. Jack enticed, seduced, tortured and mercilessly killed kids, while John pretended not to know what happened. Jack built his house of horrors on Summerdale Avenue in Norwood Township, disposed of the bodies like pieces of excrement in his crawl space, while John lived there with his wife, and told his neighbors his shit didn't stink.

Gacy was his own major accomplice. A total split person. John was the married man, the good Catholic, the guy who received a private mass before his execution; Jack was the bisexual who had sex with guys, but told those guys they were

---

[117] Serial killer John Wayne Gacy was executed in May, 1994.

not gay, they were just doing "a bisexual thing." Having your dick sucked by another guy is a bisexual thing. John was clear about that: he was no sissy. An unrepentant clown, but not a homosexual.

Jack picked up mostly marginal kids, average age a little over 17. Runaways. Kids who had left their home, family and church, also believing, like Gacy, that they were not "gay" or "sissy." They were, at times, "bisexual," but no way were they homosexual.

They fit into Jack Gacy's lifestyle perfectly. He looked like a policeman or city worker; he didn't dress or act "gay"; he had a wife at home, wore a wedding ring; and he was a private contractor who remodeled pharmacies--where the drugs are--and someday planned to build a McDonald's in London.

I probably knew eight of his victims by sight and word on the street. John, Tim, Greg and Bill--all on a shortened, first name basis. At his trial, 17--more than half--of the bodies remained unknown and unclaimed. Fourteen years later, on the day of his execution, there are still bodies lying in an anonymous grave, unclaimed. The shame is rancid. The pungent stench of fear, not of murder, but of homosex, hangs over these anonymous graves.

Chicago in the '70s was a great mecca and magnet for kids. Kids came to Chicago to crash and find their way. You could rent a room with a buddy or two in an SRO for $37.50 a week. Rent a nice studio or micro-loft for $175 a month. There were two Y's downtown. Action started at the bus depot. The parks and beaches from Oak Street to Foster, from Lincoln to Grant, were unofficially open at night, even though they legally closed at 11 p.m. There were no roaming gangs of fag bashers in the parks, and the police were cool. "Nickel and dime" referred to bags of pot for five and 10 dollars. Highs were cool and cheap.

Downtown, Bughouse Square and Rush Street, Clark and Division, Old Town, Wells, all the way up Broadway and Clark, kids hung out on corners. The drinking age was 19 (for wine and beer), and who checked, anyway? Barbacks got jobs at 14. Many kids were out on their own for their first time, living an excitement that seemed like freedom. If you got stuck, just ask a guy to take you home. A stringy-haired blond 19-year-old in a red-and-black checked jacket stopped me on Division. "Please take me home, please! Take me home and fuck me. Please, I want to crash." All Gacy had to do was open his car door and some kid would jump in.

Jack's dreams fit the kids' dreams. They wanted to work for him and join him. He could give them a job, money and drugs, and a new start in life. So he seemed a little weird. And there was that "smell" around his house that was decorated like a tasteless motel. There was also cash, a game room, uppers, hash, food and a hideaway from the rough-trade street scene in Chicago. To go with Gacy was finally to have a chance to get on top of things.

Gacy also shared the kids' attitude about gays. They were silly people. Guys you teased and laughed at. Not real men with real homes and jobs. Guys who dressed like women. Fruits. Gacy and his pickups had so much in common. He seldom went to a "fruit" bar. At times, he was seen at the Broadway Limited, a hot disco made out of railroad cars. You would sometimes see him sitting, wearing a tacky leather jacket, at the end of the bar at the edge of the scene. Trying to look tough, but nervous and out of place. He was more comfortable at the "Chicken Coop" in front of the Limited, where the kids hung out.

I would see this weird guy, who I later learned was Gacy, with his little pencil mustache driving around Bughouse Square. He would reach out of his big car and put a red light on top. Some thought he was a cop. I knew guys who went with him and worked for him, and nothing bad happened to them. They might quarrel over a paycheck, but generally he was a good guy to work for. I knew a couple of guys who got in a nasty scene with him at home, all the way up to the rope trick, but escaped. They were thrilled by it all. They had lived! After Gacy's arrest, they were too ashamed to talk on the record.

I have also run into guys who want to tell me about "their night with Gacy," but I find their stories unbelievable.

Though gay youth was often at the core of the scene, making clubs like the original Bistro or La Mere Vipere[118] go, all kids participated in the scene. The Gacy kids were particularly vulnerable to his trap, however, because he told them basically what their parents and church had taught them about gays: Don't go with "fruits," they will pervert and corrupt you. Go with a guy like Gacy, who is "straight" like you. He still goes to mass, has a wife and home, a good job, clowns for the neighborhood kids, and is a respected party worker for the Democrats. A guy with clout and know-how.

Kids on the street looked up to Gacy, and wanted to become a "responsible family man" like him. Many Gacy survivors did go on to become what they imagined he was; "straight." They all believed, as he did, that they were staying away from "that sissy stuff." Gacy proved you can make

---

[118] A popular "punk disco" In Chicago's Lincoln Park neighborhood in the 1970s.

it in this world, as the Pink Floyd anthem went, and "you don't need no education."

Gacy to the end held these beliefs. Murder is a crime, but a natural act; gay sex is a sin, a "crime against nature." Gacy was not gay; neither were most of his seductees. They did not fear anyone would call them a sissy. What they did together was all very macho.

Even worse than the smell of dead bodies in the crawl space is the pungent stench of homophobia. Fear of queer. The fear that not only makes you an easy mark--"take me home and fuck me"--but years after you have been murdered, and the clown that did it is executed, your family still leaves you unclaimed. They can adjust to the murder, but they can't cope with the fact that their kid might have hooked up with a Gacy type and actually asked him to take them home and fuck 'em.

chapter sixty-six

CLOSURE | 1994

Nineteen-ninety four brought a closure to three of the famous serial killers who worked our neighborhood. In March, Larry Eyler died on death row in prison of complications from AIDS. In April, John Wayne Gacy was executed. In November, Jeffrey Dahmer was murdered in a prison bathroom while cleaning the prison gym.

The most egregious fact about all serial killers is that we don't know much for sure about them. Our profiles are sketchy. Our ideas are mostly speculation. We picture them as monsters; but they are also a lot like you and me. We would never go home with a monster, but we would go home with someone like you and me. Knowing many of the guys killed by these "monsters," I also know that people like you and me did go home with them.

They are sick, but their sickness is often symptomless. We are as clueless as the police in apprehending them. We seem to know the danger only after the fact, when it is too late.

These monsters are, in most all cases, male, with no defining sexual orientation.

Gacy often hooked up with kids using the line that he was not a homosexual or fruit. Sex didn't seem to be the object. He liked to catch you in his trap and watch you squirm between life and death. Sometimes he let you go. Most times not. He enjoyed the power of deciding.

Eyler was a priestly type. He attracted you with a gay man's moves, offering heavy-duty leather sex. Into his truck and down the highway you would go. Once he tied you up, you were in his trap, and he performed the final priestly function of deciding how and when you should die. Dahmer got you home and gave you knock-out drops in your drink. You passed out. Then he had the power over your zombie body to determine when you would expire. He used your body parts for ritual artifacts for his personal love cult.

Dahmer used his white-male classic look as bait for minority kids. He came on like the catch and lucky break of the night. Promised to make you a film star. Photography and not sex would be involved. None of that "gay stuff" unless you were already wanting sex with him. Basically, he used the fantasies of white power to get black kids home to his building occupied by working

African Americans. He played on their fantasies in their hood to get them into his trap.

In gay life, 10 years is a generation. Gacy, Eyler and Dahmer represent three generations of our experience. Gacy was the homosexual clown of the 1970s. Closet case to the end. His split personality of John and Jack never acknowledged what John and Jack did. John was the good one; Jack the "fruit." Gacy was so full of self-denial that he had no self. He joked with us in the media, with himself and his prison guards and lawyers all the way into the injection room. I thought his execution was a fitting closure; long overdue.

Eyler represented the co-dependent code of the 1980s. He had a gay lover, partied comfortably in our bars--something neither Gacy nor Dahmer ever felt comfortable with--always had a partner to lean on; including his mentor, the library professor in Indiana. Eyler never lived alone, and probably never acted alone. He became the fall guy of the murders. No one ever believed his last testimony, so his partner(s) in crime got off. He lived a co-dependent gay man's life and died of the Gay Man's Health Crisis. A fitting closure.

Dahmer's closure caught me off base, but not by surprise. I knew that "the general population," both inside and outside of prison, wanted him dead. My first column about him was entitled

"Dahmer Be Damned!" I was mad that he entered our world in the 1990s as a Gacy copy-cat, an efficient human killer virus, at a time when all our resources were sapped fighting the real killer virus. He seemed to be asking for a quick trial and death for himself; yet, he committed his monstrous crimes in a state without a death penalty.

Dahmer wanted to die but couldn't bring himself to suicide. The state wanted him dead, but didn't have a death penalty. So they put him, under mutual agreement, to work in the "general population." Among his sworn enemies. Knowing it wouldn't take long to happen. Like sending a wounded puppy to live with wolves. Dahmer ended his curious life in a gang murder aided by a state-assisted suicide.

Outside of his parents and a couple of weird female groupies, who appeared on tabloid talk shows and in the magazines there were few tears for Jeffrey.

I have no tears for Dahmer, either. But when I listened to the psychiatric testimony at his trial and his public interviews after his sentence, I recognized there was more to Dahmer than pure monster. The Milwaukee Sentinel called him "the most hated and most fascinating man in America." Like most descriptions about Dahmer, that's overblown. He was never a figure larger than life, but always smaller than life. Never a man, but a boy.

His first murder was in 1978 when Dahmer was 18. Between that murder--done at the same time Gacy was first arrested and his story blasted all over the world in vivid detail, and he became the dark hero in the gallery of monsters--and the next murder, 12 years elapsed. In 1978, Jeff was a boy who murdered another boy, because he had never figured out he could love another boy. His upper-middle class professional parents and school counselors all sent signals that gay is bad. His father said it was "evil," and Jeff would never get to heaven if he ever did something like that. That was his sex education.

So, one weekend when his parents were away, Jeffrey decided to find out for himself. He had a private "risky business" party for another boy in his parents' home. He picked up Steven Hicks, also 18, a white hippie on the highway going to a rock concert. He took him home, to experiment with those urges his father had called "evil." He tried to make love to the other boy, but over-loved him. Smothered him; killed him. They had done evil together. So, he had to get rid of the body and the body of evidence of his evil. What did Jeffrey want? He wanted what the Beatles were singing about in those days: "I want to hold your hand." He wanted to hold Stevie's hand. But no one had ever told him how he could hold another boy's hand in an act of love. Male-to-male puppy romance turned evil. The bad seed grew for another 12 years.

The song remained the same. So he invented his signature scene of horror, his cannibal chop shop, the only way he could figure out how to get a boy to stay with him forever.

PART EIGHT

chapter sixty-seven

POINTLESS SEX | 1995

I saw *Kids*, a movie by Larry Clark, the most controversial film of the summer. It was produced by Gus Van Sant, director of *My Own Private Idaho*, another hard-to-take flick about street kids.

Half the critics think the movie is pointless and falls flat. The kids in it are no way cool, and no way chicken delight. They are mean, cruel, and heartless; mostly scrawny, boney and horny, no way porn stars.

Women, gays and Asians take it on the chin. The two white "heroes," Telly and Casper, are pretty awful. They call each other "nig" and "nigger," adopting a Hip Hop pose, steal from Black culture, but have no hesitation when they and their multiracial skateboard gang whack a Black dude. They are poseurs, not activists.

Kids is an affective, but not effective, movie. It touched me.

It tells truths without consequences. In the opening and closing scenes Telly fucks a virgin. In the intervening scenes we cut back to a former virgin he has fucked and learn she has tested positive for HIV. She got it from him. She races to tell him. Finds him after his last fuck, but they don't talk, and the movie ends.

Did the Black guy die after being beaten to a pulp? Did Telly learn his status? You don't know. The movie affects you, hits you, fucks you, and like the characters inside the movie, you exit in a daze wondering, "Jesus Christ, what happened!"

That's the point of this pointless movie. Most critics and viewers don't like the lack of show and tell. No one gets better in the movie. This "hard day's night" of the '90s is not for Beatles fans. These kids don't even go to Pearl Jam, and don't have wallets and purses bulging with credit cards. They are more likely to show up outside and crash a concert by Anthrax, Biohazard or Bad Brains.

Ray Pride, film reviewer at *New City*, offered the best assessment of the movie--"I can't figure it out." Pride is willing to wait, see it again and reflect on it for a year or so. This is an interactive movie--they give you the parts and you take them home to assemble.

One point I got: don't be too quick to judge these kids and this film. Just as they whack dudes outside their circle, so we middle-class viewers and critics tend to whack these kids. On sight, without reason. We do mental violence on them, just as they do physical violence on us.

I admit these kids scare me, I remember Jon Simmons' murder, and Ron Cayot attacked on Halsted and left with a mechanical voice box. Attackers never found. They may be the kind of "kids" who are in this movie.

Second point. I laughed to myself at their situation. AIDS education is the central adult message running through this film. They engage in pointless drugs, huffing; pointless rock, industrial sludge; pointless encounters, pointless chick searches; pointless stealing, fruit juice; pointless telling mother off; and pointless dialogue. But when it comes to sex they get serious, try to add a "family value" theme to their pointless sex.

That's the snag--they want to love, romance and have babies. Ridiculous consequences.

Why? They admit they like blow jobs. The gals like the way the guys use "their fingers." The gals kiss each other, The guys and gals like foreplay.

So why try to mix family sex with pointless street encounters? Why have babies, get AIDS and die? Why "go all the way" and fuck yourself, when kids are just supposed to enjoy themselves and their gals and pals?

chapter sixty-eight

BOTTOMS UP | 1996

At Larry McKeon's fiftieth birthday party,[119] I met a guy interested in ideas, great books, and words. We bantered around the old problem of what or which words we should call ourselves.

I said I liked "queer"; it marks and keeps the ground we have fought and won in the gay movement, preserves transgender identities, and includes women, too.

He said "queer" is good, but he always preferred "sodomite." That word bounces well off Oscar Wilde, resonates tradition, but to me always had a too narrow religious sound. Leave it to the fundamentalists.

I promised him to think more about it, because in the mid-'90s the word queer is becoming a little overused and tired. Even our queer heroes, like Jean Genet, seem to have lived in another century, a much darker mediaeval time.

---

119 Politician Larry McKeon, the first openly gay member of the Illinois General Assembly, died of AIDS complications in 2008.

Genet, according to Edmund White's biography, used the old term "homosexual," and at times had serious and pessimistic doubts about himself, his self worth, and his kind. Genet, in a reflective autobiography called Fragments, complains that "homosexuality is a curse, a life sentence that can't be lifted." The homosexual cannot shed himself of his "guiltiness." "There is no way of getting used to it, of living with it. Homosexuality cuts each homosexual off from the world--even from the world of other pederasts."

A grim view. We are men trapped in our own sin, condemned "sodomites," alone, imprisoned, without hope of forgiveness or liberation. Hardly the stuff to tell your folks about, or to camp it up and be "gay" about.

Most of our current leaders and representatives chatter about Hillary and the pillory, checks to Dole, Edgar's good intentions, and the mayor's "backing"--a phrase which never specifies who's fucking who.[120] They are taking us to the promised land of acceptance as bland as white bread. But the shadow and stigma of "the sodomite" still hangs over us. In plain English, we are uncomfortable around the guy who enjoys

---

[120] References to then-First Lady Hillary Clinton, Republican presidential candidate Sen. Bob Dole, Illinois Gov. Jim Edgar, and Chicago Mayor Richard M. Daley.

bottoms up,who is not ashamed to put his legs in the air and get fucked. The guy who knows that the so-called "woman's position" is everyman's position.

Throughout western history, however, there has been shame attached to this joyous act, and enforced conventionally and socially by the Sodomy Code.

Ancient Athens spelled it out this way: A young boy (12-18) could go out to the gym and school with a guy, man, mentor, and they could enjoy each other's naked body up to a specific point. The older guy could not put his cock inside the butthole of the younger. This was not because of the gender, but because of their civil codes. If a boy let a guy do that to him he would lose for life (a life sentence), his social class and status. In our terms he would no longer have the chance of being considered a legal straight white man. He would be considered lower class, that is with the status of "a woman, a foreigner, or slave," a guy who could never legitimately run a business, be in a profession, be a leader or own property. He would be called an outcast, sodomite, fag, sissy, queer, nigger lover, or worse a lover of a Negroes.[121]

---

[121] See footnote 44, page 249, for the source of this viewpoint, and newer scholarship which questions some aspects of it.

The laws of nature, which neither are natural nor real laws, have always assumed that men shall not squat for other men. That's what women do when they urinate. Men who squat for other men are squat, and shall not, after enjoying the act of being "the squatee," be entitled to social squat like money, land or wampum.

Genet and many gay men and homosexuals have complained about their sense of isolation. Ironically, their isolation is not really their fault. It's a socially engineered convention. Men who squat shall not have squat. As we compete for scarce and precious resources eliminating "squatters" is a neat way of keeping the whole class of young upstarts from the fruits of society.

Ironically, this social convention, enforced by the Sodomy Code, is one of the deep layers of fear buried inside of homophobia. Any mother, who senses the conventions of things, will fear that her sodomite son, her effeminate one, could be penetrated, and thusly after, in the eyes of society, never be entitled to the goods of society.

Many gays have the same fear. It often propels them, like Roy Cohn,[122] to lead a double life, to have financial success to cover over their sin. They fear someone will tell that they like to

---

[122] Conservative, closeted gay lawyer Roy Cohn died of AIDS complications in 1986.

have their bottoms up. They would rather hide that truth and put their dukes up.

From ancient times to the current U.S. Supreme Court, "sodomy" is not really a religious term. It refers to the so-called "passive male homosexual," the guy who is willing to put his bottoms up. The guy who doesn't care if he sinks into the lower class, the proletarian collective, the heaven of folks and pals.

Sodomite is a term of social order and class, much more than of sex. Ironically, it still causes disorder and upset even inside our community. For if the bottoms of the world ever united, we would kick out the white prison guards and have a true revolution.

chapter sixty-nine

MOTHER NATURE'S EUNUCH | 1996

What is the gay angle on Theodore J. Kaczynski, the so-called Unabomber? None really. In his Manifesto, he thinks gays are UNIMPORTANT in capital letters, not even worthy of a letter bomb in his private war against the modern industrial technological state.

In Section 72, he remarks that modern society is extremely permissive: "We can go to bed with anyone we like (as long as we practice 'safe sex'). We can do anything we like as long as it is UNIMPORTANT." Ted Kaczynski, like Camille Paglia, uses the tools of 19th Century scholarship in an effort to become the last great man and mind of the 20th Century. Camille often speaks with authority and the voice of Mother Nature herself. Ted has a much weaker voice, his conclusions are surprisingly tentative, his mathematically trained mind is slyly irrational. He is Mother Nature's Eunuch.

Both Paglia and the Unabomber abhor "feminists. In Section 14: "Feminists are desperately anxious to prove that women are as strong and as capable as men. Clearly they are nagged by a fear that women may NOT be as strong and as capable as men." The Unabomber manifesto-writer clearly lets his own fear show here in capital letters.

The Romans knew impotens (impotence), a sense of powerlessness, leads to violence. The Unabomber, even though his writing is engaging enough on its own, and like his Gemini sparkling eyes, has a certain charm, yet he shows his sense of impotence at every turn. He grows his own vegetables with his own shit. Then chthonian primal Nature in the form of a rabbit eats his vegetables, eats his shit, and he has to turn violent and set traps for his bunny neighbors. So much for a Waldenesque communion with Nature.

Paglia, at least, keeps her letter bombs that go off in your face inside her books. She's all words. But Ted has a weird and totally unacademic approach to the problem of publish or perish. Publish my book, he tells the *NEW YORK TIMES*, or I'll send a bomb and you will perish. Ted's glaring tragic flaw is announced in Section 96: "In order to get our message before the public with some chance of making a lasting impression, we've had to kill people." So sings the sad castrated bird! Unlike Paglia, poor Ted has no sexual personae. He probably wouldn't know what we are talking about sex for.

But, ironically, there is one homoerotic image that seems to plague him personally, namely, the face and attitude of Tim McVeigh. Tim, the soldier of modern technology, the militia warrior with industrial strength explosives, is a fantasy rival to Ted. Every time Tim appears on the cover of a major magazine, Ted sends out a bomb or manifesto. Tim is Ted's trick and hustler. Every time the Feds move Tim they shake out Ted.

And who wins? Major media, who tell their tales in overdrawn detail.

The law may grind slow, but Big Media grinds everything up. Tim's Oklahoma and Ted's Montana, their little special unconsummated love story and rival trials will play before our eyes until a dozen made-for-TV movies obliterate their faces from the scene. Today's natural born killers are taken out of their natural habitat by media invasion, techno-overkill, until all heroes become zombies and eunuchs in the service of perverse human nature.

chapter seventy

GOD'S PUNISHMENT | 1996

The anti-sodomite Christian Coalition likes to talk about God's punishment. Beware of the punishment of God that will fall on gay men and lesbians, bi and transsexuals, and queers everywhere. But they never think through the phrase "the punishment of God"--what it means.

In grammar, the of can refer to both an objective and subjective genitive. Be both the punishment She hands out, or the punishment She suffers herself, watching the foolishness of men.

The Christian Coalition will object right away to calling God "She." In their mind God must always be a He. But if God is the Creator of everyone and everything, why can't He also be a She? Is God just a male-thing? A He-man, a Superman? If, truly, She has the whole world in Her hands, why limit her reference to one gender?

Our patriarchal texts, written by the men who ruled for the men who rule, use male pronouns. But use your brain--if God is everything and everywhere; then He is not just The Father and The Son and their Holy Union. She is everywhere and everything. She suffers as well as hands out suffering.

Isidore Ducasse, the French epic poet, whom I call "Iszy," born also on 4/4 (1846), was 23 when he finished his magnum opus *Maldoror*. His poem deals specifically with an in-your-face challenge to the concept of God as The Father. Iszy reasoned that if God The Father is "the Creator of the universe and of everyone and everything in it, He is therefore the Creator of vices." He knows, for example, what it is like for the Father to get drunk, and go to a whore house.

Iszy's book caused a scandal in school and the church, got buried in a pile of literature written by the insane, and his queer work was left mostly unread in America until our time.

As Iszy sees it, God comes down from heaven to experience the ways of men, and he gets sorely punished. He goes on, a drunk. The next day, hung over, insulted by every passer-by, "reeling, he went to sit on a rock arms a-dangle like a consumptive's testicles. He looked upon the whole of nature, which belonged to Him, with lackluster spiritless gaze. O human beings, you are *enfants terribles*!"

The night before He had visited a whore house and really punished Himself. He found a woman, kissed her armpits and wanted to go on and...her, but held back. He dare not perform these sadistic acts on a woman. So he goes down the hall of the whore house and finds a young man hanging out in front of another room waiting to visit a prostitute. He makes sadistic love to the young man. But then is ashamed of what He The Great Father has done to a son-like creature. So He kills the young man to cover over the evidence of His crime.

That's how Iszy, the first queer writer, saw God the Father. A powerful man who desires to commit shameful acts on a woman, but finds a boy instead, and kills him to keep His secret. When God the Father got back to heaven, the angels, including Satan, ask him "How will anyone obey your laws," when you yourself are capable of committing acts lower than human? "His shame was as vast as eternity." He could no longer tell whether vice was his or human's. Like the Christian Coalition, God The Father was capable of extreme evil, of committing acts queerer than queer.

chapter seventy-one

SEXUAL POLITICS | 1997

Gays are known to be trendsetters. Ironically, however, we set trends for others and other worlds, before we bring those trends to ourselves and our world. There is about a ten-year lag in what we do for "them" than in what we do for ourselves.

In the 1960s, we were behind the scenes of the hippie cultural" revolution, in music and sex. Gay guys like Brian Epstein brought us the Beatles. But rock music didn't hit the gay bars until the 1970s. In our bars we were still mainly a showtune crowd.

In radical masculine and feminist politics of the 1960s, we were behind the scenes, like Bayard Rustin setting up marches on Washington, D.C., but we didn't start conducting marches for ourselves until the late '70s and early '80s.

We were the inventors of sexual politics. We were the counter-revolutionary force of the Reagan years. Now a lot of our leaders want to disjoin sex from politics, put our sexuality in a moral closet, and turn what should be the GAY '90s into a neo-Victorian age.

I am disappointed, but not surprised, when our outstanding voice and leader Larry Kramer,[123] in *The Advocate*, joins this new fashion trend and blasts gay sexuality in severe and repressive terms. He thinks "AIDS We Asked For It." "We've all been partners in our destruction. AIDS has killed us, [and here he is most confused] and while we certainly did not invite it in, we certainly did invite it in." People living with AIDS did not invite in their disease. As a guy with cancer, even though I took my shirt off my back, like my mother told me to, and got sun on my back, I didn't invite malignant melanoma in.

It's like saying those poor kids, the Tupac Amaru in Peru, "asked for it." They asked for peaceful negotiations and killed none of the hostages. At their dying moment, they raised their hands in military sign of surrender. Got their heads blown off. Till no relative could recognize their body. They were denied proper burial by their relatives. They did not ask for that!

To argue that in the Golden Age of the '70s, the Era of the Joy of Gay Sex, we were asking to get fisted by a poison bullet; to now condemn

---

123 Writer and AIDS activist who wrote the controversial 1978 novel, *Faggots*, as well as the 1985 landmark play *The Normal Heart*.

Edmund White's liberating manual, *The Joy of Gay Sex*--is pure moralistic propaganda.

Kramer is obsessed with two things: greatness and "penises." I suspect his penis has not been all that great to and for him, and his greatness has always been limited to his pen.

"Penis" and "dick" are the way straights talk about their gay tool. My cock has never disappointed me. Because as a homo-sensualist, I have always used it sensually. Never had sex I didn't feel like having. Never counted the numbers like I was on a sex drive diet. Even now, I still have all the sex I feel like having. It's part of the joy of my totally sensual gay life.

My sexuality makes me look out for kids in Brazil and Peru who want to rage against the machine. Feeling akin to the chimney sweeps of 200 years ago, who got "soot warts" on their testicles. First major out-break of urban cancer. They would have to have one ball excised with a red-hot poker. Then usually the other ball. Then agonizing death. At the same time women were having their boobs mutilated for malignant growths, one breast at a time. All done without any anesthetic.

Breasts and testes have been the markers or sexual politics. How much needless suffering have young boys and women had to endure because the capitalist pigs running our advanced societies perversely want to mutilate them. All in the name of conservative thought and science. All in the name of higher morality. All in the name of Larry Kramer's super-ego.

chapter seventy-two

90-DAY WONDER | 1997

Andrew Phillip Cunanan[124] came on to our screen April 23 and died on our screen July 23, 1997. He was a 90-day wonder. Born on August 31, THE DAY OF THE PUBLIC APPEARANCE, he could not help but continue being a "public appearance," and never could make a private disappearance.

Let's first play one sad note of grace for Cunanan and for anyone, family, friend, or foe, who was ever close enough to his flame to try to love him, and got burned or killed.

The day after he killed himself in an apparent suicide--I say apparent, for it was much more a ritual murder, a sociopathic demise, a voodoo-death with his pursuers and audience cheering for him to off himself--I walked the streets asking waitresses, bus drivers, customers and riders what did they think.

---

[124] Chicago businessman Lee Miglin and fashion designer Gianni Versace were two victims of this spree killer, who committed suicide.

To my surprise, almost everyone, like most in our own community, felt glad it was over, but sad, very sad, it happened. There is no forgiving, excusing, explaining why. I marvel at the shortness of it all. From high school, he was supposed to be "The One Never to be Forgotten." Yet, I think he too will pass soon from the scene. We want to forget him.

The media coverage both covered him in depth, and buried him in over-coverage. Too many details, too little real cogent interpretations. No label or tag fits this kind of sudden behavior. Call him serial killer, spree killer, or misname him "homosexual homicidal maniac," we are still left clueless. You might as well say he was a Catholic murderer.

His father still maintains to this day his son would not be "gay." He was a "Catholic altar boy." "He held him in his arms as a boy." He knows his Catholic son would not do such things.

One rumor has it that he called a Catholic hotline for those abused by priests, using his alias "Andy DeSilva."

Still there is no accounting for these events that cross borders of our known territory. He was so much like us, on the one hand, and so much unlike any of us that we can't get a hold on him. Almost like he was an avenging ghost before he was a dead man. A Dead Man[125] before he was a dead man.

These killers do, however, in a horrifying and perverse way, seem to re-represent the presidents and media of their specific times.

John/Jack Gacy was stuck on being Kennedyesque. He made a horror flick out of PT 109[126], slowly stalking and deciding like an emperor-clown who should die and who should live, a B-movie, or a made-for-TV movie. A self-denying homosexual trickster.

Larry Eyler, a gay man in the bars by day, killer at night on the highway. Material for an independent film. He gave true confessions, but too late. Carter's habitat for him became a killing field, a place to saw and cut up young men.

Dahmer was the queer silent type. Wedged in the nondescript Bush years. He did everything himself by hand. Hand-held camera. Video. The only trouble: his camera may have been a boy's hand, which he wanted to hold in Beatlesesque style.

Cunanan was the slickest of them all. Openly gay in high school. Call boy for the billionaire men's club. Like surfer types himself. Chameleon body that in a few days, with the right drugs,

---

[125] 1995 film directed by Jim Jarmusch and starring Johnny Depp.

[126] 1963 film about John F. Kennedy's days in the Navy.

could go from fat to thin. Slick as Slick Willie, Slick Jefferson, Slick Clinton. No moral base or center.

So surface and superficial, so modeled on MTV, high energy production, with about 30 seconds of premeditation. Perversely re-representing his times. All flash and no substance. A bull options market arbitrator, a twisted straddler, who finally shorted himself and crashed.

chapter seventy-three

GIRLCOTTING | 1997

Throughout our history, every generation, there have been gay men like Tim Miller, a local activist now living in San Francisco, and John Lewis, my political sidekick (Boy, can he kick!), who get it. They understand that being gay is socially linked to women's issues. Men who verbally bash women will physically bash sissies, because to them we are men who "look like women." Men who physically abuse and bash women will kill gay men for the same reasons.

Yet, before Stonewall, the three decades I was in the scene, I can vividly remember gay men who hated women. Viciously and sarcastically put them down in every way. Never marry one, hate their smell, and treat all of them like doormats. Basically like someone who doesn't count.

That's something I never got. To assert your identity as a gay man, why do you feel compelled to degrade and attack women? Underneath all homophobia, including the self-directed version, lurks gynophobia.

As long as women are mistreated, even if put on patriarchal pedestals, sissies will be mistreated. As long as women are downgraded, gay men will be downgraded. Neither of us will be safe, equal, or free.

After Stonewall and the Women's Liberation Movement, gay men, like all men, learned to hide their virulent anti-women beliefs in public. It's just not "politically correct." Not realizing when they say that twisted term "politically correct," the whole concept started in lesbian circles as a self-referential joke.

If you don't get the joke, I can't explain it to you. If you foolishly think lesbians have no sense of humor, you're beyond my skills to reach. You should spend time in Study Hall with Mary Daly's Wickedary Word Play and pick up the basics of her CAT-A-TONIC philosophy.

The Girlcott of the 1997 Chicago Gay and Lesbian Pride Parade[127] was well-timed, well-directed and totally media-savvy. "Their word" got out. Most of the gay men I talked to all week commented on it. Many not favorably, only proving the girls were right. Some got it, proving they too have learned some things other than the recent dance steps at the clubs.

Has a woman ever called you a faggot?

---

[127] A 1997 event focusing on gender stereotypes.

Yes, a couple of times.

But I can't count the times men have called me that, and tried to make me run and hide.

Has a woman ever beaten you up?

I've heard of that. Never seen it. Very rare. Men have. Has a woman ever gone around like a serial killer stalking and killing young boys a la Gacy, Eyler and Dahmer?

NO!

Women are not our enemies. It's sad and tragic when gay guys say, as one did at the coffee table, "I don't live by the vaginal model."

How many women and gays are forced to live by the cock-model, the phallic centric model? Almost all of us who have ever had a Big Daddy, Big Daddy Mayor, or Big Daddy Boss.

The organizers of the Girlcott have also organized their re-entry to our main parade. Still, gay guys keep asking the dumb question: What do they want?

Want? For openers, they want you to stop being such a dummy. Know your friends, know your allies, then you'll know who is really "divisive," who really wants to put an ax through your heart and your community.

EPILOGUE

chapter seventy-four

HUSTLE TOWN | 1981

Now that we are experiencing days where we feel both the last warmth of summer and the first chills of winters,it seems a good time to remind ourselves of where we are and what we are in for. We are in Chicago, a tough city, and we are probably in for another tough winter.

From Halloween to May Day, living in Chicago feels very much like you are frozen and stuck in a state prison in North Alaska. By February, everyone in Chicago goes stir crazy, and bunnies who go out to cruise the bushes in April come back with frost bit tails.

I can't offer any easy reason why anyone would want to live here in this tough, cold city. But outside of a few sunshine sissies who go to Florida, most of my friends and most Chicagoans will tough it out another year. Most Chicago people take their vacations like everyone else in the country in July and August, and get back in time to share winter with their fellow prisoners.

Nelson Algren[128] said Chicago is like a beautiful woman with a broken nose. and you have to love her to live with her. That's like saying Chicago is a pretty boy with a scared face, had some natural beauty once, got ruined, but you love him anyway.

Actually, Chicago is built on flat, cold ground, and outside of the lake, it has little natural beauty. All the beauty in Chicago is unnatural or man-made: its streets, its buildings. its cruisable towers.

Nelson Algren also said Chicago is a town of hustlers, and that may get closer to the truth of Chicago. We stay here because we are hustlers of a sort and we like the hustle. Why do hustlers hang out on Broadway or Hubbard night after night, even though the moral majorities try to make it tough for them and want to push and shove them out?

They hang there because they are addicted to the hustle, the excitement, the expectation that something grand might happen to them. They might be out there ostensibly selling their body, but they are really there to buy their soul. You could never explain it to your mother or your

---

128 Best known for his mid-20th century novels *The Man With The Golden Arm* and *Chicago, City on the Make*. The latter book focused on down and outers, alleyways and crooked politicians.

decent friends, but you stay in Chicago because you like the hustle.

Once you realize that Chicago is a tough city yes, a cold city yes, but an exciting city because it's a hustler's town, a lot of the paradoxes begin to clear up.

Politics in Chicago is not the serious business of making laws and bringing order. Politics here is a great hustle, and the police and politicians' chief function, as Mayor Daley[129] so aptly put it, is to "preserve disorder," so they can keep the game and the hustle going.

Dick and Jane,[130] our two great mayors, are also our two great hustlers. Dick used the paternal clout system to mother us all, and Jane uses the same system to step-father us all. Dick was our town Madame, and Jane is our street hustler.

What do hustlers on the streets always dream of? That they will find a John who will pay $100 to take them to a $100 for dinner only.

---

[129] Richard J. Daley, Mayor of Chicago from 1955-1976, died in office; the remark about disorder was made at the 1968 Democratic Convention in Chicago.

[130] Linking their names alludes to the on-screen couple played by George Segal and Jane Fonda who rob banks in the romantic comedy, *Fun with Dick and Jane* (1977; remade in 2005 starring Jim Carrey and Tea Leoni).

Two weeks ago, a hustler Jane found thousands of Johns who were willing to spend $100 to have dinner with her. She is by far the best little street hustler in town.

Everyone always says Chicago is the big city where diverse families live in ethnic neighborhoods. The key to Chicago is the neighborhoods. The implication is everyone lives in neighborhoods, so everyone is neighborly, pro-family, and friendly.

But that is not the way it really works in Chicago. No one is neighborly. If you walk down the street saying hello and being friendly to people, they will think you are a lunatic or a thief. When we walk the streets of Chicago we maintain at all times the hustler pose, never smile, never say hello.

We are all in the same business, we are all hustling for our existence, but we don't say hello to each other because we don't want anybody else to know our business.

That's why Chicago is such a tough city, everyone lives here with a cracked heart. You want to give out to other people, but you don't, for that would break the hustler's code.

Ironically, perhaps the friendliest people on the streets of Chicago are the real-life hustlers and senior citizens living in transient hotels, because they know what they are doing here and they are not ashamed of it. Our neighborhoods are separate turfs, and you don't cross neighborhoods here anymore than you hustle a rival gang's turf.

Gays stay in gay town (New Town), the Poles stay west. The blacks stay mostly south side, and the egg-heads in Hyde Park. And we don't mix neighborhoods. Living in Chicago, I go more often to Harvard yard and Berkeley, than I go to Hyde Park.

As for being "pro-family," look at our school system. We don't raise and educate kids in the system, we hustle kids. And the kids know it! They are out singing "we don't need no education," while the mayor and aldermen I are singing "we don't need no school system," especially if Superintendent Love[131] thinks she can hustle Jane's job away from her.

Once you realize that Chicago really is a hustler's paradise, that beneath the cold flat surface all life here goes on underground you start hustling and making the city work for you.

The enterprises that thrive well in Chicago are underground enterprises, things that go below the surface. Chicago is not for the superficial. It's not a hot spot or come on town. A

---

[131] Dr. Ruth B. Love, chosen Superintendent of the Chicago Schools, moved from the Oakland school system in 1981 to become the highest paid superintendent in America.

lot of gays, because of the romance and come on, would give their deviated sphincter to live in San Francisco!

Chicago is not that kind of town. It gives you no reason to live here. You have to hustle it out for yourself. And it helps if you know and like what's beneath the surface.

Underground activities like crime and psychoanalysis thrive here. The first thing you see upon arriving in the Loop are a lot of men in blue, and book stores like Stuart Brent's on Michigan Avenue specializing in psychiatric literature.[132] Chicago is a great city if you like to go into yourself and underground. Writers, journalists, and playwrights do well here. But not dancers.[133]

Buildings here are massive and deep-rooted because they go underground and have to endure the winters. Other cities can have pretty malls and toy-like imitations of Chicago skyscrapers. But other cities are playgrounds; Chicago is the deep rooted ground of your own being. In Chicago, bodies are thick and massive,

---

[132] Stuart Brent Books closed in late 1995.

[133] The status of dance and dancers has improved greatly since this column was written. The Joffrey Ballet moved to Chicago in 1995 and a vibrant modern dance community is featured in the annual late Fall Dance Chicago events around the city, begun in 1994.

like the buildings, to stand the nine months of winter; so our souls, here, thick and enduring--a Chicago soul is deep-dished like a Chicago pizza.

Other cities can tell you love it or leave it. Chicago is not that romantic or dramatic. It just tells you hustle and make for yourself. Which is not a bad offer, if you want to live a life that is both deep and broad. And I guess that's why a lot of us stay here--not as in California, to shine in the sunlight, but waiting through the winter to do our sting.

chapter seventy-five

ECHO AND THE BUNNYMAN | 1993

For the last six months, I have been trying to get to Foxy's[134]--especially for Steve Lafreniere's Fake Party,[135] which is now held on the first Thursday of every month. Steve is a bright and caring guy who attracts a crowd of literary wits and free spirits. He keeps the company I want to keep. So I've tried real hard to get there.

But something happens to the body rhythms at 56. With all my good intentions to go out and party, my legs ache, my body sags and I'm lucky to stay awake for Ted Koppel. It happens to you, to all of us. Rick Garcia tells me he also is feeling more like a party-pooper these days. "I used to think guys just said that because they didn't like bar life anyway, and it was a good excuse to stay

---

[134] Foxy's used to be at the corner of Belmont and Halsted, now occupied by Spin. Foxy's was where one could dance to deep house, originated by Chicagoan Ralphi Rosario.

[135] Steve Lafreniere is an arts writer and sometime DJ who was prominent in Chicago's New Wave/gay art/music world of the 1980s and '90s. He also contributed to the Chicago gay magazines *Gab* and *Babble*.

home." No, it's no excuse. Your body changes as you get on.

Not only do I go to bed earlier, but I wake up earlier. It's nothing for me to start work at 5 a.m. Can't sleep any more. A couple of times, when I feel real perverse, I'll hop out of bed around 4 a.m., twirl out to a bar and get there for last call. Then I enjoy a brief encounter with sleaze, sharp and awake, feeling like a hot-tailed bunny.

The male body goes through stages. Robert Bly, poet and generally homophobic Iron Man, in a convoluted essay (*New York Times* July 23), tries to convince the joint chiefs to admit gays into the military, and borrows categories from Mayan culture. They say that men pass through four stages: The boy, the warrior, the community man and the "echo" man. The echo man, as Bly interprets, "is not exactly man or woman but a person who hears. One could say he is all ears, all grief, all intuition, all response to sound. He does not act but rather listens to the community and to the ancestors and tries to figure out to whom our debt for living is to be paid."

Because each of us in actual living is a mixture of all these things at once, this set series of labels will not automatically fit everyone's individual life. For example, I was a man, or "little man," before I was a boy, and later a gay man, "big boy" in Boy's Town.

I told Don Eric, *Gay Chicago*'s idiosyncratic columnist, about these ideas, and his response was a quick put-down. "Mayans--they pounded nails into tongues--I would follow their culture! Besides, I'm a boy, an eternal boy." Don's right: he remains a youthful Narcissus, one of the few "man-boys" still dancing in our clubs years after his older friends like me have quit.

I see my personal history in this community as one who has left--but not abandoned--the boy stage, the warrior/activist stage, the community service-man stage. I'm now an echo man. I try in my writing to keep alive what was and now is the sound of our community. Sometimes I speak for our young ancestors who are gone, sometimes addressing those who are just coming out and into our community. I try to figure out what we owe to each other in terms of debts and respect.

But also in my personal history there is another deviation. I am a Bunnyman. Bunny still symbolizes the life-child in me. Bunny makes sure that I don't take all this echo stuff too seriously.

The bunny figure has surrounded my life. As a kid, I had a stuffed bunny to take to bed with me. And a live bunny to nose. Pink noses, white furry ears, green grass symbolize the freshness of new life. My personal fetish and predilections.

In high school, I had a Republican Zen-master teacher, Mr. Bleakney, for philosophy. Besides teaching me how to read the Wall Street Journal and how to appreciate the cycles of business--something he thought a young radical should know--Mr. B. gave each student in our class a word picture, which he said we would remember for the rest of our lives because of its crazy association. He told me to think of a rabbit with a baseball on its head. No matter how adult I have become, or sophisticated in my words and arguments, I smile like a happy kid every time I think of that magic image.

Omega and I were bunnymen. Bunnies in bed together and bunnies on the run out searching for other bunnies. That's the special way we played and talked.

The echo man takes all this in. I'm all ears. A radar and radio set all in one. The everyday conversations of everyday folk, especially queens, fascinates me. I take it in, I take it down, I spit some of it back, but I don't divide it up much in terms of right and wrong.

Except when those bunnies got arrested at Glee Club, because I identify with them. The Blue Meanies, as far as I'm concerned--are home-invaders. Justice for adults--the unbunny-kind--is a big pay-off. Pigs put the squeeze on gay bunnies so that the guys who run bunny clubs will gleefully pay back to pol pigs, so raids will stop before the next election. That's the funny game I've seen played for years in this town.

My private sense of justice is still an echo of an earlier time when I was a child/boy/ bunnyman. Adults were not let into our space or allowed to touch or pinch our bunnies with their dirty hands. In adult society--a bunnyless home--they like to single out molesters and string them up in public, not recognizing that the whole crappy adult world, with all its authoritarian law-games, molests kids more than any single individual.

Rather than become an overheated bunny--which is worse than an oversexed bunny--I drop the warrior mode and return to echo land. I am not about to tell a cop, "I'm a cop, too!" ("I'm a better cop than you.") I'm against all copping attitudes.

As an echo man, I don't try to go out every night or get engaged in every political fight and gossip-slinging feud. I prefer to stay inside my echo retirement. Not a state of action and reaction, but a state of memory and reflection, where I recreate the sound of our community past and future.

THE NEW TOWN ANTHOLOGY VOLUME 2

NOTHING PERSONAL

CHRONICLES OF CHICAGO'S LGBTQ COMMUNITY 1977-1997

Jon-Henri Damski

fire –)♡(– trap

A Firetrap Press Book www.firetrappress.com

Firetrap Press **Books by Jon-Henri Damski**

www.firetrappress.com

Nonfiction

Angels Into Dust : The New Town Anthology Volume 1

dead/queer/proud : schizoculture 1

Nothing Personal: Chronicles of Chicago's LGBTQ Community 1977-1997 (The New Town Anthology Volume 2)

Poetry

Poems for the Fo(u)rth Quarter: Virtually Incurable But Not Quite Terminal

Fresh Frozen: First Chicago Poems

My Blue Monk: Poems from Blood and Sugar

Eat My Words: More Chicago Poems from the '70s

Epigrams

Damski to Go

LaVergne, TN USA
01 October 2009
159658LV00001B/94/P

9 781891 343032